Download Forms on

You can download the forms in this book at:

 www.nolo.com/back-of-book/HDAB.html

We'll also post updates whenever there's an important change to the law affecting this book—as well as articles and other related materials.

More Resources from Nolo.com

 Legal Forms, Books, & Software
Hundreds of do-it-yourself products—all written in plain English, approved, and updated by our in-house legal editors.

 Legal Articles
Get informed with thousands of free articles on everyday legal topics. Our articles are accurate, up to date, and reader friendly.

 Find a Lawyer
Want to talk to a lawyer? Use Nolo to find a lawyer who can help you with your case.

NOLO
LAW for ALL

5th Edition

The Essential Guide to
Handling Workplace
Harassment & Discrimination

Attorney Deborah C. England

FIFTH EDITION	SEPTEMBER 2021
Editor	AMY LOFTSGORDON
Cover Design	SUSAN PUTNEY
Book Design	SUSAN PUTNEY
Proofreading	IRENE BARNARD
Index	UNGER INDEXING
Printing	BANG PRINTING

ISSN: 2769-2647 (print)

ISSN: 2769-2655 (online)

ISBN: 978-1-4133-2894-3 (pbk)

ISBN: 978-1-4133-2895-0 (ebook)

This book covers only United States law, unless it specifically states otherwise.

Please note

Accurate, plain-English legal information can help you solve many of your own legal problems. But this text is not a substitute for personalized advice from a knowledgeable lawyer. If you want the help of a trained professional—and we'll always point out situations in which we think that's a good idea—consult an attorney licensed to practice in your state.

Dedication

To my nephew, Jake, and my nieces, Isabelle and Olivia. May your world be free of prejudice, with opportunity equally available to all. And if it's not, you know what to do.

Acknowledgments

The author wishes to thank everyone at Nolo who helped with this book, including:

Lisa Guerin, for her pithy, astute, and insightful editing. Also, for her unquenchable wit and enthusiasm for this inherited project.

Alayna Schroeder, for her diligent effort to pull this book into shape and clarify its many knotty concepts.

Janet Portman and Mary Randolph, for championing the book and staying with it.

Sigrid Metson, Kelly Perri, and Tom Silva, for their strategic input.

About the Author

Deborah C. England has practiced employment law in San Francisco for more than 30 years, representing clients in litigation in state and federal courts. In addition to litigating, she regularly advises clients on employment issues, guides in efforts to informally resolve employment disputes, and has conducted discrimination and harassment training. Ms. England is the coauthor, with Lisa Guerin, of *The Essential Guide to Family & Medical Leave*, published by Nolo, and frequently writes and speaks on employment and civil rights law.

Table of Contents

Introduction

D iversity is among the great strengths of American society. Employers in this country are able to draw from a pool of workers of both genders and of all races, religions, nationalities, abilities, and ages. Diversity provides companies with the broadest base of talent, the widest range of viewpoints, the deepest reach into potential client and customer communities, and the best chance of benefitting from our increasingly global economy.

But diversity can also present vexing challenges to employers. Sometimes, differences among employees can lead to conflict, misunderstanding, and, in the worst cases, hostility. Employers that enjoy the benefits of a diverse workforce also bear the responsibility of making sure that it functions harmoniously. This task can, at times, be a daunting undertaking. This book is designed to help employers, and especially the human resources personnel, managers, and supervisors who work for them, negotiate some of the trickiest waters of the modern workplace: preventing and dealing with harassment and discrimination.

Since 2017, with the rise of the "Me Too" (#MeToo) movement of women speaking out about sexual harassment and misconduct by powerful men in various high-profile industries including film, television, theater, the arts, politics, and even on the Supreme Court, a new awareness of and focus on the problem of sexual harassment in the workplace has finally come. Women from other industries, including farmworkers, domestic workers, construction workers, and others, soon joined the campaign and reported their own experiences of sexual harassment.

The movement both highlights the continuing pervasiveness of sexual harassment and calls for a much more robust effort by employers to rid workplaces of this scourge.

A 2020 U.S. Supreme Court decision expanded the definition of "sex" as it's used in the federal law prohibiting workplace discrimination and harassment to include gay and transgender individuals. At the time of writing, a bill to amend the language of Title VII, the federal law in question, had been introduced in Congress. In short, the legal landscape of discrimination and harassment in employment is dynamic. (For updates to the information in this book, visit www.nolo.com/back-of-book/HDAB.html.)

You might have turned to this book because you want to help your company avoid problems down the road by preventing harassment and discrimination from occurring. Good for you! That kind of proactive initiative will help keep your company on the right track, using the strategies and tools provided here. On the other hand, maybe you grabbed this book because your company just got hit with a harassment or discrimination complaint or even a lawsuit. You've come to the right place, too. The chapters that follow provide clear direction on how to help your company through the process and how to prevent similar problems in the future. With these strategies, you and your company can be confident that you're doing all you can to make the workplace welcoming to all employees, so they can focus on doing their jobs.

What Are Harassment and Discrimination?

"Harassment" and "discrimination" are terms that are used frequently and loosely in everyday conversation. This book focuses on the kind of workplace harassment and discrimination that the law prohibits: mistreatment of an employee because of that employee's race, color, national origin, gender, religion, age, disability, or other characteristic protected by law.

Harassment and discrimination are related but distinct concepts. An employer discriminates against an employee when it takes an action against the employee because of membership in a protected group. For example, a company that refuses to hire Japanese American applicants is discriminating against those candidates because of their national origin.

Harassment is actually a type of discrimination, a particular way employers mistreat employees based on a protected trait. An employer harasses an employee when it targets someone in a protected category and subjects that person to unwelcome conduct that affects their job. Harassment can take the form of attempted sexual extortion, such as when a male supervisor pressures a female subordinate to consent to a physical relationship with him to keep her job. It can also take the form of conduct that poisons the working environment, such as when a coworker calls another employee racist names or displays sexual, racist, homophobic, transphobic, or other offensive materials in view of other employees.

How Harassment and Discrimination Affect the Bottom Line

The words "harassment" and "discrimination" might lead you to envision lawsuits, courtrooms, and lawyers. Legal costs are certainly among the costs of failing to prevent and remedy these problems. An employee who faced illegal workplace discrimination or harassment can sue your company. Lawsuits come with a very real price tag, from lost hours spent preparing a case to attorneys' fees to potentially huge damage awards. Of course, being sued can also have costs that are more difficult to quantify, including loss of goodwill, a poor reputation in the community, bad publicity, and poor employee morale.

How much do harassment and discrimination claims cost employers? The Equal Employment Opportunity Commission (EEOC), the agency that interprets and enforces federal discrimination laws, provides a partial answer. In 2020, the EEOC received over 80,000 complaints of harassment and employers paid claimants damages, attorneys' fees, and other penalties amounting to over $106 million. These figures don't even include charges filed with state agencies, damages paid as a result of lawsuits, or settlements reached before the filing of charges. It's clear that discrimination and harassment charges continue to cost employers a great deal of money.

But harassment and discrimination don't have to result in a lawsuit to cause serious problems for your company. Harassment and discrimination tear down morale, destroy loyalty, drain productivity, and harm your company's ability to attract and retain employees. Preventing and dealing appropriately with harassment and discrimination don't just fulfill your legal obligations; they also further your company's best interests. Employees who work in an environment that is tolerant, free of slurs and offensive conduct, and welcoming to all are more content and productive than those who don't.

How This Book Can Help

As a manager or human resources professional, you have probably heard and read quite a bit about employment harassment and discrimination. Perhaps you've even attended a training session, participated in a webinar, or taken a professional development class on these topics. If so, here's something you might have noticed: Problems can arise in innumerable ways in a real workplace, most of which don't match the scenarios presented in training.

This book will help you make the leap from abstract rules to everyday workplace situations. It will help you recognize harassment and discrimination when they arise and offer you proven strategies and tools for preventing and dealing with them. It's filled with examples, common questions, and real-world lessons that will help you apply the sometimes complicated legal principles of harassment and discrimination to the very real problems that come up in your workplace. Whether you're new to these topics or you're interested in refreshing your training, this book will help you understand the law and apply it at your company, in a way that makes sense on the ground level of a functioning business. At the time of writing, the coronavirus (COVID-19) pandemic was ongoing, with many employees working remotely. The legal principles, strategies, and tactics discussed in this book apply to remote workers as well.

Part I of this book focuses on prevention. It explains the legal ins and outs of harassment and discrimination, including what types of conduct are prohibited, when harassment and discrimination commonly occur, when your company can be held liable, and how to handle common problem areas, like conducting job interviews and managing workplace romance. This information will help you identify problems early on, so you can take quick action to stop potential misconduct.

Next, you'll learn how to develop an effective harassment and discrimination policy. You'll find out how this type of policy can protect your company, what a good policy should include, and how to distribute the policy to employees. You'll also learn about the important role that employee and supervisor training can play in preventing violations, along with some tips on setting up an effective training program, whether you do the training yourself or hire someone else to handle it.

Part II focuses on responding to harassment and discrimination complaints. You'll find information on investigations, including the importance of taking complaints seriously, how to investigate claims promptly and thoroughly, and how to document each step of the process. You'll also learn how to handle the stresses to the working environment that complaints and investigations can cause, along with practical tips for healing any rifts that might have developed so that employees can continue to function professionally and collegially. Finally, the book explains the process of responding to complaints that employees file with governmental agencies and in court.

Get Updates, Forms, and More on Nolo.com

When important changes to the information in this book happen, we'll post updates at this book's online companion page, which also includes all of the forms referenced in this book and more. You'll find a list of materials available on the companion page—along with the URL where you can access it —in Appendix B.

Although we as a society have come a long way, harassment and discrimination are still part of the landscape of the modern workplace. Armed with the information and tools provided in this book, including the resources and audio scenarios provided on the online companion page, you'll be ready to handle claims of harassment and discrimination from start to finish. And, better yet, you'll be able to prevent those claims from arising in the first place.

Part I: Preventing Harassment and Discrimination

What Is Discrimination?

Y ou might hear the word "discrimination" used rather broadly in everyday speech. People who feel wronged might say, for example, "He discriminated against me because he doesn't like people who speak their minds" or "It's so unfair that we have to go stand outside to smoke; this company really discriminates against smokers."

Statements like these get at only one important aspect of discrimination: It involves making a distinction between groups of people. But, as you probably know, discrimination is illegal only when the basis for the distinction has been declared off-limits by Congress, courts, or a state or local legislature. Not every unfair or biased decision is discriminatory. For discrimination to be illegal, it must be based on a "protected category," such as race or religion.

This chapter will cover:

- laws that prohibit discrimination
- what discrimination is, and
- how and when discrimination might occur.

This information will help you recognize the signs of discriminatory behavior. In later chapters, you'll learn what steps you can take to prevent discrimination and how to handle complaints of discrimination that has already taken place.

Laws Prohibiting Discrimination

Many different laws, both federal and state, protect employees from discrimination in the workplace. The most prominent federal antidiscrimination laws are:

- **Title VII of the Civil Rights Act of 1964 (Title VII).** This law prohibits discrimination on the basis of race, color, religion, sex (including transgender and gay individuals, as well as pregnant individuals), and national origin. Title VII applies to employers with 15 or more employees.

> ⚠ **CAUTION**
>
> **If your company had 15 employees at any time in the last two years, Title VII might apply.** Title VII applies to entities with 15 or more employees for each working day in 20 or more calendar weeks in the current or preceding year. If your company's workforce fluctuates around 15 employees, talk with a legal adviser about whether the law applies to your company. Even if Title VII doesn't apply, your state's antidiscrimination laws might; state laws often apply to smaller employers. (See "State Laws Prohibiting Discrimination in Employment," in Appendix A for more information.)

> 📘 **RESOURCE**
>
> **Looking for a lawyer?** Asking for a referral to an attorney from someone you trust can be a good way to find legal help. Also, two sites that are part of the Nolo family, Lawyers.com and Avvo.com, provide excellent and free lawyer directories. These directories allow you to search by location and area of law, and list detailed information about and reviews of lawyers.
>
> Whether you're just starting your lawyer search or researching particular attorneys, visit www.lawyers.com/find-a-lawyer and www.avvo.com/find-a-lawyer.

- **Genetic Information Nondiscrimination Act (GINA).** This law prohibits discrimination on the basis of genetic information. GINA applies to employers that have 15 or more employees.
- **The Age Discrimination in Employment Act (ADEA).** The ADEA prohibits discrimination against those age 40 or older on the basis of age.
- **The Americans with Disabilities Act (ADA).** The ADA protects workers with disabilities from discrimination in the workplace, and it requires employers to offer reasonable accommodations to help those workers do their jobs.
- **The Equal Pay Act (EPA).** This law is designed to ensure that men and women receive equal compensation for the same or similar work. The jobs don't have to be exactly the same to require equal pay, but they must involve "equal work," meaning equal skill, effort, and responsibility and similar working conditions.

- **The Civil Rights Act of 1866, 42 U.S.C § 1981 (Section 1981).** Section 1981 prohibits discrimination on the basis of race in the making, enforcing, and performance of contracts. It also prohibits discrimination on the basis of ethnicity, if that discrimination is racial in character (for example, discrimination based on physical characteristics or skin color violates Section 1981; discrimination based on surname or accent generally doesn't). Section 1981 applies to all contracts, including employment agreements, partnership agreements, and the like.
- **The Immigration Reform and Control Act (IRCA).** IRCA prohibits employers with four or more employees from discriminating against individuals on the basis of citizenship, ethnicity, immigration status, or national origin in recruiting, hiring, firing, and verifying identity and authorization to work in the U.S. The law also prohibits employers from retaliating against individuals for reporting possibly discriminatory actions to the EEOC or other federal agencies.

Most states also have their own laws prohibiting employment discrimination, and many extend greater protections than federal law. For example, they might apply to smaller employers or apply to other protected classes (such as marital status). Finally, some city or county ordinances could also provide additional protection.

 Common Questions

Q: *We are a multistate employer, and our handbook says that we don't tolerate discrimination based on sexual orientation. An employee is now complaining of sexual orientation discrimination in a state that doesn't prohibit it. Do we have to do anything about it?*

A: *Yes. First, the U.S. Supreme Court has expanded the definition of "sex" for purposes of Title VII protection against discrimination to include gay individuals. Second, arguably the company obligated itself, in its handbook, to protect employees from sexual orientation discrimination, regardless of where it occurs and whether it is illegal. And it's a good business practice, too. Following this policy uniformly shows the company's sincere commitment to treating employees fairly and protecting them from discrimination no matter where they work.*

Which Antidiscrimination Laws Apply to Your Company?

Not every antidiscrimination law applies to every employer. For the most part, whether your company has to follow these laws depends on its size and location. Federal antidiscrimination laws (listed below) apply only to employers with more than a minimum number of employees—and this minimum number is different for each law.

Name of Law:	Discrimination Prohibited on the Basis of:	Applies to:
Title VII	Race, color, national origin, religion, sex (including transgender, gay, and pregnant individuals)	Employers with 15 or more employees
Age Discrimination in Employment Act	Age (employees age 40 and older only)	Employers with 20 or more employees
Americans with Disabilities Act	Physical or mental disability	Employers with 15 or more employees
Equal Pay Act	Sex (applies only to wage discrimination)	All employers
Civil Rights Act of 1866 (Section 1981)	Race, ethnicity	All employers
Immigration Reform and Control Act	Citizenship status, national origin	Employers with four or more employees
Genetic Information Nondiscrimination Act	Genetic information	Employers with 15 or more employees

What Is Discrimination?

In general, antidiscrimination laws are designed to keep an employer from making employment-related decisions that disadvantage employees based on the categories identified above (or other categories state or local governments find worthy of protection). It is illegal to discriminate when hiring, creating or applying policies, training, promoting, firing or laying off employees, or with regard to any other terms and conditions of employment.

> **TIP**
>
> **Conduct could be inappropriate even if it isn't illegal.** This section explains how courts and legislatures define discrimination, including what an employee must prove to win a discrimination lawsuit. That doesn't mean, however, that you should ignore any behavior or conduct that falls short of these standards. For example, a supervisor might be able to show that the younger employee he promoted was truly the best qualified candidate for the position, even if that supervisor made inappropriate ageist remarks that led an older employee to mistakenly believe that the decision was based on age. However, it's still not acceptable for a supervisor to make biased comments.

The supervision should be disciplined for violating company policy, even if no law has been broken. Taking disciplinary steps will not only help you maintain a professional workplace, but also help you avoid expensive lawsuits. Even if the supervisor's conduct didn't violate the law, the ageist comments are likely to inspire the older employee to file a lawsuit. Although you might be able to eventually convince the court to dismiss the case, it will cost you plenty of time, resources, and attorneys' fees.

Discrimination can take the following forms:

- **Disparate treatment.** Intentionally treating people differently because of a protected characteristic is the textbook form of discrimination. It can mean denying a job to someone because of race, or giving promotions to men over equally qualified women based on gender.
- **Disparate impact.** Conduct that is neutral on its face but affects a disproportionate number of employees in a protected class is also discriminatory. Unless the employer has a very good, job-related reason for the different treatment—for example, a strength requirement (which could disproportionately affect women) because the job regularly requires heavy lifting—the practice or policy won't pass legal muster. Even if an employer has a valid business reason for the practice, it might still constitute discrimination if an alternative requirement exists that wouldn't disproportionately affect the protected class.

- **Failure to accommodate.** When an employer is legally required to accommodate an employee (such as an employee with a disability or an employee whose religious practices require a change to workplace rules) and fails to do so, this failure to accommodate is also a form of discrimination.

Discrimination doesn't often present itself in an extremely obvious way, like a supervisor admitting he won't promote women, he refused to hire someone because of race, or he won't consider anyone older than 50 for certain positions. The rare occasions when something like this happens are called "smoking gun" cases because employers will have a hard time refuting such direct evidence of discrimination.

Much more often, however, an employee will have only an inkling or hunch that something isn't right. The employee might look at several different pieces of suggestive information (called "circumstantial evidence") and decide that discrimination is the logical conclusion. For example, an employee who claims that she didn't receive a promotion because of her gender might present evidence that her supervisor made sexist statements shortly before denying her the promotion, offered the promotion to a man whose qualifications were not as strong, and has a history of promoting only male employees.

 Lessons From the Real World

Sexist comment about an employee's rate of pay could support the employee's Equal Pay Act claim years later.

When an Indiana academy hired Cheryl Kellogg in 2006, the academy director told her that she didn't need a higher starting salary "because her husband worked." Cheryl sued the academy in 2018 for unjust compensation, alleging it paid her less than comparable male teachers.

The trial court dismissed the case but the federal appeals court reversed that decision, holding that Cheryl could rely on the 2006 comment to dispute the academy's claimed gender-neutral explanations for her lower pay.

Kellogg v. Ball State University, Case No. 20-1406 (7th Cir. 01/05/2021)

An employee can't win a discrimination case simply by claiming discrimination on the job. If an employee's discrimination case goes to court, the employee will have to show all of the following:

- **The employee was qualified for the job in question.** An employee or applicant can't claim discrimination unless he or she had the necessary skills, qualifications, and experience to do the job.

- **The employee is a member of a protected class.** Although this requirement might seem fairly straightforward, that isn't always the case. For example, an employee who claims discrimination based on religion will have to show that the religious belief in question is "sincerely held."

- **The employee or applicant suffered an adverse action.** It isn't enough for an employee to claim that someone is prejudiced toward, or holds particular beliefs about, certain groups of people. The employee must also show that his or her job was affected negatively by these biased beliefs. For example, a female employee couldn't sue simply because her manager is a member of a private, male-only golf club; she would have to show that she suffered a negative employment action based on her gender.

- **There's some reason to suspect that the employer had an improper motive.** Essentially, it's up to the employee to show that there is some connection between his or her membership in a protected class and the adverse action the employer took. In other words, an employee who is fired and happens to be African American doesn't have a legal claim; an employee who is fired because he is African American does. One exception: an employee claiming a violation of the Equal Pay Act (EPA) does not have to prove that the employer intended to discriminate based on gender. If your company pays men and women differently for the same or a substantially equal job, it has violated the EPA.

Even if the employee can prove these elements, the employer has the opportunity to show that it took the job action for a legitimate business reason. For example, you could show that you didn't hire a qualified applicant in a protected class because another applicant was more qualified. If you're able to do that, the employee will have to show that your rationale wasn't the real reason for the action (in legal terms, that it was just a "pretext" for discrimination). For example, if you claim that you never promote anyone with fewer than two years of experience, and an employee bringing a gender discrimination case shows that several men with less experience were promoted, that might be proof of pretext.

Being a Jerk Isn't Illegal

Not every type of discrimination is illegal discrimination. Differences in personality, temperament, and taste can lead to friction in the workplace. If unfair treatment arises out of a personality dispute that is not based on membership in a protected class, it is not illegal. That means the "undiscriminating jerk"—the manager who treats everyone badly—isn't discriminating illegally if he's mean to everyone just because he's, well, mean. Even obvious favoritism or bias, such as refusing to hire fans of a particular baseball team, isn't illegal as long as it isn't actually based on race, gender, or some other protected status.

Of course, that doesn't mean the company has to put up with obnoxious behavior and foolish rationales for employment decisions. After all, it can affect employee morale and productivity. You'll probably want to put a stop to it; even though the company shouldn't risk legal liability for it, it's hardly conducive to a good work environment.

Also, be aware that many states have enacted laws prohibiting bullying. If an employee's conduct is not discriminatory but fits your state's definition of bullying, your company might be liable under state law for not taking action to address and prevent that conduct. Check with an employment attorney in your state to find out if any anti-bullying laws apply.

Sex-Based Discrimination

Sex discrimination means making decisions based on sex or adopting policies that appear to be neutral but disproportionately affect one gender. An employer discriminates when it gives men the plum assignments or gives women more paid leave than men, for example. Sexual harassment is also a type of sex discrimination, as explained in Chapter 2.

But there are more subtle ways to discriminate based on sex, too. Here are some other forms sex discrimination might take.

Sexual Orientation and Transgender Discrimination

The U.S. Supreme Court ruled in 2020 that the term "sex" as used in Title VII includes sexual orientation and transgender status. (*Bostock v. Clayton County, Georgia*, 140 S.Ct. 1731 (2020).) So, gay and transgender individuals are protected against employment discrimination. Also, many states offer explicit protection for such individuals in state laws. (See Appendix A for information on the law in your state.)

In addition, federal laws prohibit discrimination based on sex stereotyping, as discussed below. Treating people differently because they fail to live up to gender norms—for example, because a man acts feminine or a woman acts masculine—can be illegal sex discrimination.

Sexual Stereotyping

Sexual stereotyping, that is, holding men and women to different standards based on historic or traditional sex roles, is also sex-based discrimination. In one famous case, a female manager in an accounting firm was denied promotion to partner due to her "interpersonal skills," among other reasons. The partners making the decision wanted her to walk, talk, and dress more femininely and to wear makeup and jewelry. The Supreme Court recognized that this challenge to her "interpersonal skills" and appearance was really just another way of saying she didn't conform to the partners' stereotypes of how a woman should look and act, which is sex discrimination.

Common Questions

Q: *An employee complained that her supervisor always gives lead projects to men. When I asked the supervisor about it, he told me that it's because he happens to be more comfortable working with the men in the department. He doesn't mean to discriminate; it's just a personality issue. Is this discrimination?*

A: *Most likely, yes. Discrimination doesn't have to be a series of calculated decisions intended to harm one group of people: It just means treating people in the same situation differently because of a protected characteristic. The supervisor's personal comfort level with the men who report to him doesn't justify giving them the lead assignments. It looks like his personal preference is clouding his professional judgment, and female employees are suffering as a result. Whether or not gender is playing any role in his decisions—that is, whether he is comfortable only around men generally or he just happens to be more comfortable with these particular fellows—this situation needs to change.*

Dress Codes

In most cultures, including ours, men and women traditionally dress and appear differently from one another. For example, it is customary for women to wear skirts, but not men. Courts have generally allowed dress codes or grooming standards that recognize these social differences, but not if such codes impose a greater burden on one gender or the other. For example, it is probably okay to have a rule that men can't wear their hair longer than collar length. But a rule that requires only female employees to wear uniforms is likely illegal, as it imposes a greater burden on women.

CAUTION

Dress codes can cause problems if they impose a greater burden on members of a different protected class. For example, "no-beard" policies may be illegal as applied to African American males who suffer from pseudofolliculitis barbae, a painful skin condition caused by shaving. So, your company might have to make an exception for these employees if it has such a policy.

Favoring a Paramour

Everyone is affected in an environment where the boss dates a subordinate. It can quickly create feelings of distrust and discomfort and, worse, it can put the company at legal risk.

As explained in Chapter 2, workplace relationships can lead to claims of sexual harassment, particularly if the relationship ends or one person has less power at work than the other. These relationships can also lead to claims of discrimination where, for example, a supervisor gives her boyfriend better work assignments than she gives his peers. While a court might not find the existence of a relationship alone to be illegal discrimination (because everyone not in the relationship is equally affected, men and women alike), it's not a risk worth taking—and it's a bad business practice. No one wants to believe a relationship with a supervisor or manager is a prerequisite to professional success. If you allow this type of behavior to happen in your company, you will likely face high turnover and general feelings of dissatisfaction. For more information on handling workplace relationships, see Chapter 2.

 Lessons From the Real World

Employee who was fired after complaining about false rumors that she was sleeping with her boss could proceed with her lawsuit.

Evangeline Parker was horrified to hear rumors being spread at work by a lead warehouse manager that she was sleeping with another manager. After Evangeline formally complained to the company's human resources manager, the company issued warnings to her and ultimately fired her. Evangeline sued the company for violating Title VII.

The federal trial court dismissed Evangeline's case, but the Fourth Circuit Court of Appeals reversed that decision and allowed Evangeline's case to proceed, holding that the company discriminated against her by punishing her but not the manager who spread the rumor.

Parker v. Reema Consulting Services, Inc., 915 F.3d 297 (4th Cir. 2019).

Unequal Pay

Paying men and women different wages or salaries for the same or a substantially equal job is a violation of the federal EPA. As noted earlier in this chapter, an employee claiming she was paid less than a man for the same job doesn't have to prove that her employer intended to discriminate; if she shows a wage differential, the employer is liable for violating the EPA. Basing an employee's pay rate at the time of hiring on earnings history at prior jobs, while a common practice, can lead to problems. Certain courts have held that employers may rely on such information when setting pay at hire without violating the EPA, but some states, including California, prohibit employers from using earnings histories at prior employers as a justification for paying men and women differently for the same job.

Pregnancy Discrimination

Treating employees differently on the basis of pregnancy, childbirth, or medical conditions related to pregnancy or childbirth (including abortion) is also prohibited, sex-based discrimination. The employee doesn't have to be pregnant to be protected, however. For example, a federal court allowed a pregnancy-based lawsuit to proceed when an employee alleged she was fired because she was undergoing in vitro fertilization to try to become pregnant.

If an employee is temporarily unable to work due to pregnancy you must treat her just as you would any other employee who is in a similar position in his or her ability or inability to work. Put another way, you should treat pregnant employees as you would any other employee with a temporary disability. If you'd give an injured employee a flexible schedule to attend medical appointments, for example, do the same for pregnant employees.

CAUTION

Employers might have to accommodate pregnant employees under state law or the ADA. Many states have laws that grant additional leave and accommodation rights to pregnant employees, beyond what federal law requires. And, if a pregnant employee has a disabling condition related to her pregnancy, you might have a duty to provide reasonable accommodation under the Americans with Disabilities Act (ADA) or similar state disability laws.

Common Questions

Q: *I have a pregnant salesperson whose job requires her to travel a lot. She's had a lot of complications in the pregnancy, and I am worried about whether it's safe for her to travel. I have an administrative position opening up—she won't make commissions anymore, but at least she'll be close to home and she won't have to take any unnecessary risks. Can I offer her the position?*

A: *You can offer her the position, but you can't require her to take it. Even though your intentions are good, forcing the employee to take the position would be discriminatory. Because the position you want her to take sounds like it pays less and is less prestigious, requiring her to take it would be demoting her because she's pregnant, a clear violation of the law. It's up to the employee and her medical care provider to decide whether she's able to continue traveling.*

Breast-Feeding Accommodation

The federal health care reform law (and some state laws) requires certain employers to provide breaks for women who need to breast-feed or express breast milk. The federal law requires employers to provide a private area, other than a restroom, for nursing women to express breast milk. These employers must allow nursing women to take reasonable breaks for that purpose for up to one year after the birth. Employers with fewer than 50 employees are not subject to the requirement if it would impose an undue hardship by causing significant difficulty or expense relative to size, financial resources, nature, or structure of the business. (29 U.S.C. § 207(r).)

In addition, many states have their own laws requiring employers to provide breaks for nursing women, some of which offer greater protections to new mothers. See Appendix A at the end of this book for a summary of state laws on breast-feeding breaks.

Gender Identity Discrimination

As noted above, the U.S. Supreme Court issued a decision expanding the definition of "sex" as used in Title VII to include transgender status. And, in recent years, many states and local governments have begun to include "gender identity" in their lists of protected classes. Gender identity refers to one's self-identified gender, as opposed to one's anatomical gender at birth. (See the chart in Appendix A for the rule in your state.) An employee need not have undergone sex reassignment surgery to be protected by these laws.

In addition, the EEOC—the agency that interprets and enforces federal antidiscrimination laws—has ruled that Title VII's prohibition of sex discrimination also bars discrimination on the basis of gender identity and transgender status. And, as noted above, employers can't discriminate based on stereotypes about how men and women should behave, which could include holding employees to stereotypes of their anatomical gender.

The EEOC has taken a proactive role in putting a stop to transgender discrimination. In 2015, it held that the Department of the Army's restrictions on a transgender woman's ability to use a common female restroom was discrimination on the basis of sex in violation of Title VII.

In 2014, the EEOC filed lawsuits against two employers alleging that they had discriminated against transgender employees in violation of Title VII's prohibition against sex discrimination. These were the first lawsuits ever filed by the EEOC on behalf of transgender employees. One case settled in April of 2015, with the Florida employer agreeing to pay $150,000 to the transgender employee. In the other lawsuit, against a Michigan employer, the Sixth Circuit ruled in favor of the transgender employee (reversing the district court's dismissal of the case) and sent the case back to the district court for further proceedings.

Q: *Our bookkeeper, Jim, just announced that he is undergoing a sex change transition, wants to be called Jamie, and insists on being treated as female from now on. He's just started the medical transition and won't be finished for many months or longer. It's a big hassle to change all our records, figure out bathroom arrangements, and make sure Jim's coworkers and supervisor are handling this in a way that doesn't offend him. Can't we treat him like a man until he isn't one anymore?*

A: *Definitely not. Part of Jamie's transition is living as a woman, the gender with which she identifies. It's no more of a burden for your company to change Jamie's records than to add new employees or adjust records to reflect changes for other employees. Demanding that you be allowed to treat Jamie "like a man" could be considered gender stereotyping and might also violate your state law if it protects against gender identity discrimination.*

Race Discrimination

Race discrimination occurs when an employer makes a job decision based on an employee's race or adopts a policy that appears neutral, but disproportionately affects members of a certain race. For example, in the first Supreme Court case to establish the concept of "disparate impact," an employer required laborers to have a high school diploma. This rule disproportionately screened out African American employees. Even if the employer's intent wasn't to discriminate, the policy had this effect. Employers with policies that have a disproportionate impact on members of a protected class must be able to show that there is an important work-related reason for the requirement. In this case, it was difficult for the employer to show that a high school diploma was necessary for the job of laborer.

Common Questions

Q: *I'm the HR manager at a garbage collection company, and we conduct background checks on all applicants, including getting credit information. Recently, the company rejected an applicant for a driver position after learning that he had bad credit (due to some late credit card payments). He's African American and was otherwise qualified for the job. I'm convinced his race had nothing to do with the rejection, but he filed a charge of discrimination with the state human rights commission. Are we at risk?*

A: *Maybe. Credit report information, while neutral on its face, could have a disproportionate negative impact on African American applicants, as the U.S. Supreme Court has recognized. And your company will have a hard time showing that an individual's credit report is necessary to being a garbage truck driver. Better to drop the practice and avoid the problem.*

National Origin and Citizenship Status

Under Title VII, employers are prohibited from discriminating on the basis of national origin (also sometimes called "ancestry"). National origin refers to the country in which someone was born, where his or her ancestors came from, or the ethnic group to which that person belongs. It does not have to refer to a country. Citizenship in another country is not in and of itself a protected status.

The Immigration Reform and Control Act of 1986 (IRCA) bans discrimination based on national origin and citizenship by any employer with four or more employees or by any employer not covered by Title VII, such as those employing seasonal workers. All employees who are authorized to work in the United States (such as those holding valid "green cards") are protected by this provision. Employers may legally choose to hire a U.S. citizen rather than an equally qualified lawful permanent resident. However, employers may not choose a U.S. citizen over an equally qualified lawful permanent resident for termination. And, an employer may not have a blanket policy of always selecting U.S. citizens over qualified, lawful permanent residents or others who are authorized to work in this country.

English-Only Rules

Some employers would like to require that everyone in the workplace speak English. Unless they're necessary for a job, however, these English-only rules are illegally discriminatory. If a business necessity for the rule exists—speaking only English to English-speaking customers, for example—and employees have advance notice of it, such a rule is usually allowed. But rules that are unnecessarily restrictive (not allowing employees to speak their native languages on their breaks, for example) can cause problems.

 Common Questions

Q: *An employee in our accounting department is excellent at what he does, but has a very thick accent that makes it difficult for people to understand him. This isn't usually a problem, except when he has to give a presentation at the monthly manager's meeting. Would it be discriminatory to demote him to a junior position that doesn't require the presentations?*

A: *In all likelihood, yes. Discriminating against someone because of an accent can be considered national origin discrimination.*

That doesn't mean you can never take an adverse action against an employee because an accent affects his or her work. When an accent materially interferes with an employee's job performance, it isn't discriminatory to take appropriate action. But it doesn't seem that you would meet that standard here. The employee's accent doesn't interfere with his primary job tasks; it only interferes with his ability to communicate at a monthly meeting, and there might be other solutions that can overcome this. For example, consider asking the employee to bring handouts to the meetings or to prepare presentation materials that communicate the bulk of relevant information, so that others can read along as he speaks.

Besides the possible legal risks if you demote the employee, you risk losing a high performer who might soon look for a job elsewhere. Replacing a competent employee could prove much more costly than trying to find a solution to the situation you're currently in.

Age-Based Discrimination

The ADEA protects employees age 40 and over from age-based discrimination. It is illegal for employers to discriminate against employees who are 40 and older in favor of employees who are under 40. It is also illegal for employers to favor younger members of the protected class over older members, based on age. For example, it's illegal to hire a candidate who is 45 years old instead of an equally qualified candidate who's 65, based on age.

> CAUTION
>
> **State laws may expand protections beyond those granted by federal law.** Some states prohibit age discrimination by smaller employers than those covered by federal law. And, some states even extend age discrimination protections to employees who are under 40.

Common Questions

Q: *We recently promoted a younger employee into a more senior technical position that requires detailed knowledge of a computer application he learned in college. An older coworker has worked at the company for years and says he should have been offered training in the application; if he had been, he claims he would have been the best choice for the promotion. He says this is age-based discrimination. Is it?*

A: *It doesn't sound like it. The company can't make decisions based on a person's age, but can make decisions based on a person's qualifications. Here, the younger applicant was more qualified. While there's certainly nothing to prevent you from offering specialized training to help promote a current employee, you're not legally required to do so (of course, you can't offer the training only to younger workers). And there's nothing to prevent the older employee from seeking that training himself, to increase his career opportunities.*

One part of the ADEA regulates benefits offered to older employees. The Older Workers Benefit Protection Act (OWBPA) prohibits employers from denying benefits to workers age 40 and over. Because it costs more to provide certain benefits to older workers, the OWBPA does permit employers to reduce benefits based on age as long as the cost of providing the benefit to older workers is the same as the cost of providing the unreduced benefit to younger workers. However, this defense applies only to certain benefits and only in certain situations.

SEE AN EXPERT

The OWBPA also regulates the waiver and release of age discrimination claims by employees 40 and older. A release that doesn't meet these requirements isn't valid, and your company can't enforce it. Whenever your company wants to secure a release from any employee, consult with an employment attorney to make sure the release satisfies the OWBPA requirements.

Religious Discrimination

Title VII also protects employees from discrimination based on their religious beliefs. Discrimination based on religion occurs when an employer treats an employee differently, based on religion, or takes action that disproportionately affects employees of a particular religious faith. Discrimination against employees because they don't adhere to a particular, or any, religious faith is also illegal.

An employee's religious beliefs don't have to be associated with a mainstream religion, such as Islam or Catholicism. According to the EEOC, a belief is protected if it is "'religious' in the person's own scheme of things." So long as the belief is "sincere and meaningful," occupies a place in the believer's life "parallel to that filled by ... God," and concerns ultimate issues of life, purpose, and death, it is irrelevant that it might not be affiliated with any particular religious group.

Common Questions

Q: *An employee who describes himself as an evangelical Christian approaches coworkers on breaks to discuss his and their religious beliefs. A couple of employees told their supervisors they're offended. I know we're not supposed to interfere with his religious beliefs, but he's bothering other employees—what about their beliefs?*

A: *You aren't legally required to put up with conduct that offends employees or disrupts the workplace simply because the offending employee's conduct is part of a religious practice. But you do need to examine whether his religious practice can be accommodated in some way that doesn't impose a hardship on your company and its other employees. For example, you could propose that he advise his coworkers that they can come to him to discuss religion during breaks, away from their workspaces. This would permit him to engage in his religious practice but would also prevent him from confronting other employees about religion if it offends them.*

Religious observances are defined broadly as well, and include, for example, attending worship services, praying, wearing religious clothing or symbols, displaying religious objects, adhering to certain dietary rules, proselytizing or other forms of religious expression, or refraining from certain activities.

RESOURCE

Looking for more guidance on what constitutes religious discrimination and how to prevent it? In January 2021, the EEOC issued a revised *Compliance Manual on Religious Discrimination.* You can find this compliance manual on the EEOC's website at www.eeoc.gov/laws/guidance/section-12-religious-discrimination.

Reasonable Accommodations

Under Title VII, an employer has a duty to accommodate an employee's religious practices and observances, as long as doing so doesn't create an undue hardship. An undue hardship means an accommodation that imposes more than a "de minimis," or very slight, burden on the employer. For example, an employer might be required to relax a uniform requirement if doing so wouldn't affect the employee's safety and ability to do the job.

 ## Common Questions

Q: *During the COVID-19 pandemic, the local restaurant chain I own instituted a requirement that all employees receive one of the vaccines. One of my newer servers recently told me that her religious beliefs prohibit her from getting vaccinated. Can we tell her she has to get the vaccine or we will be forced to let her go?*

A: *Whether you may require her to get the vaccine depends on two things: (1) whether her vaccine resistance is practiced as part of a sincerely held religious belief, and (2) whether her request that she be exempted from the company vaccine policy is reasonable and doesn't create an undue hardship for you. If you doubt that her beliefs are sincere or that they are truly religious in nature, you are allowed to ask her for further information that substantiates the practice. For example, if she had rejected getting vaccinated because of health or ethical reasons, rather than because of her religion, you probably don't need to accommodate her request.*

The more common question most employers have is whether the requested accommodation is reasonable. If it's going to create an undue hardship for the company, you do not have to agree to it. Given that a server's job is to serve food and have close contact with both the public clientele and kitchen and floor staff, your restaurant reasonably needs her to be vaccinated. And, because an alternative way to protect your other employees and the public isn't available, her accommodation request would likely be viewed as an undue hardship.

But, while you are within your rights to exclude the employee from the workplace, best practice is not to just terminate her. Be sure to examine all federal, state, and local laws that could apply to this employee.

For more information about your responsibility and rights with respect to COVID-19, review the EEOC's December 2020 guidance. You can find it on the EEOC website at www.eeoc.gov/wysk/what-you-should-know-about-covid-19-and-ada-rehabilitation-act-and-other-eeo-laws.

The EEOC advises employers to "ordinarily assume that an employee's request for religious accommodation is based on a sincerely held religious belief." But, if an employee requests a religious accommodation that you have an objective basis for questioning, either as to its religious nature or the sincerity of a particular belief or practice, you may ask the employee for additional supporting information.

Lessons From the Real World

A cashier's insistence on wearing facial jewelry for religious reasons imposed an undue hardship on her employer.

Three years after being hired by Costco, Kimberly Cloutier began wearing an eyebrow ring. The next year, Costco modified its dress code to prohibit all facial jewelry. Cloutier protested, claiming that her eyebrow piercing was part of her religious belief as a member of the Church of Body Modification, which requires that members display piercings at all times.

After firing Cloutier for refusing to comply with the dress code, Costco offered to let her return if she would cover the piercing with a Band-Aid while at work, an accommodation that Cloutier herself had earlier suggested. Cloutier refused.

The court noted that the accommodation offered by Costco was reasonable, which Cloutier had essentially conceded when she offered it originally herself. The court held that Costco had a legitimate interest in its public image and that exempting Cloutier from the dress code would have imposed an undue burden on the company.

Cloutier v. Costco Wholesale Corp. 390 F.3d 126 (1st Cir. 2004).

Exceptions for Religious Employers

Title VII provides an exception for religious entities, which may limit employment "connected with carrying on its activities" to members of its own faith. In 2012, the U.S. Supreme Court decided that Title VII also includes a "ministerial exception" for religious employers. The Court ruled that the First Amendment bars employment discrimination lawsuits by employees terminated from ministerial positions with religious organizations. The Court's rationale was that requiring a religious employer to keep an unwanted minister to preach its beliefs would constitute government intrusion into church administration, in violation of the Constitution.

Discrimination Based on Disability

Under the Americans with Disabilities Act (ADA), an employer can't discriminate against a qualified employee with a disability. A qualified worker is someone who is able to perform the essential functions of the job in question, with or without reasonable accommodation.

Person With a Disability

Under regulations promulgated by the EEOC, which enforces the ADA, an employee has a disability if that person has a mental or physical impairment that "substantially limits a major life activity" (such as seeing, hearing, breathing, sleeping, reading, standing, sitting, walking, thinking, or learning). A major life activity also includes major bodily functions (such as immune, neurological, digestive, respiratory, eliminatory, and circulatory functions). A major life activity is substantially limited even if the limitation can be mitigated or corrected with medicine or devices (such as diabetes is by insulin treatments).

Employees are also protected if they have a history of such an impairment, or if the employer regards the worker—even incorrectly—as having a disability. So, for example, an employee diagnosed with epilepsy has a history of that impairment, even if the employee hasn't had an epileptic seizure in several years. And, an employee who is openly gay and is treated differently by an employer who wrongly assumes that he is HIV positive faces discrimination because the employer regards him as having a disability.

CAUTION

COVID "long-hauler" employees might be entitled to ADA or FMLA provisions. If an employee suffers long-term health consequences from a prior COVID-19 infection, that employee might be considered disabled under the ADA and entitled to protections under that law. And, even if the employee's "long-haul" conditions might not qualify as a disability under the ADA, they could constitute a serious health condition under the Family and Medical Leave Act (FMLA). You can get more information about your obligations under the FMLA, as well as forms and sample policies, in *The Essential Guide to Family & Medical Leave* by Lisa Guerin and Deborah C. England (Nolo).

Lessons From the Real World

Employer who didn't know about an employee's disability when it fired him for recurrent absenteeism did not violate the ADA.

Antonio Alamillo worked as a locomotive engineer for BNSF Railway. He worked on the "extra board," which required employees to go to work only when called. During the time he was employed, Alamillo missed several calls from BNSF to report for work. After suspending Alamillo twice for absenteeism, the company terminated him. Following the termination, Alamillo received a diagnosis of obstructive sleep apnea, which might have caused him to oversleep and miss work. Alamillo sued BNSF for disability discrimination.

However, the Ninth Circuit Court of Appeals affirmed the district court's granting of BNSF's motion for summary judgment, finding that the company did not violate the law because it did not know about Alamillo's condition when it terminated him.

Alamillo v. BNSF Ry. Co., 869 F.3d 916 (9th Cir. 2017).

Otherwise Qualified

Only qualified people with disabilities are protected under the state and federal laws prohibiting disability discrimination. A person is qualified if that person has the qualifications for the job in question and is able to perform the essential functions of that job with or without accommodation (discussed below). So, the employee has to meet the employer's requirements for the job, including education, skill level, experience, and other merit-based standards. And, the employee must be able to perform the job's basic duties and requirements. As discussed below, if the employee can meet these standards only with an accommodation, the employee is still qualified for the job.

 Common Questions

Q: *I recently interviewed a candidate for the "Action News" videographer job at Channel 2 News here in our city. The candidate told me that he'd recently had a "very close call" while on a heli-ski trip and, as a result of his stress from this scare, he is "disabled" from flying in helicopters. Our Action News video feeds are sent live from our chopper as it flies over the city, checking out calls to the police and fire departments, high-speed chases, etc. The candidate asked very insistently that we accommodate him by letting him work a camera in the studio or live on location on the ground. The problem is that we don't have any openings in either of those positions. Could he make us hire him?*

A: *No. Flying in a helicopter is not a major life activity, and he's only limited from performing the particular job of in-air videographer. Very few jobs actually require an employee to fly in a helicopter—although yours sounds like one of them—so he's not prevented from working more broadly. So, his condition isn't a disability under the ADA. (Check with your company lawyer to see if state law has a broader definition of disability than the ADA.)*

Even if his condition qualifies as a disability, it prevents him from performing an essential job function: flying in a helicopter. Therefore, he likely isn't qualified for the job, as defined by the ADA.

Reasonable Accommodation

A "reasonable accommodation" is a measure that would enable an employee with a disability to do the job in question. Reasonable accommodations can include things like adjusting work hours, installing access ramps, providing special furniture or other work equipment, providing voice-activated software, or providing qualified readers. A requested accommodation is unreasonable if it imposes an undue hardship on the employer, as discussed below.

Lessons From the Real World

A single failure to accommodate leads to victory for an employee.
An Albertsons checkout clerk had cancer of the larynx. As a result of radiation treatment, the clerk suffered from a very dry mouth and drank a lot of water. As a result, the clerk needed to take frequent bathroom breaks, which Albertsons knew about and had agreed to allow after engaging in the interactive process with the employee. One night, the floor lead, who did not know of the accommodation, denied the clerk's request for a break, and the clerk urinated on herself at the check-out stand. A jury awarded the clerk $200,000 for the failure to accommodate her disability, and an appellate court upheld the verdict.

   A.M. v. Albertsons, LLC, 178 Cal.App.4th 455 (2009).

!   CAUTION
    Physical capacity tests violate the ADA. When the accommodation an employee needs includes time off from work, some employers have required returning employees to take physical capacity tests upon returning from leave. While your company might want to make sure that an employee can perform physical aspects of the job after returning from an ADA leave, some courts have viewed such tests as medical examinations, which violate the ADA. Your company is, however, allowed to ask an employee to provide a fitness for duty certification from their doctor, stating that the employee is able to return to work.

Lessons From the Real World

Employer who terminated an employee returning from maternity leave because she failed a physical strength test had to produce names, other "pedigree information," and reasons for firing other employees whom it made take the strength test.

Damina Ochoa worked as a cigarette selector for McLane Company. Ochoa took maternity leave and, when she tried to return to work afterward, McLane made her take a physical strength test. After she failed the test, McLane fired her and she filed a claim with the EEOC for pregnancy discrimination. During the EEOC investigation, the EEOC subpoenaed McLane's records of employees whom McLane required to take the test. McLane produced some information, but not the names, phone numbers, addresses, and other "pedigree information" (such as the employees' Social Security numbers) nor the reasons for termination of those fired after taking the test.

The EEOC went to court to ask that the subpoena be enforced but the district court denied this request. The EEOC appealed the case all the way up to the U.S. Supreme Court, which sent it back to the Ninth Circuit. The Ninth Circuit Court of Appeals then ruled that the lower court had erred in denying enforcement of the subpoena, thus forcing McLane to produce the full information.

U.S. E.E.O.C. v. McLane Company, Inc., 857 F.3d 813 (9th Cir. 2017).

Common Questions

Q: *Our company has a strict policy against employees eating at their desks. An employee who was recently diagnosed with Type 2 diabetes has asked that he be allowed to snack at his desk to keep his blood sugar stable. This seems like a reasonable request, but my boss is worried about other employees demanding to be allowed to eat at their desks. Will we have a problem if we bend the rules for this one employee?*

A: *No. You are not bending the rules; you are following the law. As long as the employee meets the definition of a qualified employee with a disability (and it sounds like he does), this is a reasonable accommodation. Unless they require a similar accommodation, other employees are not entitled to a waiver of your company's rule. As an alternative, you could give the employee permission to leave his desk to snack in private. And you shouldn't explain the reason for the different treatment to other employees; the information is confidential medical information that you aren't allowed to reveal to people who don't need to know it.*

Undue Hardship

An employer doesn't have to provide an accommodation if doing so would create an undue hardship. An "undue hardship" means significant difficulty, disruption, or expense to the employer.

Whether a needed accommodation is an undue hardship depends on several factors, including the cost of the accommodation, the employer's ability to absorb the cost, the impact of the accommodation on the worksite, the size of the employer, and the type of business. For example, a change that might be reasonable and inexpensive for a large employer might be completely impossible for a small employer.

Genetic Discrimination

Federal law bars discrimination on the basis of an individual's genetic information. The Genetic Information Nondiscrimination Act (GINA) prohibits employment discrimination based on an individual's genetic tests, genetic tests of family members, or the manifestation of a disease or disorder in an individual's family members. GINA is not limited to discrimination based on the medical condition of blood relatives; it also includes adoptive children and spouses.

Many states also have statutes that prohibit genetic discrimination, and some of these laws provide more protection for employees than GINA does.

To comply with GINA (and any applicable state laws), an employer should:

- Make sure that company policies prohibit the gathering, use, and disclosure of genetic information.
- Make sure that employee genetic and medical information is maintained in confidential files, completely separate from other employee records, and that access to genetic and medical information is strictly limited to only those who are authorized. Most importantly, ensure that managers, supervisors, and others with authority to make decisions about employees' terms of employment do not have access to such information.
- Include language on forms for employee medical care providers (such as those issued for ADA or FMLA leave requests) warning the providers not to disclose genetic information on the forms. (You can find more information at the EEOC's website, www.eeoc.gov; under the "Employers/Small Business" tab, choose "Genetic Information.")
- Train managers and supervisors on what questions not to ask, what information not to seek, and what not to do on social networking or other sites in order to avoid learning genetic information.

- Make sure any company wellness or other programs do not inadvertently or otherwise violate GINA.

When and How Discrimination Occurs

Discrimination has the potential to taint any stage of employment. This section discusses some of the key points in the employment relationship where discrimination commonly occurs. Chapters 3 and 4 cover the steps you can take at each juncture to prevent it.

Hiring

Discrimination can occur even before the employment relationship has officially begun. Claims brought by applicants alleging that they were discriminated against in the hiring process are relatively uncommon, perhaps because applicants typically don't know who else was in the running or even who ultimately got the job. But, if you give an applicant reason to think that a protected characteristic played a role in your decision, through job postings, interview questions, or otherwise, you could run into some problems. Here are several ways employers, sometimes unknowingly, can create legal liability for themselves in the hiring process:

- **Advertisements.** Language in job descriptions, postings, and advertisements can violate the law. Usually, employers get into trouble by using words that are really codes for certain protected classes, or by including criteria that aren't necessary for the job but that screen out people in a protected class disproportionately (for example, a height requirement for a bus driver, which could screen out women or Asian or Latino men but isn't really a requirement to do the job).

Common Questions

Q: *I handle hiring for a national music publication. We need to hire a photographer. Our CEO has instructed me to post the job on a few websites using the language "recent graduates preferred." I'm a little uneasy about this wording, but he says he just wants to be sure we draw applicants who will "fit in" with the musicians and fans they'll be photographing. Should I push for a rewording?*

A: *Yes. The term "recent graduates preferred" violates the ADEA (29 C.F.R. § 1625.4). Instead, the ad should emphasize the skills you're looking for—it doesn't matter what age the person is, if he or she has those skills. (And perhaps you can gently remind the CEO that preeminent rock photographer Annie Leibowitz is hardly a "tween.")*

- **Applications.** Employers can also cause problems by asking inappropriate questions in their job applications. Applications that ask about an employee's gender, age, disability, or other protected status might seem benign to you, but they raise red flags about whether you are making hiring decisions based on these impermissible factors. For example, it's appropriate for an application to ask for confirmation that a person is 18 years of age or older because employees who are not adults are subject to child labor restrictions. But asking for the applicant's date of birth is not appropriate, because it means you have information that could allow you to make a decision about a person based on age.
- **Screening.** Applications should be screened based on the applicant's ability to do the job. It's important not to focus on protected class information to draw conclusions about an applicant's suitability for the job—even information voluntarily supplied by the applicant, such as membership in clubs or organizations that suggest membership in a protected class.
- **Testing.** While job-related-skills testing is permissible, testing that doesn't serve a job-related function or that is required only of certain applicants raises suspicion. For example, if a company requires only applicants with foreign-sounding surnames to submit a writing sample or requires only applicants with obvious disabilities to show

how they would perform the job's requirements, that requirement would be discriminatory.

- **Interviewing.** It's easy to inadvertently ask an improper question that delves into an applicant's protected status such as age, ancestry, or religious beliefs—even when you're talking to a candidate you like and want to hire. Questions like, "What year did you graduate from college?" or "Where are you from?" might seem like simple conversation starters, but they bring you into dangerous territory, exploring age or national origin, neither of which is probably relevant to the job. Keep interview questions job related. For example, instead of asking, "Do you have child care?" you can simply ask, "Are you available to work Monday through Friday, from 8 a.m. to 5 p.m.?" The best practice here is to avoid asking questions if you are legally prohibited from considering the applicant's answer in your decision making.

 Common Questions

Q: *During an interview, a colleague nonchalantly asked the candidate what her necklace symbolized. The candidate replied that it was a gift from her mother, but she evaded the question and seemed uncomfortable. I happen to know that it is a symbol for a Hindu deity.*

The candidate isn't the most qualified person for the job, and we aren't planning to offer it to her. But in light of what my colleague said here, I'm a little worried about whether this creates an appearance of discrimination. What do you think?

A: *This is a good example of a well-intentioned interviewer going a bit astray. Your colleague probably didn't mean to go into off-limits territory, but that's what happened.*

Even though you'd have preferred that your colleague not bring up the necklace, the error doesn't mean you have to hire the candidate if she isn't the most qualified person for the job. While she's unlikely to challenge your hiring decision, if she does and you have ample evidence that she wasn't selected because she's not the best candidate, you should be in the clear. It sounds like your colleague might need more direction about what kinds of topics are appropriate for interviews, though.

Decisions During Employment

Many employment discrimination complaints arise out of decisions that occur during the course of employment. Unlike job applicants, who know little about the company, how it operates, and how its individual managers and supervisors behave, employees who have been with the company for some time have a basis for comparison. They can more easily recognize when they're being treated differently from their coworkers, and they might have more experience and facts to suggest an improper motive at work.

> **CAUTION**
>
> **Your company might be liable if a biased manager influenced the employment decision.** If your company makes an employment decision that negatively affects an employee, make sure that the decision was not influenced by any manager or supervisor with a discriminatory intent. The Supreme Court has found that if a biased manager's discriminatory intent played a role in the action taken against the employee, the company is liable, even if the actual decision maker didn't know about it or intend to discriminate. Courts have also found that the discriminatory comments of HR managers or supervisors who were not directly involved in making decisions about a particular employee can be introduced as evidence to support the employee's discrimination claim in court. This is one reason why thorough training of supervisors and managers is so important, as explained in Chapter 4.

Discrimination during employment can occur at many stages, such as:

- **Training and mentoring.** Opportunities to advance through training and mentoring should be available to all employees, and no one should be excluded or neglected because of race, gender, disability, or another protected trait. It's easier to recognize overt opportunities, such as which employees are tapped for major training programs, than informal opportunities, such as which employees are invited to socialize with key clients or assist on important projects. However, you need to be aware of both.
- **Job assignments.** Even assignments that employers claim are designed to protect or help employees—for example, not allowing pregnant women to do physically arduous tasks—can be discriminatory,

and they are particularly problematic when tied to promotional opportunities.

- **Benefits and pay.** Pay disparities might be obvious from the beginning, or they could develop over time. Your suspicions should be raised any time two similar employees receive different compensation or benefits. For example, if two employees who started around the same time and perform similarly get different raises or bonuses, that discrepancy should raise a red flag.
- **Performance evaluations.** Performance evaluations or appraisals are a good opportunity to communicate to employees how they're doing and what they can do to improve. However, if you treat employees differently or make any statements that suggest discrimination (for example, noting that an employee who is sporadically unavailable for staff meetings due to a disability is "not a team player"), you could run into trouble.
- **Promotions.** When it comes time to promote employees, decisions should be made based on job-related experience and performance only.

 Common Questions

Q: *A male employee recently complained that his manager always takes a female subordinate out to "mentoring" lunches—the manager's business receipts support this characterization—but none of the other employees in the department get the same treatment. The coworker who gets asked out to lunch is the only woman in the group. A promotional opportunity is coming up, and the employee who came to me wants to apply for it, but he feels like his coworker has an unfair advantage.*

A: *He might be right. The manager's one-on-one mentoring of the only female employee might put everyone else at a disadvantage: They might not acquire the same skills or institutional knowledge, which could affect their promotional opportunities. You need to find out why the female employee is getting this special attention. Absent more information, it appears that the supervisor could be singling her out because she's female. Even if the supervisor's actions have nothing to do with gender, it's not a good managerial practice to play favorites like this.*

- **Imposing discipline.** When imposing discipline, make sure it's done fairly—not just within the department, but within the entire company. Use your company's policies to establish appropriate levels of discipline, then apply these guidelines uniformly.

RESOURCE

Need help creating or implementing a discipline policy? You can find detailed information on tailoring an effective discipline policy to meet your company's needs, along with sample policies, forms, and examples in *The Employee Performance Handbook* by Margie Mader-Clark and Lisa Guerin (Nolo).

Common Questions

Q: *An employee claimed that his supervisor disciplined him for tardiness, while a friend in his carpool has had no such repercussions. This employee is Caucasian, and his friend is Asian. He believes this is race based.*

I looked into it further, and it appears the employee was written up according to company policy. There's no documentation that his friend, who works in a different department and has a different supervisor, was ever late. Should I stand by the discipline?

A: *Before you can make this decision, you have more work to do. If the employee was disciplined according to company policy, the supervisor was doing what he was supposed to. But if another employee in the same circumstance wasn't disciplined, you need to find out why. Because they carpool together, you can assume that they arrive at work at the same time, as long as one of them doesn't routinely make an extra stop (for example, to get a latte or make a five-minute phone call).*

If they both actually start work at the same time, it sounds like the other employee's supervisor either doesn't know what time he arrives or isn't following company policy. As you can see, either one puts the company at legal risk. Even if neither supervisor is making a decision based on race, inconsistent enforcement of the rules leads to poor morale, hard feelings, and, as you've seen, suspicions of discrimination.

- **Development of a protected trait.** The potential for discrimination might also change during an employee's tenure, for example, if an employee becomes pregnant, develops a disability, turns 40 years old, or adopts new religious beliefs.

CAUTION
Customer bias is no excuse. It is no defense to a discrimination claim for an employer to claim that its customers or clients insisted that only employees of a certain race, gender, or religion service them, or that only younger or fully able-bodied employees do. If your company is asked to make such discriminatory decisions by a client or customer, firmly refuse.

The End of Employment

The end of an employee's tenure is the most fraught transition in employment and the one most likely to lead to lawsuits, including allegations of discrimination. Claims might arise out of:

- **Termination, layoff, reorganization, or reduction in force.** Despite your best efforts, employees who are fired or otherwise involuntarily lose their jobs might question your motives. Even if your company has acted in strict compliance with the law, it might have to justify its decision and provide supporting documentation.
- **Resignation.** If an employee is forced to resign because of discriminatory treatment (for example, to escape racial slurs or abuse), that might be viewed as a "constructive discharge"—basically, that the employee was forced to quit because any reasonable person in the situation would have. And even if an employee is not forced to resign, he or she may recover damages suffered during employment as a result of illegal discrimination (such as lost pay due to denial of promotion or compensation for emotional distress).
- **Providing a reference.** To avoid claims that you said something discriminatory or even defamatory (a false statement that harms the employee's reputation) when called by a prospective employer for a reference, you might want to recommend that your company

provide only content-neutral information like the employee's title, rate of pay, and dates of employment. If you adopt such a policy, make sure to apply it consistently to all former employees.

RESOURCE

Want more information on terminations? Terminating an employee can be difficult and can present a number of legal risks. For details on how to end the employment relationship, including entire chapters on making the decision to fire and how to deal with the aftermath, see *Dealing With Problem Employees*, by Amy DelPo and Lisa Guerin (Nolo).

TIP

Conduct exit interviews of all employees who leave the company, for any reason. Ask departing employees whether they feel that they were treated fairly by the company and if not, why not. Follow up any report of unfair treatment as you would a complaint of discrimination, by investigating the claims of the employee as discussed in Chapter 5. If an employee has responded that he or she felt fairly treated, this response can be a useful piece of information with which to respond to a later claim of discrimination.

TIP

Check out employee reviews of your company online to get insight into potential problems. Employees and ex-employees review their employers on several online sites, such as Glassdoor, Indeed, and Vault. Check out your company reviews, especially those written by ex-employees, to see if anyone mentions potential discrimination or harassment issues. While the reviews are anonymous and might not be accurate, you could learn valuable information about employee experiences at your company.

Dos and Don'ts

Do:
- Know which antidiscrimination laws apply to your company.
- Treat employees consistently, fairly, and equally, regardless of their membership in a protected class.
- Provide reasonable accommodations when the law requires you to do so.
- Conduct exit interviews, and investigate any reports of unfairness.
- Give out only neutral employment data to prospective employers.

Don't:
- Set job requirements that aren't tied to the requirements of the position.
- Make decisions—even well-intentioned ones—based on an employee's membership in a protected class.
- Hold different employees to different standards or provide different working conditions to similarly situated employees, unless it's justified by legitimate business demands.

What Is Harassment?

Like the word "discrimination," some people use the term "harassment" loosely, often to describe anything they perceive as unfair or overly critical, from a manager's insistence that all employees arrive at 9 a.m. precisely to a company rule that prohibits employees from using the company postage meter for personal packages. Whether or not you consider rules like these to be sensible, they don't qualify as harassment.

Illegal harassment is a form of discrimination, and it occurs only when an employee is mistreated because the employee is a member of a protected class. Although sexual harassment is probably the most widely publicized form, employees might also be harassed on the basis of other characteristics, such as race or disability.

This chapter explains what constitutes illegal harassment, so you can recognize real problems when they come up and respond appropriately to employee concerns and complaints. It covers:

- which laws apply to your company
- how to identify illegal harassment
- who can be a harasser or a victim of harassment, and
- what doesn't qualify as illegal harassment.

Which Laws Apply to Your Company?

Because harassment is a form of discrimination, the same laws that prohibit discrimination—including Title VII of the Civil Rights Act of 1964 (Title VII), the Americans with Disabilities Act (ADA), the Age Discrimination in Employment Act (ADEA), and the Genetic Information Nondiscrimination Act (GINA) also prohibit harassment. (For more information on each of these laws, see Chapter 1.)

Most states also have laws that prohibit employment discrimination, including harassment. Some of these statutes expressly prohibit sexual harassment, separate from discrimination, and a few explicitly prohibit harassment and discrimination based on other protected characteristics, such as obesity.

If your company is subject to both state and federal law (as many are), it must follow both, which can be tricky because state and federal laws aren't always exactly alike. Here are some of the most significant ways state laws often differ from federal law:

- **Size of covered employer.** As explained in Chapter 1, federal discrimination laws apply to employers with several employees—15 under Title VII and the ADEA, and 20 under the ADA. But state laws might prohibit discrimination—and especially harassment—by smaller employers. For example, in California, even the smallest employers—those with only one employee—are subject to the state's harassment laws.

- **Protected classes.** Many states extend protections against discrimination and harassment to more protected categories than federal law. For example, state laws might prohibit discrimination or harassment based on marital status, medical marijuana user certification, lawful off-duty activity, domestic violence, or stalking victimization. See Appendix A to find out what characteristics your state protects.

- **Amount of recovery.** Title VII limits how much an employee can collect in certain types of damages after winning a lawsuit. While no limit applies to how much the employee can collect in lost wages, a collective limit does apply to the employee's award for compensatory damages (out-of-pocket costs, such as medical bills, and compensation for emotional harm caused by the harassment or discrimination—sometimes called "pain and suffering") and punitive damages (a sum awarded to punish the employer). The limit varies depending on the size of the employer, but ranges from $50,000 to $300,000. Many state laws prohibiting discrimination and harassment do not have similar caps on damages.

- **Training requirements.** Some states require employers to provide antiharassment training, and more states are considering this type of requirement. As a practical matter, for reasons explained in "Avoiding Liability," later in this chapter, many employers provide harassment training to their managers and employees, even if training isn't legally required in their state.

- **Who is a "supervisor."** Federal law and some state laws hold employers liable for harassment by supervisors, high-level managerial employees, or officers regardless of whether the employer knew about the harassment. However, the definition of supervisor differs from state to state. Some states include anyone who has the authority to transfer, suspend, promote, demote, assign duties, impose discipline, or recommend such actions to the decision maker. As a result of this difference, your company might be legally liable for an employee's actions under state law, but not under federal law.

- **Individual employee liability.** Under some states' laws (but not federal law), individual employees who engage in harassment might be *personally* liable for that harassment. So the employee can be sued, and the employee's personal assets will be at stake in the lawsuit.

- **Protection for nonemployees.** Many states extend protection against harassment beyond employees and applicants to other individuals, such as independent contractors.

Your company must follow every law that applies to it. In general, you must follow the rule that is more favorable to the employee. If an employee sues the company, the employee may bring claims under both state and federal law. For example, if an employee in Colorado claims she was sexually harassed, she may be able to file claims under both federal and Colorado law.

SEE AN EXPERT

If your company has employees in more than one state, get some help to figure out your obligations. As noted above, employees are entitled not only to federal protections, but also to the protection of the laws in the state, city, and county in which they work. You should consult a local attorney with experience in discrimination and harassment to make sure you comply with all applicable requirements.

RESOURCE

Looking for a lawyer? Asking for a referral to an attorney from someone you trust can be a good way to find legal help. Also, two sites that are part of the Nolo family, Lawyers.com and Avvo.com, provide excellent and free lawyer directories. These directories allow you to search by location and area of law, and list detailed information about and reviews of lawyers.

Whether you're just starting your lawyer search or researching particular attorneys, visit www.lawyers.com/find-a-lawyer and www.avvo.com/find-a-lawyer.

Common Questions

Q: *My company employs people in several states. I think we should have one company-wide harassment policy. Is this a good idea and, if so, what is the best way to go about it?*

A: *Even though federal law sets out the mandatory minimum level of protection against harassment for employees anywhere in the country, state laws are often more protective. For example, your company might do business in several places, only one of which prohibits discrimination based on personal appearance, like the District of Columbia.*

In this situation, you have a couple of options. Some companies voluntarily commit to protecting employees from discrimination even if they aren't legally required to do so. For example, a company in the personal care products market might want to adopt a policy that prohibits discrimination based on personal appearance, even in states where this isn't a protected category.

This could help your company attract and retain employees, market itself to its customers, and generally build a positive brand. If you do adopt a policy that isn't legally required, however, remember that you'll have to follow it. A court could very well find that your commitment in a handbook is an enforceable contract, giving employees the right to sue if they face discrimination based on personal appearance, even in states whose laws don't recognize personal appearance as a protected category.

If you don't want to commit your company to anything beyond what the law requires, the best way to structure your policy is to make it clear that your company prohibits harassment based on the categories protected by federal law. Then, identify which states or cities protect additional categories. For example, after listing the federally protected categories, your policy could state, "Employees in the District of Columbia are also protected from discrimination and harassment based on personal appearance."

What Is Harassment?

"Harassment" is unwelcome conduct that is a condition of continued employment or that creates an intimidating, hostile, or offensive work environment. But the conduct is illegal only if it is based on an employee's protected status—that is, on one of the characteristics that federal or state law protects. So not all harassing behavior breaks the law. It isn't illegal harassment to berate and belittle all your employees just because you're a mean-spirited person and don't like anyone, for example.

> **CAUTION**
>
> **Just because conduct doesn't meet the legal definition of harassment doesn't mean it's appropriate workplace behavior.** If an employee is being rude to coworkers or a manager belittles every employee on the team, you'll want to put a stop to it. Whether or not this behavior constitutes harassment, it's unprofessional and inappropriate, and should result in discipline. And, such behavior might violate state anti-bullying laws, which the majority of U.S. states have on the books.

Any conduct that meets the definition above is illegal harassment. However, courts have divided harassment into two categories, for which the employer has different levels of legal responsibility:

- **Supervisor harassment that results in a "tangible employment action."** When an employee suffers a tangible employment action at the hands of a supervisor—an actual adverse effect on the job or working conditions, like a firing, demotion, or undesirable transfer—the employer will always be liable for the harasser's conduct. This is true even if your company took steps to try and prevent or correct the behavior, and even if your company didn't know about the behavior (for example, because the employee never reported it). From an employer's perspective, this is the more serious and dangerous type of harassment. You can prevent future problems by taking immediate action as soon as you learn about the problem, but you'll still be held responsible for harassment that's already taken place.

- **Hostile work environment harassment.** If an employee is subject to a hostile work environment, but doesn't suffer a tangible job action like firing or demotion, the employer's liability depends on its response to the situation. If a company can show that it took reasonable steps to try to prevent and correct the behavior, and that the employee unreasonably failed to take advantage of internal complaint procedures to deal with the problem, it may be able to limit or avoid legal responsibility for the employee's complaints, as explained below.

Tangible Employment Action

An employee's job should never be conditioned on submitting to inappropriate workplace behavior but, unfortunately, it happens. And when a supervisor's unwelcome harassing conduct results in a tangible employment action, the employer can be "strictly liable" for the harasser's behavior, meaning the company is legally responsible for the supervisor's act, even if it was unaware of the situation or did everything within its power to prevent harassment. The logic here is that supervisors are agents of the employer and act on its behalf, so the supervisor's actions are seen as the actions of the company.

Problems often arise when a supervisor conditions some aspect of an employee's work—such as getting hired or promoted, getting chosen for plum assignments or opportunities, or just keeping a job—on submitting to the supervisor's sexual advances (traditionally called "quid pro quo" harassment). The conditions don't even have to be explicit—sometimes, they're just implied. For example, if a supervisor begins making sexual advances right before an employee is due for a promotion, the employee could infer that getting the promotion is linked to putting up with the sexual advances.

A tangible employment action is an actual, adverse job effect from the harassment. It includes firing, failing to promote, or any other decision that causes a significant change in the employee's job status. Threats to an employee's continued employment can also be a tangible employment action. And job or duty changes that result in a perceived demotion or less desirable shifts or hours can constitute a tangible employment action.

Sometimes, harassment makes an employee's working conditions so intolerable that any reasonable person would resign. In that situation, an employee can claim he or she was "constructively discharged." If an employee is constructively discharged due to harassment, then the forced resignation constitutes a tangible employment action just like a traditional firing. The idea behind constructive discharge is that it's unfair to require employees to put up with intolerable working conditions.

 Common Questions

Q: *I work in human resources, and I recently saw a manager at my company giving a subordinate a neck massage while he read a document over her shoulder on her computer screen. When I told him in private it wasn't appropriate, he told me that if she isn't complaining, he doesn't think I should either. When I talked to the employee about it, she said she knows the manager likes to do it, it isn't a "big deal" to her, and she doesn't want to "make waves" because she is up for a promotion at her next review. Where, if anywhere, do I go from here?*

A: *You started down the right path. You need to stay on it because it looks like the employee doesn't really welcome the conduct: She tolerates it because, based on the manager's position of authority, she believes it will affect her job prospects. This perception could lead to legal troubles for your company, which can be held strictly liable for the supervisor's behavior if the employee decides to sue. And, it's just not right to tolerate a situation where an employee feels she has to let her manager touch her.*

An employer will be strictly liable for this type of harassment only if the harasser is a supervisor. After all, the threat to the employee's job is real only if the employee believes that the person making it actually has the ability to carry it out. For more information on who qualifies as a supervisor, see "Supervisor Harassment," later in this chapter.

Common Questions

Q: *Because of the "#MeToo" movement and the exposure of sexual harassment by so many celebrities and politicians, our firm is very concerned about potential sexual harassment, or even the appearance of it. At a recent partners' meeting, the managing partner recommended that male partners not conduct one-on-one mentoring with female associates to avoid even the appearance of harassment. Is this a wise practice?*

A: *While the managing partner's concerns are understandable, the suggested approach is not a best practice and could itself lead to a claim of gender discrimination by women denied mentoring opportunities. Instead, here are a few approaches that serve the purpose of preventing harassment but don't violate the law:*

- *Conduct mentoring in a group setting.*
- *Hold mentoring sessions in a glass-enclosed conference room during work hours, rather than behind closed doors or after hours.*
- *Elevate more women to partner.*
- *Have a female partner handle the mentoring.*

And, of course, make sure your firm provides sexual harassment prevention training to everyone annually.

Hostile Work Environment

The more common type of harassment, hostile work environment harassment, doesn't depend on whether the harasser is a supervisor or whether the harassment is based on sex. A hostile work environment is created when an employee is subject to unwelcome conduct that:

- is based on the employee's protected characteristic (such as race or age)
- is so severe or pervasive that it alters the terms and conditions of the victim's employment, and
- creates a hostile or an abusive environment.

Unwelcome Conduct

Conduct is unwelcome if the employee doesn't invite it or want it to happen. It can take many forms beyond touching or slurs. It may include cartoons, photos or other visual depictions, social media posts, comments, jokes, nicknames, symbols, pranks, insults, or gestures. Pretty much any way that people communicate can be a medium for harassment.

Conduct can be unwelcome even if an employee submits to it or puts up with it. Employees might not complain about conduct because they're concerned about not making trouble for the harasser or they're unsure of how to handle the situation, for example. But merely putting up with conduct isn't the same as welcoming it.

 Common Questions

Q: *During a break in a meeting of the IT group I manage, Anna, one of my technicians, told an off-color joke about sorority girls. All of the other techs laughed, including Gerilyn, the only other woman. One of the men then told a slightly raunchier dirty joke and, again, everyone laughed. No one objected to the joking and, after a couple of minutes of banter, we resumed our meeting. Now Gerilyn has complained to me that she felt the jokes were inappropriate and offensive. But, Anna, a woman, started the whole thing, and Gerilyn laughed right along with everyone else. Her complaint seems bogus to me.*

A: *You shouldn't brush this off so quickly. Anna might have started the joking, but she isn't the one complaining (if she were, she'd have a hard time claiming that the next joke was unwelcome). However, Gerilyn didn't tell a joke, and laughing along in a group setting doesn't necessarily mean that she found the joking welcome and not offensive. People go along to get along in group settings, where peer pressure can be strong. Better take Gerilyn's complaint seriously and respond to it appropriately. And the next time you're in a group of subordinates telling dirty jokes, remember that it's much easier to put a stop to it at the time than to wonder whether anyone was really offended by it later.*

Email, Social Media, "Sexting," and More

Statements, gossip, slurs, and photographs that employees post on social networks and transmit via electronic communications, including emails, texts, and tweets, can be considered harassment. Courts and juries have found employers liable for offensive communications even on sites that are operated by a vendor rather than the employer.

It might seem daunting to satisfy the requirement that your company prevent and address harassment on social networking sites or other websites, or in emails, texts, or blog posts, without violating employee privacy. However, court cases provide some guidance. Courts have consistently held that the more related an electronic means of communication is to an employer's interests, business, or functioning, the greater the responsibility the employer has to make sure its employees are not harassed through that medium. For example, an employer must step in if an employee is harassing a coworker via the company intranet. On the other hand, if the employee is making lewd comments about a coworker on a private blog, the employer doesn't necessarily have the same duty to step in. Of course, if the targeted employee or other coworkers learn of the blog posts and begin accessing or discussing them at work, the employer might have to take action because the harassment has entered the workplace.

It is also important to have sound policies in place regarding electronic communications and to make sure that all employees know and understand those policies. We discuss antiharassment policies in Chapter 3 and employee training programs in Chapter 4.

Protected Status

Harassment is illegal only if it is based on the employee's protected status. Many hostile work environment claims are sex based, but that is not the only type of illegal harassment. Harassment may also be based on characteristics such as race, religion, national origin, age, disability, sexual orientation, or transgender status.

Lessons From the Real World

Employer might be liable for harassing comments posted on an Internet bulletin board.

Tammy Blakey, a pilot for Continental Airlines, sued Continental for hostile work environment harassment after some of her male colleagues posted derogatory comments about her on an Internet bulletin board called "Continental Forum," which was administered by CompuServe, an Internet service provider. Continental tried to get the case thrown out of court based on the fact that it did not administer the bulletin board, but the New Jersey Supreme Court ordered the lower court to determine whether Continental was liable for the harassing comments on the site.

The court held that Continental had a duty to remedy harassment on an electronic bulletin board that was not physically located on its premises or even administered by the company, if the site was closely related to the workplace and beneficial to Continental and its employees. The court reasoned that harassment occurring on the site could be regarded as part of the workplace. While recognizing the privacy concerns associated with employer monitoring of employee communications, the court held that employers have a duty to prevent harassment in settings related to the workplace if they know or have reason to know that harassment is occurring.

Blakey v. Continental Airlines, Inc., 741 A.2d 94 (1999).

Hostile conduct doesn't always explicitly refer to the employee or the employee's protected status. Stereotyping, visual images, or inappropriate jokes are just a few examples of behavior that can be based on a protected status, without specifically referring to a particular employee. For example, coworkers who tell racist jokes and post racist cartoons might create a hostile work environment for employees of a certain race, even if none of those employees are the target of the misconduct.

Also, conduct targeting employees in a protected category can still be harassment, even if the harasser "means well." For example, repeated comments to a female employee about her appearance, intended to be complimentary, can be harassing.

Common Questions

Q: *A female sales manager is much harder on female subordinates than male subordinates, often yelling at and berating them. She says she does this because women have a harder time in this business and need to be tougher to succeed. She had a strong female mentor and wants to give her female mentees the same "gift." I see her point, but I'm wondering if I still shouldn't step in.*

A: *You should step in. Her "gift" is going to keep on giving—in this case, giving her female reports ample fodder for a harassment lawsuit. Even though her motives might be understandable, it looks like she is singling women out for particularly negative and potentially harassing treatment, based on gender. She must treat men and women equally.*

Keep in mind that coworkers who share the victim's protected status might also engage in hostile environment harassment. It doesn't matter whether harassers are in the same protected status as their targets. For example, women can harass women and African Americans can harass African Americans.

Lessons From the Real World

Employee who alleged harassment based on her Mexican heritage could go forward with those claims.

Mercedes Hernandez sued her employer, Bank of America, alleging that a manager's demeaning comments about her heritage amounted to illegal harassment. The bank sought dismissal of the harassment claims, and the trial court granted its motion. But, the California State Court of Appeals reversed that decision.

The Court of Appeals held that the manager's comments referencing Hernandez's Hispanic heritage were offensive and sufficiently severe or pervasive to create a hostile work environment to allow the case to go to trial. *Hernandez v. Bank of America*, Case No. B289499 (Cal. Ct. of App. 09/24/2019).

CAUTION

Retaliation is illegal, too. When an employee is retaliated against for making a complaint of harassment, that's also illegal. This is true even if it turns out that there was no illegal harassment taking place, as long as the employee made the complaint in good faith. For more information on retaliation, see Chapter 7.

Severe or Pervasive

Not all "bad" behavior is illegal harassment, even if it is unwelcome and based on an employee's protected status. After all, most employers would be put out of business if they were held legally responsible each time an employee made an inappropriate joke or said something insensitive.

Instead, to be illegal, the conduct must be so severe or pervasive that it "alters the terms and conditions" of the victim's employment. What does that mean? A severe act is one that is extreme, such as a physical assault or the use of a particularly offensive term. Pervasive means multiple, continuous offensive acts. For example, if an employee is teased or taunted daily by her coworkers, that's pervasive. Generally, the more severe the behavior, the less pervasive it must be to meet the definition of harassment, and vice versa. Although one severe act can be enough to be harassment, it's more typical for harassment to consist of multiple offensive acts over a period of time.

But whether conduct actually alters an employee's working conditions can be anyone's guess. After all, one person might think a teasing comment is no big deal; another might find it so distressing that she can't concentrate on her work. To account for these differing perspectives, the law requires the conduct be both objectively and subjectively severe or pervasive. Objective means that a reasonable person in the victim's position, considering all of the circumstances, would find that the conduct created a hostile work environment. Subjective means that this particular victim really did feel harassed.

Lessons From the Real World

A court's finding that offensive conduct has to be severe *and* pervasive to constitute harassment was erroneous and applied the wrong standard.

Victoria Zetwick worked as a correctional officer for Yolo County, California. She sued the County, alleging that the County Sheriff had created a sexually hostile work environment by greeting her with chest-to-chest hugs and attempting to kiss her on the lips. Zetwick noted in her allegations that the sheriff did not hug or kiss male employees. The County filed a motion for summary judgment in its favor, arguing that the sheriff's conduct was "innocuous" and that differences in hugging men and women were genuine differences in the way people interact with members of the same or opposite sex. The district court agreed, finding that the alleged conduct was not "severe and pervasive" and thus did not amount to sexual harassment.

The Ninth Circuit reversed this ruling, finding that the district court had applied the wrong standard. The correct standard for determining if conduct is harassing is whether the conduct is "severe or pervasive." The Ninth Circuit also noted that hugging and similar conduct was not necessarily innocuous.

Zetwick v. County of Yolo, 850 F.3d 436 (9th Cir. 2017).

Common Questions

Q: *A female employee, Kerry, told me that Sterling, a coworker, had started hanging around her desk and asking her out. She declined and he backed off, but a few days ago, he put a love letter on her car. The letter expressed his feelings, but it wasn't sexual. From my point of view, Sterling seems pathetic and harmless, but Kerry is very upset. She told me she'd been attacked getting out of her car several years ago, and finding the note on the windshield reminded her of the assault. Though she feels Sterling's behavior is threatening, it seems to me that she's overly sensitive. Am I wrong?*

A: *Even though you don't think the situation is threatening, Kerry feels it is. You should consider her position as a female victim of an assault that occurred in similar circumstances. Is it reasonable for a woman in that position to be upset when she receives an unsolicited love letter on her car, after making it clear she wasn't interested romantically? From this position, Sterling's behavior could be seen as harassing. At any rate, this behavior is clearly bothering Kerry, and it's not appropriate. She asked him to stop and he needs to do so.*

Avoiding Liability

As explained above, an employer is legally responsible for a supervisor's harassment that results in a tangible employment action. A company is an entity, not a person; it can act only through the people who represent it. A supervisor's actions toward employees are considered to be the actions of the company, from a legal perspective.

In hostile work environment cases, however, your company isn't automatically liable. Even if an employee is subjected to illegal harassment, your company can avoid liability if:

- your company exercised reasonable care to prevent and correct the harassment, and
- the complaining employee unreasonably failed to take advantage of your company's antiharassment policies and procedures.

This is called an "affirmative defense" to the employee's harassment claim: Even if the employee really was harassed and really suffered harm as a result, the company will not be held liable for it. The purpose of this rule is to give the company a chance to correct the situation. An employer that doesn't take action, despite having an opportunity to do so, will be held legally responsible for harassment; an employer that never learns of the harassment may not be liable.

An employer may raise this defense, sometimes referred to as the *Ellerth/Faragher* standard (after the two Supreme Court cases that first established it), only if the following are true:

- the company had an effective policy banning harassment at the time the alleged harassment occurred (this means not only that the company had a policy, but also that the company actually followed its policy), and
- the policy included an effective procedure for employees to report harassment (the procedure must also result in appropriate action by the employer, including an investigation), and
- the employee failed to take advantage of the company's antiharassment policies and procedures, or
- the employee made a complaint, and the company thoroughly investigated the complaint and promptly remedied any harassment found (for example, by imposing discipline on the harasser).

This defense is one reason why it's so important to have an antiharassment policy (see Chapter 3), training program (see Chapter 4), and investigative procedure (see Chapter 5): These measures reflect your company's commitment to preventing and correcting harassment. Once your company has these protections in place, an employee who wants to hold the company liable for harassment has a responsibility under the *Ellerth/Faragher* standard to use the procedures you've established to put your company on notice.

Your company will learn about possible problems more quickly if it has a good policy that encourages employees to report potential violations. In turn, your company will have the opportunity to deal with anticipated problems before they get out of hand, not only protecting your company's interests, but also promoting your employees' interest in a comfortable, harassment-free working environment.

Common Questions

Q: *My company has a written harassment policy that includes a procedure for reporting harassment to any managerial-level employee. One of our employees has filed a complaint of racial harassment with the EEOC, even though he never reported any harassment to me or any other supervisor or manager. The employee claims that he didn't read the policy and didn't know about the complaint procedure. He also says he was too intimidated to report to his supervisor in any event. Are we in the clear on this?*

A: *Maybe, depending on a couple of key questions: Did you have the employee sign an acknowledgment form when he received the policy? If so, it shows he knew or should have known about the policy and had the opportunity to follow it. And does your policy explicitly state that employees may report harassment to any supervisor or manager? If so, his discomfort talking to his own supervisor likely doesn't explain his failure to complain to others.*

Of course, your duty doesn't end there. Now that you know about the complaint, you should promptly investigate. You'll want to make sure the employee's reluctance to report the matter isn't a company-wide concern. That is, you should make sure that employees aren't hesitant to report harassment generally and that this employee's failure to report doesn't reflect a deeper problem with the company's management or culture. And then you'll need to figure out whether there's any basis for his claim.

Who Is a Harasser?

The law imposes a duty on employers to maintain a workplace free of harassment, including harassment by their employees, contractors, and others they hire, or even their vendors, customers, and clients. As explained above, however, the extent of the employer's financial and legal responsibility depends on who's doing the harassing.

Supervisor Harassment

As explained above, when a supervisor takes some tangible action that affects an employee's job, the company is liable for the harassment even if it didn't know about it or tried to prevent or correct it. But the term supervisor is interpreted fairly broadly. For example, you may think a supervisor has to have a certain job title, level of responsibility, or pay. But a supervisor can include any manager, officer, or other employee or agent in a superior position to the employee, or anyone else who reasonably appears to be in a position to grant or deny, or influence the granting or denial of, job benefits to the employee. That includes anyone with the authority to hire, fire, set work schedules, or set pay rates. Some courts also include any employee who assigns work, supervises shifts, or directs employees. And, many states have defined the term supervisor even more broadly, to include, among other things, anyone with the authority to transfer, suspend, assign work to, discipline, or reward employees.

Even if the harasser doesn't actually have the authority of a supervisor, the company can still be held liable if it reasonably appears to the employee that the harasser has supervisory authority. For example, an employee may honestly believe that a coworker who's assigned to head a project can carry out a threat to have her removed from the team if she doesn't comply with his advances. Even if the coworker couldn't actually kick her off the project, he will qualify as a supervisor if the employee reasonably believes otherwise.

A supervisor's empty threats don't constitute a tangible employment action if the employee rebuffs the sexual advances. If a supervisor says he's going to fire an employee if she doesn't submit to his advances, but then doesn't fire her after she turns him down, the employer won't be held strictly liable. However, the supervisor may still have created a hostile work environment, as discussed above, and the company could be liable on that basis. On the other hand, if the employee submits to the conduct because she believes the threat and later alleges harassment, the employer will be strictly liable even if the supervisor didn't actually intend to fire her.

TIP
Review your company's organizational chart to confirm that authority matches job titles. For example, if an employee has the title "vice president" but doesn't really have the authority of an officer, your company might want to change the title to more accurately reflect the employee's authority and prevent confusion among fellow employees.

Lessons From the Real World

An employee's reasonable belief that she had to submit to her boss's advances supported her sexual harassment claim.

Holly D., a financially strapped single mother, worked as a senior administrative secretary for Professor Stephen Wiggins at the California Institute of Technology. Holly alleged that Professor Wiggins made sexually provocative comments to her, stared at her breasts and buttocks, and displayed pornographic websites to her. She asked him to stop and rebuffed his advances. Shortly thereafter, he gave her a negative performance evaluation.

Even though Professor Wiggins never directly or indirectly threatened her job, Holly believed her job could be on the line if she did not submit to his advances. As a result, she alleged, she began a sexual relationship with him. Then, she sued the school and Professor Wiggins.

The trial court found for the school and the professor, but the appellate court reversed the ruling and gave Holly another chance to argue her claims. Holly could go forward with her harassment claim if she could show that a reasonable woman in her position would have "believed that her job depended on fulfilling Wiggins's demands."

Holly D. v. California Inst. of Technology, 339 F.3d 1158 (9th Cir. 2003).

Common Questions

Q: *Our company hired a prominent local lawyer, Jerry Johnson, to work on a complicated merger agreement. Though he insisted on the title "vice president," he doesn't oversee any employees. An employee in accounting overheard Vice President Johnson asking a trans-female employee of ours working with him on the agreement if she "still stood to go number one." I think this might be a problem, but I'm not sure how serious.*

A: *This could be very serious. Because Jerry Johnson is being held out as an officer of the company, regardless of his actual authority, an employee could reasonably infer from his title that he is in a supervisory position. And, as an apparent supervisory employee of your company, Johnson may be creating a hostile work environment and that's a potential harassment problem.*

Finally, supervisors are different from other employees in another important way: In some states, they can be found personally liable for harassing behavior. That means employees can sue them individually, in addition to suing the company, for their behavior.

Coworker Harassment

The law views hostile work environment harassment by the victim's peers or coworkers differently than it does tangible employment action harassment by a supervisor. In general, the best way for an employer to avoid liability for coworker harassment is to take all reasonable steps to prevent it and stop it as soon as the employer knows about it, whether through an employee complaint or otherwise. But don't just close your eyes and assume everything will be okay. Employers are also liable for harassment if they should have known about it because it was readily apparent in the workplace.

An employer should have known of harassment if it is aware of a history of harassment by the same harasser, evidence of harassment is readily apparent (such as where there are pictures, graffiti, or other readily observable conduct at the job site), or supervisors or others with authority have seen sufficient evidence of harassment to trigger a duty to investigate. For example, if a supervisor overheard an inappropriate workplace remark and observed that an employee seemed upset by it, the company has a duty to investigate the situation, even if the employee doesn't make a formal complaint.

Harassment by Nonemployees

Even people who don't work for your company can create a hostile working environment for your employees. Your company has the same responsibility to protect employees from harassment, whether it's committed by employees or outsiders. If you have a client who makes inappropriate comments to female staff members, for example, you will have to put a stop to the behavior. Unfortunately, sometimes the only way to do this is to end the working relationship, because you don't have the same control over outsiders as you have over employees.

Why Supervisors Get Sued

You might be wondering why an employee would ever sue an individual supervisor; after all, unless the supervisor chose to continue working after winning the lottery, the company is likely to have much more money ("deeper pockets," as lawyers say). Two primary reasons generally explain why a supervisor might be dragged into court.

The first is emotional. Typically, the supervisor is the person who actually mistreated the employee, and the employee feels that the supervisor should be held responsible. Employees might want the supervisor to pay, whether in time, money, or stress. Some employees simply want to make sure that the supervisor understands exactly how much damage was done, and requiring the supervisor to sit in the courtroom day after day certainly might accomplish this goal.

The second reason has to do with our federal system of government. An employee can sue under state law, federal law, or both, whether the employee brings the lawsuit in state or federal court. But in some states, the state judges —and juries—are perceived as more sympathetic to employees than those in the federal system. So, employees who have a choice often sue in state court.

Employers can have these cases transferred to federal court, but only if the federal court has jurisdiction over the case. Federal courts don't have the authority to hear every type of case. In discrimination and harassment cases that include state law claims, a federal court can hear the case only if all of the named parties to the lawsuit are from different states (called "diversity jurisdiction"). If any two parties are from the same state, diversity doesn't exist, and the federal court can't take the case.

Back to our supervisor: The employee suing and the supervisor are almost always residents of the same state. So, by suing the supervisor, the employee avoids getting hauled into federal court, even if the company's headquarters or official offices are in another state (as is often the case for corporations, many of which incorporate in Delaware, regardless of where they do business). For more information on lawsuits against supervisors, see "If You Are Sued Personally," in Chapter 9.

Who Can Be Harassed?

Just as many different people within your company can be harassers, many different people can be harassed, too. Behavior doesn't even have to be directed at a particular employee for it to be harassing: Any conduct that affects an employee's working environment could potentially be harassment. For example, if an employee personally witnesses offensive conduct aimed at another employee or group of employees, the witnessing employee might still suffer from a hostile environment. This is true even if the witnessing employee isn't a member of the protected class on which the harassment is based.

Of course, male employees can be the victims of sexual harassment, as well as female employees. And, female supervisors may be harassers, too.

 Common Questions

Q: *A lesbian employee recently reported to her supervisor that she witnessed a male coworker coming on to another female employee and using very lewd, inappropriate language. She said that the female employee didn't seem offended, but as a witness to the behavior, she was offended by it. Do we have to treat this as a harassment complaint?*

A: *You do because the employee was offended by gender-based conduct. It's irrelevant that the employee was neither the target of the conduct nor heterosexual. Because she observed the inappropriate conduct, it can still create a hostile work environment.*

What's more, you don't know for certain that the employee to whom the comments were made really didn't find them offensive. Although the employee who complained didn't think the target was offended, you should talk to the other employee to make sure. And, even if the other employee thought the conversation was harmless, you'll probably want to caution the lewd Lothario that he needs to observe professional standards of conduct at work.

Lessons From the Real World

Employer failed to stop a female employee from harassing a male employee.

Rudolph Lamas worked at a Las Vegas airport as a passenger service assistant for Prospect Airport Services. Another passenger service assistant, Sylvia Munoz, began making sexual overtures to Lamas, passing him love notes at work and telling coworkers of her sexual interest in Lamas. The overtures made Lamas, who was a recent widower at the time, distressed and uncomfortable.

Lamas told Munoz, who was married, that he was not interested and asked her to stop. She continued passing notes and making comments to and about Lamas. Lamas went to his supervisor and asked him to intervene. The supervisor said he did not want to "get involved" in "personal" matters but said he would talk to Munoz. However, Munoz's overtures not only continued, they increased. Lamas's job performance suffered as a result of his stress, and he went over his immediate supervisor's head to his manager and pleaded for action to be taken. Munoz's conduct not only continued, other employees began gossiping that Lamas was gay.

Prospect disciplined and then fired Lamas because of problems with his job performance. The EEOC sued Prospect for sexual harassment on Lamas's behalf. A trial court granted judgment in Prospect's favor. The federal appeals court reversed and ordered the case to trial, noting that Prospect did not take Lamas's complaints seriously enough and did not act to stop the harassment.

EEOC v. Prospect Airport Services, 621 F.3d 991 (9th Cir. 2010).

What Is Not Harassment?

It would be nice if all the complicated situations that lead to harassment claims could be completely banned from the workplace—but it's hard to do in practice. Let's face it—you don't want to create an oppressive work environment where people are afraid to have friendly conversations. And not everyone has the same idea of what's offensive.

Consensual Relationships

Get ready, because you *will* encounter consensual relationships between coworkers in your company. The numbers speak for themselves: According to a survey by vault.com, 47% of professionals report that they have dated at least one coworker and, according to a survey by the American Management Association, 30% of all managers and executive-level employees report that they have dated at least one coworker.

A truly consensual relationship between employees who are not in a reporting relationship (for example, peers who are not in each other's chain of supervision) needn't concern you, as long as workplace repercussions don't happen. But it's often not so tidy. Sometimes, dating employees bring their romance into the workplace with comments, gestures, or the like, which can affect employees who observe the behavior. Relationships that end badly may have consequences at work, as well.

Some employers adopt antifraternization policies prohibiting all relationships between coworkers at any level. Barring coworker dating may seem like the easiest approach. But you must ask yourself this: If you have such a policy, how will you enforce it? In all likelihood, such prohibitions will just lead to secret relationships, reducing your ability to control how employees in those relationships behave. And employees may reasonably feel that such a prohibition infringes on their privacy.

In most cases, your best approach to coworker dating is not to prohibit it, but to make sure employees know that they still have to conduct themselves professionally at work. That means making sure they understand appropriate workplace behavior—for example, that public displays of affection aren't acceptable or that the company's email system is only to be used for work-related purposes. It's prudent to include a general requirement of professional workplace conduct in your company's personnel policies, with examples of violations (such as rude or disparaging comments, unprofessional conduct, public displays of affection, and so on).

Common Questions

Q: *Tony and Kamela work in different departments and report to different supervisors. They are dating and often spend breaks together, in one or the other's cubicle. Employees in neighboring cubicles have reported to me that they often overhear Tony and Kamela talking about their sex life. And others have told me that they've seen the two kiss at work. I've spoken to Tony and Kamela, who both assured me that their relationship is totally consensual. Am I out of the woods here?*

A: *No, because others are being affected by their conduct. You need to talk to Tony and Kamela and tell them in no uncertain terms that they need to cool the public displays of affection and discussions about their sex life in the office. Even if their conduct hasn't yet risen to the level of illegal sexual harassment, it is unprofessional and inappropriate in a place of business.*

When Relationships End

Even the best relationships can turn sour when they end. Sometimes the blowback from a failed consensual relationship between coworkers creates an uncomfortable environment for one of the employees in the relationship, or for their coworkers if the animosity of the former couple spills over into their jobs.

One of the most difficult aspects of a failed relationship is the possibility that one person in the relationship will complain that the other has harassed or is harassing him or her. An employee might deny that the relationship was consensual or complain about being contacted by the former partner. Although these might seem like personal matters for the former couple to resolve, that's not all they are: The hard feelings that might be left behind after a workplace romance ends can lead to harassment claims if either partner is unwilling to let things go. You'll have to step in if one employee complains or if you notice personal behavior that's unprofessional (or worse).

? Common Questions

Q: *I just learned that two coworkers used to be romantically involved. Apparently, the relationship ended, but one of them had hard feelings. He has started to publicly snub her at work, for example, by talking over her at meetings. She's complained about it. Is it harassment?*

A: *He might be creating a hostile environment by showing hostility toward her at work and by interfering with her ability to participate at work meetings. But, even if he isn't, he's creating a distraction and probably not just for the complaining employee. At the very least, you'll have to talk to him and tell him to behave professionally and leave the personal stuff at home. And if further investigation leads you to conclude the behavior is harassing, you'll have to follow your company's policy for handling it.*

Relationships With Subordinates: Proceed With Caution

When a supervisor dates a subordinate, it creates a particularly delicate situation for an employer. The supervisor is in a position to affect tangible aspects of the subordinate's employment, which leaves the door open for serious employer liability. And, of course, even if the supervisor doesn't misuse the position of authority, the relationship can create a sense of impropriety to other employees.

While it's hard to control or prevent coworkers from dating each other, it's much easier—and makes more sense—to prohibit supervisors from dating their subordinates. Courts around the country have upheld such policies in recognition of an employer's legitimate interest in preventing harassment. And your supervisory employees should understand that their positions of authority come with the responsibility to avoid even the appearance of impropriety. Given that they can be held personally liable for harassment in many states, they should be motivated to keep working relationships professional.

If you don't have such a policy and don't want to implement one, we nonetheless recommend that you act immediately when a supervisor and subordinate begin dating. The best approach is to remove the supervisor's authority over the employee, for example, by reassigning the employee to a different supervisor.

Relationships between supervisors and employees don't just affect the two parties involved—they also have an impact on others in the workplace. Even that can lead to legal trouble for the employer. Under some state laws, coworkers of an employee who is intimately involved with a supervisor can claim harassment based on the supervisor's favoritism toward his or her paramour. This type of claim can happen when a coworker doesn't receive the same job benefits as the supervisor's boyfriend or girlfriend and claims it's based on sex. The EEOC has said that this conduct is not only discrimination, but also a form of harassment because other employees might believe that they have to be intimately involved with a supervisor to get ahead at the company.

Conduct That Is Not Related to Work

Conduct that occurs off the job and has no connection to work or the workplace won't subject the employer to legal liability. However, if any connection at all exists between an off-work event or location and the employment, the employer might be liable for harassment that occurs there.

 Common Questions

Q: *A group of account reps and their bosses went out to dinner to celebrate landing a major account. Apparently, a company VP and several employees left together and had an "after party" at a nearby dance club. Now one of the female employees says the VP fondled her during the dancing and grabbed her in a hallway and kissed her. She wants to file a formal sexual harassment complaint under the company policy. We didn't organize or sanction the after party; we didn't even know the team members had gone out until this complaint. Are we responsible?*

A: *Though it might seem unfair, you could be. Because the incident had some connection to the team's work, you will have to accept the complaint, investigate it, and treat it as you would any claim of employment harassment. Your company can argue that it should have no liability if the complaint goes to court, because it wasn't a company-sanctioned or associated event, but this is not a clear-cut case. The wise course is to investigate and respond promptly. Besides, if the VP did what the employee says he did, he needs to be reminded of the risks he creates for the company and himself.*

Even where the alleged conduct doesn't occur at a company function, it might amount to harassment if the off-site encounter between the alleged harasser and the victim is work-related, such as a social get-together on a business trip. The same is true if off-duty conduct spills into the workplace—for example, if an employee brings to work an inappropriate and offensive photograph taken of a coworker in a social situation or posts the photo on his Facebook page and tells all of his coworkers to check it out.

 Lessons From the Real World

An employee's sexual assault by a coworker in a hotel room occurred in a "work environment."

Penny Ferris and Michael Young, both flight attendants for Delta Air Lines, worked a flight from New York to Rome and stayed overnight in a hotel there. While there, they shopped together, and later in the evening, Young invited Ferris to sample a bottle of the vintage wine that he had purchased. Ferris agreed. After one sip of wine in Young's room, Ferris felt dizzy and lost consciousness. She partially awoke to find Young sexually assaulting her; she told him to stop but then blacked out again. Delta had received previous complaints from female employees about Young.

When Ferris sued Delta for harassment, the company argued that the court should dismiss the case because the assault did not occur at work, on duty, or during work hours. However, the court disagreed and found that the assault had occurred in a "work environment."

Ferris v. Delta Air Lines, Inc., 277 F.3d 128 (2nd Cir. 2001).

Dos and Don'ts

Do:

- Know the protected classes in every state in which your company operates.
- Understand the difference between tangible employment action harassment and hostile work environment harassment.
- Consider whether conduct is harassing from the perspective of a reasonable person in the victim's position.
- Determine which employees are supervisors, as that term is defined under harassment law.
- Establish a policy to deal with consensual workplace relationships.

Don't:

- Assume that conduct is welcome just because an employee submits to or puts up with it.
- Hesitate to correct harassing behavior as soon as you know about it.
- Try to police employees' private lives; just be ready to step in if their personal relationships start to adversely affect the workplace.
- Automatically assume relationships (especially between superior and subordinate employees) are consensual.
- Assume that the company won't be liable for harassing behavior that happens off company premises.

Policies Prohibiting Harassment and Discrimination

P eople sometimes do the wrong thing because they don't know that it's wrong—or sometimes because they believe they can get away with it. Wise employers make clear to employees that certain types of conduct cross the line and won't be tolerated. One of the most effective steps your company can take to prevent harassment and discrimination is to develop a clear policy explaining what constitutes inappropriate behavior, how employees can report problems, and how the company will respond.

This chapter explains the benefits of an effective policy. You'll learn what a good policy should look like, with examples, so you can make sure your company's policy will be a powerful tool in preventing harassment and discrimination. And, because a policy works only if employees know about it, this chapter also explains how you can ensure that employees receive the policy and read it.

Benefits of an Effective Policy

Even the smallest company should have a policy prohibiting harassment and discrimination, for a number of reasons. An effective policy helps employees understand appropriate behavior, gives them an avenue for raising concerns and complaints, and shows them that the company takes those complaints seriously.

FORM

Don't have a policy? If your company doesn't have a harassment and discrimination policy, don't worry—you can use the information in this chapter, and the sample policy on this book's online companion page, to develop one of your own. If you already have a policy, don't skip this chapter: Read on to make sure your policy gives your company all the legal protection possible. (For information on accessing the companion page, see Appendix B.)

A good policy provides clear standards of conduct that everyone has to follow, as well as procedures for handling complaints and conducting investigations, ensuring that employees are treated consistently and fairly. Your policy should also tell managers how to handle complaints and incidents, so they don't waste time trying to figure out next steps or deducing what others in the company have done in the same situation. And, once all of your managers and employees understand what harassment and discrimination are, they are more likely both to keep an eye on their own behavior and to notice and report problems, which will go a long way toward helping your company maintain a positive working environment.

Another benefit of an effective policy is that it might provide your company with a valuable defense to lawsuits. As explained in Chapter 2, your company can defend itself in a hostile work environment lawsuit if it can show that it took reasonable care to prevent and promptly correct harassment. And one of the things a court will look at when determining whether your company took reasonable care is whether it had an effective policy in place at the time the alleged harassment occurred.

 Common Questions

Q: *An employee called in today saying she is quitting because a coworker is sexually harassing her by making "daily comments" about her body. This employee never reported the harassment to her supervisor or to me, the HR manager, as our policy says she should. Now that the employee is leaving, do I need to worry about her bringing a lawsuit for this?*

A: *She might consider a lawsuit, but it sounds like your company should be on solid ground. If your policy was clear and given to the employee, she had an opportunity to report the harassment to you before it got so bad that she felt she had to quit. She had more than one avenue for making the complaint and didn't use them. Unless your company has a history of ignoring complaints or a supervisor witnessed the harassing behavior and did nothing to stop it, you should have a legitimate defense.*

Now that you know about the complaint, however, you should investigate. If her coworker really did harass her, you want to make sure he doesn't do it to someone else. And you want to apply your antiharassment policy consistently, which means you should discipline him according to company policy, even if the complaining employee no longer works for you.

While we're on that topic, if you conclude that the employee really was harassed and quit for that reason, you might want to ask her to reconsider after assuring her that you have investigated her complaint and taken appropriate action against the wrongdoer. After all, even though she didn't follow the proper reporting procedures, reinstating her could be an appropriate way to remedy the harm the harassment caused—and allow her to get past this misconduct and back on track.

One final recommendation is to check your policy to ensure that it is clear employees may report harassment to any manager or supervisor if they're uncomfortable reporting to the HR manager.

In a discrimination lawsuit, an effective policy can show that the company made a good faith effort to prevent discriminatory behavior from occurring. Under federal law, that good faith effort means the company won't be held responsible for punitive damages—damages intended to punish the employer for bad behavior—even if it is found to be legally responsible for the discrimination. This is sometimes referred to as the *Kolstad* defense, after the U.S. Supreme Court case that first recognized it.

Elements of an Effective Policy

The exact language of your policy will depend on your company's culture and industry, but all good policies have a few elements in common. An effective policy should do all of the following:

- **Establish that the company is committed to preventing harassment and discrimination.** The fact that you have a policy shows this commitment, but you should also come right out and say it explicitly. A primary policy goal is to inform employees of the company's sincere intent to keep inappropriate behavior from occurring in the first place. So, start with a firm, clear statement that the company doesn't discriminate and won't tolerate any harassment or discrimination (sometimes referred to as a "zero tolerance" policy).

Sample: Company Commitment

The Company is committed to providing a workplace free of discrimination and harassment for all employees and employment applicants. The Company has a policy of zero tolerance for discrimination and harassment, which means that we will not tolerate workplace discrimination or harassment of our employees by any coworker, company officer, manager, supervisor, contractors, vendors, customers, clients, or other person.

- **Explain whom the policy covers.** Your company's policy should list all applicable protected categories—that is, the characteristics, such as race, gender, sexual orientation, and transgender status, that can't legally be the bases for employment decisions. In addition to the categories that federal law protects, be sure to include categories protected under applicable state and local laws (city or county ordinances), such as marital status or receipt of government benefits. If a category is protected only in certain states where you operate, you can include a supplemental statement that lists the states in which the category is protected. For example, you could say, "Employees in California and Colorado are also protected against discrimination and harassment based on their status as a victim of domestic violence." Be sure to monitor changes to the discrimination and harassment laws in each state in which you have employees and update your policies to reflect those changes.

TIP

Check state laws. To find a handy chart of state-by-state antidiscrimination and harassment laws, go to the National Conference of State Legislatures website (www.ncsl.org), search for "State Laws on Employment-Related Discrimination," and follow the link.

- **Inform employees of prohibited conduct.** In addition to saying that harassment and discrimination are illegal and won't be tolerated, your policy should give actual examples of prohibited behavior, such as slurs, insults, commentary, cartoons, pictorials, or symbols that denigrate any protected status or anyone in a protected category. This will help employees understand more fully the types of conduct you're trying to eliminate. The policy should make clear that these are just examples, however—you can't reasonably list out every potentially harassing or discriminatory act.
- **Identify prohibited conduct outside the traditional work environment.** As mentioned in Chapter 2, employees must be instructed not to send or post offensive comments via emails, blogs, texts, Twitter, or other social media or Internet services. Employees should be instructed that behavior at work-related events, even offsite, must not cross the line, either. Most importantly, managers and supervisors should be instructed not to "friend" subordinates (or vice versa) and to carefully monitor all electronic communications and posts to avoid violating company policy.
- **Alert employees to any monitoring.** Tell employees in writing if your company monitors certain types of communications for particular policy violations (such as the posting or sharing of confidential, proprietary information; and of harassing commentary or pictorials regarding any coworker, contractor, vendor, customer, and so on).

CAUTION

Don't ask for employee passwords to personal social media accounts. Some companies have begun asking for applicant and employee passwords to personal Facebook accounts, Twitter accounts, Instagram, and other social media sites so that they can review any posts, photographs, or other information supplied by that person. Nearly half of U.S. states have passed legislation barring employers from requiring applicants or employees to disclose usernames and passwords to, or otherwise allow employers to access, their private electronic or social media accounts. Many states are considering similar bills. Because this area of law is rapidly changing, you should check with your company's lawyer before deciding whether and how to access employee's social media pages.

Sample: Prohibited Conduct

All discriminatory or harassing acts, behavior, and conduct are prohibited, including, but not limited to, comments, jokes, gestures, unwelcome physical contact, drawings, cartoons, videos, emails, texts, namecalling, slurs, or use of derogatory terms directed at anyone's race, color, national origin, religion, sex (including pregnancy, sexual orientation, and/or transgender status). Prohibited sexual harassment includes all of these prohibited actions as well as other unwelcome sex-based conduct, such as unwanted sexual advances, requests for sexual favors, or sexually suggestive gestures, jokes, and propositions. Such conduct is prohibited whether it occurs in person; via email, text, or instant messaging; or on social media sites. These lists are intended as illustrations only. Conduct not listed may be considered discriminatory or harassing if it otherwise meets the definition above.

- **List the types of employment decisions that cannot be based on any protected status,** such as hiring, firing, layoffs, discipline, and granting or denying raises, promotions, leaves, work assignments, or transfers. Also make clear the list is not exhaustive and that discrimination in any aspect of employment will not be tolerated.
- **Set the company standard for how employees are to be treated.** A good policy clearly states that employees can expect a workplace free of harassment and discrimination and that the employer will work to make sure this happens. It's also a good idea to include a general statement about standards of conduct, specifying that all employees are expected to act professionally and treat each other with respect at all times.
- **Advise employees of the repercussions of failing to meet the standard of behavior.** The policy should make clear that prohibited conduct will not be tolerated and can result in disciplinary action, up to and including termination. Reiterate that employees might also face discipline, including possible termination, for failing to act professionally and respectfully, even if their conduct doesn't amount to harassment or discrimination.

- **Include the company's employee complaint procedure.** As covered in more detail below, the policy should explain how employees may report violations, including a statement identifying the managerial employees to whom employees may report prohibited conduct. This should include the human resources manager, if any, and any other managers whom your company deems appropriate. Be sure to give employees more than one person to bring complaints to, in case that person is the one accused of misconduct. The policy should also make clear that the procedures will be applied consistently to all employees.
- **Describe the investigation process.** Give a general outline of the steps that the company will follow in response to reports of violations; this is covered below.
- **Assure confidentiality to the extent possible.** Inform employees that the company will disclose any complaints only to those who have a need to know and will otherwise keep the complaint and related information confidential. Caution, however, that complete confidentiality can't be guaranteed.
- **Make clear that retaliation is prohibited.** In a direct, firm statement, inform managers and employees that those who report possible violations will not be subject to retaliation and that retaliatory conduct of any kind will not be tolerated.

Sample: Retaliation

The Company will not engage in or tolerate retaliation against any employee who makes a good faith complaint or participates in an investigation of prohibited discrimination or harassment, regardless of the outcome of the investigation. If any employee believes that he or she is being subjected to any kind of negative treatment because of making a complaint, assisting in a discrimination or harassment investigation, or filing an administrative charge or lawsuit alleging discrimination or harassment, the employee should report the conduct immediately to his or her immediate supervisor, the Human Resources Director, any department head, or any Company officer.

Common Questions

Q: *Our small start-up has grown to a staff of 30. The founders are very progressive and promote diversity and tolerance. We've never had an employee complaint, and we have an open-door policy so employees can freely take concerns to their supervisors. Do we still need a written antiharassment and antidiscrimination policy?*

A: *Yes. A written policy ensures that all employees are held to the same standard of behavior, know what is expected of them, and know that they can expect the company's support if they feel harassed or discriminated against. Your current method of dealing with potential problems doesn't provide any standards: No one, including your supervisors, will know exactly what the company expects them to do if someone complains, which can lead to inconsistent (and therefore confusing) responses to complaints.*

Just because you haven't heard a complaint doesn't mean one isn't lurking. Because you don't have a policy, employees might be unsure what to do in the face of a problem. Without clear guidance, they could opt to go straight to the state's fair employment agency without trying to resolve the problem internally. While normally, employees can be expected to go through company procedure first, this isn't the case if there is no stated procedure.

Finally, it really doesn't matter that you think the company's founders support diversity and tolerance or that there have never been any reported problems. Neither of these facts will protect your company if it is sued. And, even if you're right, that doesn't mean that there won't be problems in the future, as new employees come on board and the founders move on to other endeavors.

Complaint and Investigation Procedures

Many companies have a policy stating simply that harassment and discrimination are prohibited, and nothing more. To make your policy effective, however, the company must enforce it by promptly responding to and investigating complaints. That's why your policy must describe the complaint process, including how employees may report possible violations, what the company will do in response to a complaint, and how the company will investigate.

Complaint and investigation procedures are the key to your company's "on the ground" response to harassment and discrimination. After all, you can't resolve problems until you know about them, through employee complaints or reports from managers who witness potentially inappropriate behavior. Your complaint procedure will encourage employees to come forward as soon as possible and tell managers exactly what to do if they receive a complaint or learn about misconduct.

You can't just take action on the basis of a complaint, though: You need to know all the facts before you can decide what to do. This is the purpose of the investigation procedures. It gives employees a general idea of what to expect when they make a complaint, and it makes clear that your company intends to get to the bottom of every complaint.

Of course, once you put these procedures in your policy, you must follow them. If you don't, you might lose the opportunity to find out about problems early on, because employees will come to believe that you don't take complaints seriously. You'll also lose the opportunity to defend your company by claiming that an employee who files a lawsuit should have taken advantage of your internal complaint procedures. If you don't enforce your policy, a court will likely find that the employee's failure to use it was justified.

The Complaint Process

The complaint portion of your policy should describe:

- **Where to report violations.** As already explained, an effective policy absolutely must tell employees how and to whom they should report violations. Choose more than one person to receive complaints, so employees will have somewhere to go if they have a complaint about one of the designated complaint takers or if they just aren't comfortable talking to a particular person. Never require employees to report violations to their own supervisor or manager. In harassment and discrimination cases, the employee's direct supervisor is often the very person accused of wrongdoing. A good approach is to identify several individuals to whom employees can report possible violations to, including the human resources manager or department (if you have one).

Sample: Complaints and Reporting

Any employee who experiences or observes any incident that he or she believes might constitute discrimination or harassment should immediately report the incident to his or her direct supervisor, the Human Resources Director, any department head, or any Company officer.

Managers or supervisors who observe, learn of, or receive complaints of possible discrimination or harassment must promptly inform the Director of Human Resources.

 Common Questions

Q: *I'm the VP of my company, and I'm responsible for handling all of the HR issues. The only person above me in the company hierarchy is the president. I'm drafting our complaint procedures, and I need to decide where employees should go if they don't feel they can complain to me. The president told me she doesn't have time to deal with personnel issues (that's why she hired me, as she puts it). Who else can handle a complaint?*

A: *As you rightly note, the complaint procedure must give employees the option to report violations to someone else if they don't feel comfortable reporting to you. Even if the president isn't available to take complaints directly, any other company executive who reports directly to the president can take on this task, which prevents any appearance of impropriety because you won't be in the chain of command.*

However, the president needs to understand that she might eventually need to be involved in handling complaints, against you or others, in order to protect the company from legal liability.

- **Confidentiality concerns.** Your policy should make clear that complaints will be kept as confidential as possible. Often, it won't be possible for you to keep all of the information in the complaint, or the complaining employee's identity, secret. The accused employee should have the opportunity to respond to the allegations, which will require you to provide some details. In addition, you can't conduct meaningful witness interviews without revealing at least some of the information in the complaint.

 Common Questions

Q: *An employee reported that he saw his male boss grab and kiss a female coworker after she closed a major deal. According to the employee, the female coworker had a "creeped-out" expression on her face during the incident. The reporting employee doesn't have any problems with his boss, and he doesn't want to seem like a snitch, so he asked me not to reveal his identity. I plan to talk to both the boss and the woman he kissed. How can I avoid revealing the male employee's identity?*

A: *It's a good idea to respect confidentiality to the extent practical. Employees will feel more comfortable bringing problems like this one to your attention if they know you're not going to be sharing the details at the water cooler.*

In a situation like the one you've described, it's perfectly reasonable to keep the employee's identity confidential—for now. You can simply tell both the boss and the coworker that someone reported seeing this inappropriate activity. Who saw it isn't important at this juncture; what is important is whether it occurred and how the alleged victim felt about it.

Investigation Procedures

In addition to explaining the complaint process, your policy should briefly describe how your company will investigate complaints. You don't need to provide every detail of the process, because every complaint is different, and your company needs flexibility to respond to each particular situation. Instead, your purpose here is simply to tell employees what to expect after making a complaint, so they'll understand how the process works and see that the company takes complaints seriously. This part of the policy also tells other employees who might be involved in a complaint—such as potential witnesses or those accused of misconduct—what to expect in the investigation stage.

Though procedures might vary from company to company, effective procedures include several important elements, including:

- **A neutral investigator.** Your policy should state that the investigation will be conducted by an unbiased third party, someone who is not involved in the situation at hand. Many companies have human resources staff conduct investigations; some companies train supervisors or managers to handle these tasks, while others hire consultants or outside lawyers to conduct investigations. Although the latter approach is more expensive, it might make employees feel more confident that the person performing the investigation really *is* neutral.

> CAUTION
>
> **Don't plan on hiring the same attorney to investigate and defend against an employee complaint.** If you hire a lawyer to investigate a complaint, consider hiring someone else if the case lands in court. Some courts have found that the work done by a lawyer acting as an investigator isn't protected by attorney–client confidentiality laws, which can lead to problems in the courtroom. Your company probably will want to reveal the investigation's results to show that you met your obligation to conduct a thorough, fair review. On the other hand, you probably don't want your lawyer to have to take the stand in the middle of trial to testify about the investigation. Make sure you know the rules in your state—or are willing to hire a different attorney to litigate the case—before hiring your usual employment attorney as an investigator.

- **Interviews and other investigative procedures.** Your policy should explain that the investigator may talk to the complaining employee, the accused employee, and any others who might have relevant information, such as witnesses. The policy should also state that these interviews will be conducted separately and privately. Likewise, you should briefly mention other steps you may take to investigate—for example, reviewing emails or talking to clients or other outsiders.

- **Corrective action.** Your company also has to tell employees what will happen at the end of an investigation. For example, the policy should explain that appropriate disciplinary action will be taken if the investigation reveals that an employee violated company policy. Don't limit the type or extent of discipline that may be imposed; this could inhibit your company's ability to respond appropriately to each situation as it comes up. A good approach is to state that appropriate discipline, up to and including termination, will be imposed.

 Common Questions

Q: *After being disciplined for tardiness several times, an employee complained that the supervisor who disciplined him had made discriminating "racial comments." No other complaints have been made against this supervisor, no witnesses to the alleged comments, and one of the employee's coworkers told me that the employee had threatened to make the supervisor "sorry he messed with me." I think this employee made the complaint up to get even with the supervisor and needs to be disciplined, but I'm worried he might claim he's being retaliated against. Am I safe?*

A: *Not until you perform an investigation and find out what actually happened. You're right that an employee is protected from retaliation by a supervisor when he reports a claim of discrimination—and that can be true even if the complaint is unfounded. But there's a catch: Even an unfounded complaint must be made in good faith, meaning the person making it believes it to be true. Trying to sabotage a supervisor doesn't fall within this rule, so disciplining the employee wouldn't be retaliation if you can show that he acted to get even with the supervisor.*

However, even with the coworker's statement, that can be hard to prove. You're better off making sure you fully investigate the alleged victim's claim and reminding everyone that retaliation is prohibited. At a minimum, you must ask the reporting employee if he made the "he'll be sorry" remark. If he did (and if the investigation reveals that the complaint was groundless), warn the employee that a false accusation can lead to discipline.

Sample: Investigation Procedure

The Company will immediately investigate all alleged complaints of discrimination or harassment. All complaints will be handled as confidentially as possible by a neutral investigator appointed by the Company. The investigator will take all necessary steps to ensure a complete investigation, including interviewing employees or others who might have relevant knowledge and reviewing physical evidence related to the complaint. When the investigation is complete, the Company will take corrective action as described in this policy, if appropriate.

Communicate the Policy to Employees

Of course, even if your company has a great policy in place, it won't do any good if employees don't receive, read, and understand it. Employees won't know what's expected of them, where to go with complaints, or even what conduct is prohibited. And that could mean big trouble for your company because, if an employee files a lawsuit without reporting it to the company first, you'll have a hard time arguing that he or she should have relied on a company policy that wasn't clear and readily available.

Use Acknowledgment Forms

Make sure that all employees receive a copy of the complete policy. The easiest way to do this (and to have a record that it was done) is to include the written policy in the employee handbook, then ask all new employees to sign a form acknowledging that they have read and understood the policy. Keep that signed acknowledgment form in each employee's personnel file. If your company distributes its handbook and policy via its intranet or otherwise makes such documents available electronically, create a dialog box or another electronic confirmation form for employees to click to indicate that they have read and understood the policy.

FORM

Need an acknowledgment form? You'll find a sample acknowledgment form in this book's online companion page; see Appendix B for more information.

Reinforce the Policy in Other Ways

We all know that employees sign forms (usually quite a few forms) when they're hired, often without reading every word. So you might want to do more to ensure that employees know about and understand the policy. You have several good opportunities to reiterate the policy's message:

- **Training.** If your company conducts regular diversity, antiharassment, or other training for its employees, this is a prime opportunity to redistribute and discuss the company's policy. Training is covered in Chapter 4.
- **Performance evaluations.** Managers can remind employees of the policy during performance evaluation sessions and ask them to review it at least annually. A box on the written evaluation form can indicate that this was done and record the date.
- **Annual reminders.** Calendar an annual company-wide email or memo reminding everyone about the policy and send it every year at the same time. Make sure managers know that they should direct employees to the handbook or the human resources department when issues or questions arise.

Lead by Example

A policy is just words on paper without actions to back it up. You are in a key position to show managers and employees how the words translate into reality in the workplace. In addition to always meeting the standard of professional, collegial behavior, keep an open door (and open eyes) so that you're aware of what's going on in the work environment. If you learn of potential violations or even of conduct that might start to move in that direction, step in early to address the situation before it escalates into a real problem. And always make yourself available to employees who have questions, concerns, or complaints.

Common Questions

Q: *Our company has an antiharassment and antidiscrimination policy that prohibits offensive conduct and requires employees to follow the Golden Rule. Jamie, who's responsible for HR matters at our company, overheard Mark say to his peer David, "You're just having a blonde moment." Other employees were working with them, including two women. David laughed in response. One of the female coworkers also laughed, but then said, "Hey Mark, that's sexist." Another male coworker piped up with "or maybe racist." Then the employees all laughed. Jamie figured it was just good-natured ribbing and shrugged it off. He didn't take any action or talk to any of the employees involved regarding the incident. Are we in the clear on this?*

A: *Not quite. Jamie should have spoken to all of the employees present individually to see how they felt about the remark because Mark's statement might violate the company's standard of behavior. It's not too late, however, so step in and talk to all present to make sure that no one was offended or uncomfortable. And, if any employee present says yes, follow up with Mark and instruct him not to engage in such banter in the future.*

Review the Policy Regularly

Congress, legislatures, governmental agencies, city councils, and the courts make frequent changes to harassment and discrimination laws and regulations. A relatively recent example is the U.S. Supreme Court's extension of Title VII protections to gay and transgender individuals in 2020. Protected categories are added, new violations are recognized, and employer and employee obligations change as the law develops to address issues that arise in an increasingly diverse workforce.

As a result, your company's policies can become outdated and inadequate if you don't revise them to incorporate developments. Meet with your company's employment lawyer at least annually to go over the policy and make sure it's current. An outdated policy is almost as bad as no policy at all. It doesn't serve the purposes of setting standards for employees that comply with the law, informing employees of their rights and how to assert them, and protecting the company's interests. Worse, it can give the impression that your company makes only a superficial, half-hearted attempt to prevent harassment and discrimination—that it's all show and not a very good one at that!

Keeping your company's policy up to date is part of your commitment to create a workplace free of discrimination and harassment.

Dos and Don'ts

Do:

- Make sure your company's written policies, especially the complaint and investigation procedures, comply with the law and are consistently applied.
- Distribute the policy to all employees, and make sure they acknowledge, in writing, that they have read and understood it.
- Ensure that human resources personnel, supervisors, and managers all follow the company policy for receiving and investigating employee complaints.
- Prevent harassment and discrimination by leading by example.
- Intervene early whenever you learn of possible harassment or discrimination and urge other managers to do the same.
- Maintain an "open door/open eyes" approach so you can learn of problems as soon as possible.

Don't:

- Hesitate to push for a strong policy. Your employer is relying on you to make sure the company is protected.
- Assume supervisors and employees are familiar with the company policy just because it's in writing and available to them.
- Forget to review the company policy regularly to make sure it complies with the law.

Training

Most employers today know that creating an effective policy prohibiting harassment and discrimination isn't enough to protect them or their employees. Employees might not fully understand what's written on a piece of paper; they need more context to understand how issues play out in the real world.

That's where training comes in. You might have already been trained in this area, particularly if you work in one of the states that requires it. Even if you don't, however, your employer might choose to provide this type of training to help protect employees from inappropriate conduct and to reduce the likelihood of complaints and lawsuits.

Benefits of Training

Federal law generally doesn't require employers to train employees in harassment or discrimination prevention. In some cases, however, a company might be required to provide training as part of a settlement of an EEOC charge or a lawsuit. And, a few states require employers to provide at least certain employees with sexual harassment training—currently, California, Connecticut, Delaware, Illinois, Maine, and New York. And, some cities also require training.

Training offers a number of valuable benefits. It establishes standards of acceptable and appropriate behavior, and it tells employees how to proceed if they think they've experienced harassment or discrimination. It also reinforces the message that the company is serious about preventing and correcting violations, which both communicates your company's commitment to employees and bolsters your company's ability to defend itself from lawsuits. If there has already been a workplace incident, training can help defuse the situation and alleviate stresses employees could be feeling.

Some employers resist training employees because it costs time and money, without an immediately apparent benefit to the business's bottom line. However, investing in training is a cost-effective preventive measure that protects both employers and employees from the greater damage (in terms of money, emotions, and productivity) that harassment or discrimination can inflict.

By training supervisors, an employer prepares its frontline responders to watch for, prevent, and address potential problems early and effectively. This will promote a work environment that's comfortable, functional, and compliant with the law. By training employees, an employer gives everyone the information they need to meet company standards of conduct and to report any violations they observe to the appropriate managers. As discussed in Chapter 3, your company can take advantage of the legal defenses afforded by having an effective policy only if employees are informed of the rights and obligations the policy contains.

 Common Questions

Q: *My company operates in a state that doesn't require harassment training. Some members of the board of directors want us to institute it anyway, mostly as a PR device. I'm concerned that it might backfire by making it look like we have a problem when we don't and also that it is an undue expenditure at a time when our budget is tight.*

A: *Because training can help the company defend itself in a lawsuit by showing that you took steps to prevent and correct illegal behavior, your company has a very good reason to conduct training even absent any existing problems. Also, training will help supervisors recognize and resolve problems and this, in turn, will help your company promote a healthy workplace and avoid lawsuits. Finally, training is more likely to enhance than hurt your company's image. It shows that the company is committed to preventing harassment and discrimination complaints—not just reacting to them.*

Although it makes sense to train everyone, supervisors and employees should receive some of their training separately. Because the law confers more responsibility—and liability—on supervisors, and because supervisors are responsible for acting on your company's behalf, they will need more detailed information about what the company and the law expect of them in their managerial capacity. However, general information about harassment and discrimination can be conveyed in a joint training session for both supervisors and employees, with the two groups receiving additional training in separate sessions.

State Training Requirements

You can find a summary of each state's laws prohibiting discrimination in Appendix A. Here is a quick rundown of the training provisions in several states that currently require it:

- **California:** Employers with 50 or more employees must provide two hours of interactive (question and answer format) harassment training by "qualified" trainers (typically employment lawyers or HR professionals) every two years to all supervisors. Employees newly hired or promoted to supervisory positions must be trained within six months. Employers must retain records of trainings for at least two years. As of January 1, 2015, harassment training in California must include "prevention of abusive conduct," which is defined as conduct in the workplace that a reasonable person would find hostile, offensive, and unrelated to the employer's legitimate business interests. Abusive conduct does not need to be based on a protected characteristic and includes insults, derogatory remarks, verbal abuse, and threatening or humiliating physical conduct of any kind, regardless of the reason. (Cal. Gov't. Code § 12950.1.)

- **Connecticut:** Employers with 50 or more employees must provide two hours of sexual harassment training to all supervisors. Employees newly hired or promoted to supervisory positions must be trained within six months. Retraining is encouraged (but not required) every three years. Qualifications of trainers are not specified. Employers are encouraged to retain records of trainings, but not required to do so. (Conn. Gen. Stat. Ann. § 46a-54(15)(B).)

- **Delaware:** Employers with at least 50 employees must provide "interactive training and education to employees regarding the prevention of sexual harassment." Training must be provided to all employees within one year of hiring and every two years thereafter. Training must include direction on how to contact the state Department of Labor. Supervisors must be trained on their specific responsibilities to prevent and correct harassment and on the legal prohibition against retaliation. (Del. Code. Ann. tit. 19, § 711A.)

State Training Requirements (continued)

- **Illinois:** Illinois employers must provide annual sexual harassment prevention training to all employees; restaurants and bars must establish and disseminate a written policy on sexual harassment prevention training and provide "supplemental" sexual harassment prevention training. Training must be provided to all employees at least once each year. The State of Illinois has developed a model training program for employers to use. (Ill. Comp. Stat. § 5/2-109.)
- **Maine:** Employers with 15 or more employees must provide sexual harassment training to all new employees within one year of hire. No retraining is required. Qualifications of trainers are not specified. No records are required. (Me. Rev. Stat. Ann. tit. 26, § 807(3).)
- **New York:** Every employer in New York must provide interactive sexual harassment training to all employees once each year. The New York State Department of Labor and Division of Human Rights developed a model training program for employers to use. (N.Y. Exec. Law § 201-g.)

TIP

Put your training program in writing. If your company will require training, whether to comply with state law or on its own initiative, it's a good idea to put the training policy in writing—in fact, some states require it. The policy should set out who is required to attend, how often training will be required, who will conduct the training, and what topics will be covered. This policy will help you ensure that your company's trainings are consistent over time, and it will tell employees what to expect from the training program.

Combined Training Session for Supervisors and Employees

The content of training programs will vary depending on the law governing them (if any), who provides them, and what format they're presented in. Regardless of minor variations in content and style, however, a good training program must hit the highlights, which include:

- **The laws prohibiting harassment and discrimination.** Supervisors and employees alike need to understand which laws apply; these laws are the foundation of employee rights and employer responsibilities.
- **What harassment and discrimination are.** All supervisors and employees need to know what types of conduct are prohibited, so that they know what not to do and what kinds of behavior they should report.
- **Which characteristics are protected.** Your training should tell employees which traits (such as religion or disability) are protected under applicable federal, state, and perhaps local law.
- **When and how harassment and discrimination might occur.** The best training puts information in context, by providing examples of the ways that bias or inappropriate conduct might come up in the workplace.
- **Company policy.** Training gives you a great opportunity to go over the company's policy (see Chapter 3) and to reiterate that violations will result in discipline, up to and including termination.

Separate Sessions

In addition to a combined training session covering the topics discussed above, supervisors and employees also need separate training. Supervisors and employees have different roles in the company regarding harassment and discrimination. Supervisors represent the company and act on its behalf. So they should receive special training on what to do if they see misconduct, how their actions (or failure to act) can expose both themselves and the company to legal liability, and what to do if they receive a complaint. Employees, by contrast, need to know how to make a complaint and how the company will respond.

Supervisor Training

Supervisors have a special role to play in preventing and addressing potential violations by other employees. They are the eyes and ears of the company, and many antiharassment and antidiscrimination policies direct employees to report violations to supervisors. And, supervisors might not only face personal liability for their own actions, but also create liability for the company. Supervisors need training tailored to these special responsibilities.

In addition, California, Connecticut, Delaware, Illinois, and New York require employers in those states to provide supervisors with sexual harassment training. The stringent requirements of the California training law, especially, call for close attention when designing a training program.

Even if it's not legally required, you should train managers and supervisors so they know how to deal with complaints and understand their responsibility to always act professionally and appropriately when dealing with employees.

Supervisor's Own Conduct

In addition to learning the types of conduct that can constitute harassment or discrimination, supervisors should be informed that their own actions can, in some situations, expose them to lawsuits by the victim. This risk of individual liability is unique to supervisory employees and gives them a powerful incentive to avoid inappropriate behavior.

An employer also has greater exposure to liability for the acts of its supervisors because the law views supervisory employees as agents acting on behalf of the company. This means that a company can be held liable for a supervisor's actions even if it doesn't know what the supervisor is up to. By contrast, an employer is typically liable for the conduct of a lower-level employee only if it is aware of that conduct and fails to do anything effective to stop it.

(?) **Common Questions**

Q: *One of our managers was accused of discriminating against an older worker. Part of the company's out-of-court settlement requires us to provide antidiscrimination training to this manager. The company is now considering requiring training for all managers, but I'm not sure this is a good idea. We are not legally required to provide training to anyone but the accused manager. Doesn't this make it look like we have a bigger problem than we really do?*

A: *When a workplace incident results in a complaint and a settlement, it's a good indication that some training is in order. After all, you want to make sure other managers don't repeat the same mistakes this manager did. Providing training can convert a costly settlement into a valuable teaching tool.*

However, some delicacy might be called for here, particularly if the other managers know about the situation that inspired the training in the first place. If the accused manager senses resentment or judgment on the part of his peers, he might not fully participate in the training. Likewise, if the other managers are caught up in the "back story" of the alleged violation, they might not be able to focus. Separate trainings are an option to consider if you think a group session might prevent some employees—especially the accused employee—from fully engaging and grasping the material.

Prevention and Response

Supervisors are responsible for taking prompt action in the workplace to prevent harassment and discrimination and to address these types of misconduct if they occur. This is easier said than done, however, as the dynamics of real-life human interaction often make it hard for a supervisor to gracefully intervene before conduct gets out of hand. Training can provide supervisors with effective methods for intervening early and responding to actual violations.

In general, the earlier a potential problem is caught and dealt with, the less damage done. In harassment and discrimination situations, your company wants to create sharp-eyed supervisors and managers who notice potential issues and step in to prevent them from escalating. This can be a delicate operation, though, because it calls for supervisors to step in before anyone has clearly done anything wrong. Effective training explains how supervisors can intervene without overreacting, including:

- **Leading by example:** By not telling off-color jokes, and by not responding favorably when employees do so, a supervisor sends a strong message that such conduct is not appropriate.
- **Changing the subject:** Heading off topics that could devolve into uncomfortable or inappropriate discussions is a time-tested way of avoiding problems.
- **Discouraging conduct:** A simple, terse word or two suggesting an employee might be entering into an area that is off-limits could be enough to prevent a problem from developing.
- **Expressing disapproval:** If subtler methods won't work or a situation is more serious, a firm statement that the conduct or comment is not appropriate often does the trick.

If these methods don't work, supervisors should be instructed to escalate to a more formal response, starting with a report of the violation, followed by investigation and response, as explained in Part II of this book. So supervisors should be trained in the company's complaint, investigation, and response procedures. The trainer should go over the steps set out in the company's policy and cover the supervisor's responsibilities at each step. For example, supervisors may be identified as company representatives to whom employees can bring complaints, as participants in the investigation of complaints, or in some other role. Give supervisors a full description of their role under your company's policy.

Employee Training

Employees need to know what types of conduct are prohibited and how to deal with violations they experience or observe. In contrast to supervisors, employees needn't, and shouldn't, be trained on investigating and responding to complaints, nor should they be trained on when the company or supervisors can be held liable for harassment and discrimination.

Practically speaking, these areas aren't the employee's concern—and being told how the company can escape legal responsibility for any misconduct they might suffer is likely to alienate or even anger employees.

Employees' Own Conduct

Although your combined training session will explain the types of conduct that violate company policy, you should separately emphasize to employees their responsibility to abide by the company policy and treat one another in a professional, respectful way at all times.

Reporting Violations

Another area in which employees should receive training is how to report potential violations. An employer's policy is effective only if employees know how to use it. Your training program should refresh employees on the company complaint policy, reiterating the pertinent points:

- **Whom to report to.** Tell employees which managers or supervisors they can report violations to, if they aren't comfortable reporting to HR or their immediate supervisors. It's best to identify these individuals by title (for example, "any manager," if that is your company's policy), so that the reporting structure stays consistent as individual managers come and go.
- **How to report.** Let employees know that they can speak informally and confidentially, to the extent possible. But be sure employees also know that the company has a duty to put a stop to inappropriate conduct, which might require the investigator to reveal some details of the complaint.
- **When to report.** Urge employees to immediately report any conduct that they believe might violate the company's policy against harassment or discrimination. Even if the conduct doesn't actually rise to the level of a violation, they should err on the side of making a report.

- **No retaliation.** Emphasize that the company will not tolerate any retaliation against an employee who has reported a possible violation, even if the company finds that no violation occurred. Instruct employees to immediately report any act that they believe might be retaliatory.
- **Participation in investigation.** Remind employees that they have an obligation to cooperate with anyone who is investigating an employee complaint. Reiterate that confidentiality will be maintained to the extent possible and that the company will not allow retaliation for their participation.

Bystander Intervention

An essential element of employee training involves teaching and empowering employees to step in when they observe what might be harassing or discriminatory behavior. Bystander intervention takes courage and can lead to uncomfortable confrontations, but when trained sensitively, employees will learn how to speak up to stop and/or immediately report potential misconduct. Good training techniques include showing employees how to derail improper conduct when they encounter it and how to deflect conflict while giving the victim a chance to exit the situation. Training should emphasize that intervention, while important, does not take the place of reporting any possible harassment or discrimination observed.

How to Conduct Training

The most effective training isn't just a dry lecture that marches through each required topic. As with any presentation, it's important to engage attendees and keep their attention through the use of visuals (such as PowerPoint presentations, whiteboards, or blow-ups that set out key concepts); videos (a variety of commercially produced training videos are available, or you can create your own); scenarios presented by the trainer, followed by a guided discussion; and quizzes and exercises, which help the trainer assess how well employees are understanding the concepts.

California, Delaware, Illinois, and New York require that sexual harassment training be "interactive," which means that attendees must have the chance to talk to the trainer about the concepts covered, ask questions, and answer hypothetical questions. The techniques described above are all interactive and, as such, fulfill that state's requirement. Even if interactive training is not legally required in your state, it helps ensure that the training session is interesting and productive.

Training can be conducted in a variety of ways that include:

- **In-person training:** Traditional classroom training with the trainer and attendees all in the same room is a popular option. It allows for questions and answers and for lively discussions of the issues.
- **E-learning:** Computer-based training is a growing trend. Typically, the attendee logs in individually but can participate in some way (for example, by receiving instructions on how to contact a trainer who will answer questions or provide guidance or assistance within a reasonable time period). This training method is a popular choice because it allows employees to complete training on their own schedules.
- **Webinars:** Many companies now opt for a seminar that is transmitted via the Internet or company intranet in real time. Attendees are given an opportunity to participate in real time by either emailing questions or answers or by telephone conference.

No matter which training method your company uses, be sure to have each attendee sign a form confirming that they attended the full training. E-learning programs and webinars usually have a box for attendees to click beside their names to record their attendance.

Who Conducts Training

Many companies hire outside consultants or lawyers to run their trainings. You can also use in-house HR professionals. No matter whom you use, make sure the trainer is qualified to conduct an effective training. California, for example, requires that training be presented by individuals with knowledge and expertise (such as employment lawyers or HR experts) in harassment, discrimination, and retaliation prevention. (You can find California's regulation discussing trainer qualifications at www.dfeh.ca.gov.) If your state requires training, and your company decides to hire an outside trainer, check the laws and regulations in your state for any required qualifications for trainers.

RESOURCE

Need help finding a trainer? The EEOC Training Institute offers harassment prevention and respectful workplace training. For more information, go to the EEOC website (https://eeotraining.eeoc.gov).

Beyond having the minimum qualifications and experience, the trainer needs to be right for your company and its employees. You or another manager might be the right choice, or your company's particular situation or needs could persuade you that an outside trainer is preferable. HR consultants and attorneys experienced in harassment and discrimination cases who've done prior trainings are all good candidates.

TIP

Get referrals. Ask company employment lawyers, HR specialists, and other company HR professionals for recommendations of good trainers. You can also ask others in your professional network or membership organizations.

Once you've gotten some names, ask trainer candidates for references and find out if their other clients were pleased with their training. You can also ask other clients about the trainer's methods and style, to make sure the trainer's approach is right for your company. For example, if your company believes strongly in workplace democracy, you will need a trainer who can handle outspoken employees and vigorous debate and discussion. Trainer candidates should also give you a description of training techniques upon request.

Give the chosen trainer a summary of any recent complaints or issues at your company, any particular difficulties you anticipate that the trainer might confront, and the particular goals your company has in providing the training to employees. For example, if a company employee recently complained of sexual harassment, and the investigation revealed that sexual jokes and teasing were fairly widespread, you might want the trainer to carefully focus on sexual harassment, what constitutes a hostile work environment, and what types of comments and conversations violate the company's standards of appropriate workplace behavior.

 Common Questions

Q: *My company just settled a religious discrimination lawsuit brought by a Sikh employee. We've retained a consultant to provide diversity training to our employees. We have other Sikh employees on staff besides the plaintiff in the lawsuit, and I'd like the trainer to address employee tolerance of that religion and culture. Is this advisable or even appropriate?*

A: *It makes sense to include religious tolerance and sensitivity in the training, given the recent lawsuit. However, the trainer needn't refer specifically to the Sikh religion or to any particular religion. In fact, the trainer shouldn't do so, as that might embarrass the Sikh employees and make them feel singled out. A general discussion of religious tolerance will cover the necessary ground without spotlighting any particular employees.*

Diversity Training

Many employers today conduct diversity training for all employees, in addition to harassment and discrimination training. Diversity training can foster sensitivity to, and tolerance of, differences among employees, and it can build employee confidence in the company's commitment to a diverse and collegial working environment. Most importantly, it can remind employees of their role in helping to create and maintain that environment.

Diversity training can be especially useful in healing workplace dysfunction after a harassment or discrimination complaint, because it is forward looking. Diversity training reinforces the need for employees to respect the differences among them, rather than focusing on legal definitions and obligations. Although diversity training should refer to those definitions and obligations (and specifically to company policy), its main goal is to explore the motivation behind those legal imperatives: how to create a workplace where employees from different backgrounds can all be comfortable and productive.

One way to do this is by discussing scenarios drawn from cases or situations in the news. For example, an accusation of harassment or discrimination against a public figure can form a framework for part of the training.

> **EXAMPLE:** The coach of the New York Knicks was accused of sexual harassment. Among other allegations, a female employee said that the coach had frequently commented upon and complimented her appearance. She also said he put his arm around her shoulder on several occasions. She said that she told him she was uncomfortable with the conduct, but he continued, insisting that he was just being nice. This part of the real case could be used to highlight the fact that unwelcome conduct, even if it's intended to be flattering, can make the recipient uncomfortable and can lead to a charge of harassment.

Diversity training can accomplish two difficult goals: It can provide a way to talk about the challenges posed when employees of different genders, races, religions, ages, and abilities work together; and, it can give employees a broader, less personal perspective on such challenges. Some of the anecdotes in diversity training can focus on how these challenges are confronted and overcome in various settings. For example, the group could discuss experiences recounted by a female executive during her career in a male-dominated industry as drawn from her memoir.

> **CAUTION**
>
> **Don't allow diversity training to devolve into a discussion of negative stereotypes or biased beliefs.** Believe it or not, diversity training can provide fodder for a discrimination lawsuit—not to mention heated discussions and deeply hurt feelings—if participants are asked to discuss or reveal personal biases. It's appropriate to discuss some of the reasons why antidiscrimination laws exist—for example, that some groups in our society have been historically disadvantaged. Once participants begin sharing their own biases and beliefs, however, the discussion can quickly become uncomfortable or even hostile. Do you really want a company manager "confessing" that he believes women are too emotional to conduct hard-nosed business negotiations? Once that session ends and he denies a promotion to a female employee, you can bet you'll hear those words echoed back in a complaint.

A question and answer session can also be an effective tool during diversity training. A typical session starts with a scenario laid out by the trainer, who then asks employees questions about the conduct and the response to the conduct in the scenario.

> **EXAMPLE:** Using the allegations of unwelcome comments and touching made by the female employee of the New York Knicks, the trainer then asks the employees at the diversity training the following questions:
> - How many times should an employee have to object to behavior before it's clear that the behavior is unwelcome?
> - Assuming that he was sincere, is it relevant that the coach thought he was being nice?
> - Should the employee have to do or say more than, "I'd rather you didn't do that" before the coach should have understood that he was making her uncomfortable?
> - Is it wise for someone in the coach's position to err on the side of caution and just not compliment a female employee's appearance?

The point of this kind of dialog is to spur employees to think about situations from one another's point of view and to understand that something they think is harmless—or even flattering—can cause insult, offense, or discomfort to another person. This will help employees increase their sensitivity to the differing perspectives of their coworkers and understand that everyone benefits when possible harassment or discrimination is reported and addressed.

In a perfect world, all employees would always show respect for their coworkers, regardless of any differences between them. Unfortunately, that ideal is probably some way off. Fortunately, perfection is not required by the law. The goal of training, and of all the measures we've discussed in this chapter, is to bolster employee confidence in your company and its policy; to prevent violations; and to make the workplace a professional, collegial, and respectful environment for all employees.

Dos and Don'ts

Do:

- Familiarize yourself with the training requirements, if any, of each state in which your company operates.
- Consider training all employees even if it's not required, in order to provide guidance to supervisors and employees and to limit damages in case of a lawsuit.
- Provide training to supervisors and employees that is tailored to their different roles.
- Use scenarios, quizzes, and exercises to encourage attendees to participate and test their knowledge.
- Choose a training method that's effective and interactive.
- Choose a trainer who's qualified, experienced, and suits your company's needs.
- Consider diversity training, especially if your company has had some problems with discrimination or harassment in the past.

Don't:

- Bypass the option of training in order to cut costs; it will pay for itself by preventing lawsuits and limiting damages.
- Forget to have each attendee at training submit a form confirming attendance.
- Limit training to a dry lecture—it needs to be interactive.
- Neglect to distribute the company policy and do refer to it frequently during training.
- Leave out a discussion of informal methods of intervention when training supervisors.

Part II: Dealing With Harassment and Discrimination Claims

Investigating Complaints

B eginning in 2017, women—and some men—were inspired and empowered by the #MeToo movement to report their experiences of sexual and other types of harassment in industries and workplaces as varied as movies and television, state and federal legislatures, hospitality, agriculture, construction, and the tech industry. Many victims spoke of being ignored, receiving warnings to keep silent, and getting blackballed for attempting to report incidents and get help.

The failure of employers to respond effectively to address and prevent harassment created the pressure that ultimately exploded into public view as the #MeToo movement. Had employers followed the law and the steps recommended in this book, many victims would have been helped, much harassment would have been prevented, and the need for such a movement might not have arisen. A crucial step for any employer to take to avoid becoming a deserving casualty of this movement includes developing a robust, effective investigative procedure.

Your initial response to a harassment or discrimination complaint could well determine whether the underlying issue is resolved successfully or ends up in court. Employees who file lawsuits often say something like: "If someone at the company had taken this problem seriously in the first place, I never would have sued." At the very least, a company's inaction or sloppy investigation convinces the reporting employee—and others— that the company doesn't take complaints seriously. Even worse, problems can escalate as the inappropriate behavior continues and the harm caused by discriminatory treatment mounts.

A prompt, effective response can also limit your company's liability if a lawsuit is filed. Courts have held that an employer may avoid liability in harassment or discrimination cases by showing that it promptly, thoroughly, and fairly investigated an employee's complaint of harassment or discrimination and took immediate, effective action to end any harassment or discrimination uncovered in the investigation.

This chapter explains how to respond to a potential harassment or discrimination complaint effectively, from the moment you first hear about it. You'll learn:

- what to do when you receive a complaint

- how to interview the reporting employee, the accused employee, and other witnesses, and

- how to evaluate what you learn and decide what action to take once the investigation is complete.

Receiving a Complaint

You might find out about a potential problem in any number of ways—from the employee who feels harassed or discriminated against, from a coworker who sees or hears something fishy, from your own observations, or at worst, by receiving a complaint that the employee filed with a government fair employment agency. Or, you might find out about a problem indirectly, without any formal complaint. A current employee might report a potential violation during a performance evaluation, at an exit interview, or even anonymously.

No matter how you first become aware of a problem, your responsibility is the same—to investigate quickly, impartially, and thoroughly. Usually, your first step will be to talk to the reporting employee.

Treat the Reporting Employee Respectfully

Because employees often feel emotional about these situations, your job is a tough one. To be effective, you must respect the employee's emotions while working to get the information you need. You'll find that easiest to do if you follow these strategies:

- **Show that you take the complaint seriously.** Harassment and discrimination complaints are serious business. When you meet with an employee to discuss a complaint, you might be tempted to lighten the mood by engaging in small talk or avoiding the most pressing questions. You might worry that, if you're too serious, you could scare the employee off and not get the full story. But resist the temptation. Making light gives the impression that you don't take the complaint seriously. At worst, the employee might not share the full story with you or might hesitate to report further incidents.

Common Questions

Q: *A Korean-American employee complained that her Caucasian manager frequently asks her for recommendations of "Asian" restaurants in the cities he travels to for our business. She's annoyed by this because, as she told me, "I'm Korean, not 'Asian,' and my favorite food is pizza!" I know the manager socially, and I know his heart is in the right place. But when I said as much to the employee, she accused me of "taking sides" and stalked out of my office. Should I let it be, or should I try to discuss it with the employee again?*

A: *You need to go back to the beginning. Your statement and belief that the manager's "heart was in the right place" told the reporting employee that you didn't think her complaint was serious, even if you believed it was true. You should ask the employee to meet with you again and make clear that you're ready to listen and objectively apply the company's policy on harassment and discrimination. If the employee is still reluctant to deal with you, have another qualified manager step in to handle the complaint.*

• **Don't pass judgment.** When you receive a complaint, it's natural to want to draw some conclusions, especially if you know the employees involved. But don't—it prevents you from getting the full story. Instead, listen carefully and ask for all relevant facts. You shouldn't make any decisions about what happened until the investigation is fully complete.

 Common Questions

Q: *A hypersensitive employee (she even objected to the type of bottled water in the break room!) complained that her manager makes her uncomfortable by commenting on her appearance, saying things like "That looks nice" or "Green is a great color for you." These sound like simple compliments and, in her usual way, she's making a big deal out of them. Do we really have to treat this as a harassment complaint?*

A: Absolutely, yes. That the employee has a history of complaining—either about harassing behavior or water in the break room—doesn't tell you whether she is being harassed right now. You need to get the full story before you draw any conclusions. While the statements might seem harmless at first blush, you could find other facts that suggest there's more to the story. And, the question of whether she's experiencing harassment must be examined from her perspective, not yours or the manager's.

- **Don't get caught up in emotions.** Employees who come to you to complain about harassment or discrimination could be dealing with a host of different emotions—and some might be occurring simultaneously. They could feel angry, hurt, humiliated, or even ashamed. But it's important not to let these emotions cloud your ability to hear the complaint objectively. Your job is to get the full story and draw a conclusion based on the facts.

 TIP

You can treat the employee kindly without getting emotional. You don't have to act like an unfeeling automaton when an employee expresses strong emotions. Just maintain a professional, respectful demeanor. If the employee is crying, for example, it's perfectly acceptable to offer a tissue or glass of water. But don't cross the line: Too much sympathy implies that you have already decided that the employee's accusations are true, which compromises your neutrality in the investigation. You want both the reporting employee and the accused employee to feel that they've gotten a fair hearing. This makes it much more likely that they'll accept the conclusions you draw and the steps you take to resolve the situation.

- **Be patient.** People in a charged emotional state often have difficulty articulating their thoughts. Be prepared to sit back calmly and give the employee time to explain what's happened.

- **Don't promise confidentiality or anonymity.** Many complaining employees do not want to be identified when you conduct an investigation, but that might not be possible. The accused employee deserves to hear the accusations and respond to them. For this reason, you shouldn't promise anyone you interview that you will keep information confidential. Instead, offer to keep things as confidential as possible, and assure the employee that you won't reveal information to people who do not need to know it.

Get the Information You Need

Even as you're careful about how you treat the employee, keep in mind that your primary objective is to get the full story. You can best do this by showing the employee you are a good listener. Use active-listening strategies, such as repeating back what the employee is saying, to make sure you are hearing correctly. If the employee gets upset, acknowledge those emotions directly, by saying something like, "You seem upset. Do you want to take a break?" And keep your tone professional: The more businesslike you are, the easier it will be for the employee to keep his or her emotions in check. That will help both of you stay focused on the task at hand.

Checklist: What to Say to a Reporting Employee

When you meet with a reporting employee, use this checklist to make sure you start your investigating on the right foot.

- ☐ Thank the employee for coming forward.
- ☐ Explain that you're going to initiate an investigation immediately.
- ☐ Remind the employee to bring further complaints to you and to let you know if the employee later remembers additional information.
- ☐ Tell the employee you're going to follow company policy—and provide a copy of it.
- ☐ Reiterate that retaliation is illegal.
- ☐ Confirm that you'll only share information on a need-to-know basis, but don't promise confidentiality.

Reiterate what the employee can expect, based on what's in your company policy. Even if the employee has read it, your confirmation that the policy will be followed provides reassurance and stability. Also, tell the employee that retaliation is prohibited, and ask the employee to come to you immediately if any negative treatment occurs as a result of the complaint or investigation.

 Common Questions

Q: *I happened to walk into the break room just in time to hear an employee heatedly telling his manager, "I can't believe you said that." As soon as I came in, the employee left. The manager quickly said, "We were just discussing last weekend's big game—he's mad his team lost." This explanation could be plausible, and I didn't say anything at the time, but now I can imagine something much worse going on, too. Should I follow up?*

A: *You don't need to make a big deal of it, but you should, at a minimum, find out what the manager said that upset the employee. You can start by meeting individually with each of them and asking what happened. You don't have to do anything extremely formal at this point, but it's a good idea to make sure you have the full story before you start drawing conclusions, good or bad.*

Before you conclude your meeting, ask the employee what he or she thinks should be done to resolve the complaint. This allows the employee to express his or her perspective, and you can consider it later when you have to come up with a solution. This is also your opportunity to address the employee's unreasonable expectations—for example, if the employee expects you to immediately fire the accused employee, you can explain why it's important for you to investigate before any disciplinary action is taken.

Of course, you'll need to make it clear that you can't promise any particular response or outcome. After all, the employee might ask that you do nothing or that you do something that isn't consistent with company policy or your legal requirements. Your primary duty is to take all reasonable steps to end the illegal conduct and to prevent it from occurring again, not necessarily to please the reporting employee.

(?) Common Questions

Q: *I recently found our receptionist hiding out in the women's room. She explained that she was dodging one of the delivery men. She says he hangs over her desk to ogle her and makes suggestive sexual comments. When I told her I'd be contacting the delivery service, she said she didn't want to make a big deal of it. It's not really a problem to have someone else deal with the delivery man, and this solution seems reasonable. Is this a workable approach?*

A: *No. Although the receptionist's approach might help her avoid the delivery man, it doesn't relieve your company of the obligation to deal with the situation. First, the receptionist shouldn't have to hide in the restroom during her work hours to avoid harassment. This doesn't do anything to address the harassment she's already suffered, it doesn't prevent her from later claiming that you should have taken steps to protect her, it could itself be considered degrading, and it's a waste of her work time. Also, this delivery man might harass other employees. Now that you know about his behavior, you have to step in and address it.*

One way to do this is to let the delivery company know that its employee is engaging in behavior that violates your company's policy. Then, ask that they send a different worker in his place. If they want your business, they'll comply. There is no need to even mention the receptionist in this exchange. Be sure to tell the receptionist that you've spoken to the delivery company, and ask her to report further incidents to you.

Conducting an Investigation

A thorough, prompt investigation is essential to the successful resolution of an employee complaint. It enables you to collect evidence while it's still fresh, before witnesses' recollections fade, documents get lost, or emails are deleted. It wards off speculation and gossip. And it inspires employee confidence in your company's policies and practices.

Although you might certainly hope your investigation will yield the absolute truth, it's often more complicated. You might have little evidence beyond "he said/she said" allegations, with no witnesses to corroborate either side's story. Even if you can't reach a solid conclusion, however, an investigation shows that the company did all it could to prevent and correct inappropriate behavior—which, as explained in Chapters 2 and 3, has the important legal consequence of either providing a defense to a hostile work environment case or avoiding punitive damages in a discrimination case. The law protects you as long as you investigate in good faith, even if you aren't ultimately able to draw a conclusion about what happened—and even if your conclusion turns out to be wrong. And, at least as importantly, your good-faith, thorough investigation tells employees that your company takes complaints seriously.

Nevertheless, you should do everything you can during the investigation to get the full story. Sometimes, you'll have clear physical evidence—a series of emails or photos, for example—that will help you reach a conclusion. But more often, the majority of your evidence will come from the accounts of the reporting employee, the accused employee, and other witnesses. So you'll have to find out what happened primarily through interviews.

Preparing to Investigate

Once you receive a complaint, you will want to jump in quickly to protect the company. But don't be too hasty. Spend some time creating an investigatory plan. The plan should cover:

- **Whom you need to interview.** This list might grow as your investigation proceeds, but start with anyone who could have relevant information. Then, decide the order in which you'll interview employees. For reasons explained below, after speaking with the reporting employee, it usually makes sense to interview the accused employee before moving on to other witnesses.
- **What you need to ask.** You don't need to write out every question, but you should take some notes to make sure you address the key issues with each witness. Create a rough outline of topics you need to cover. And, make sure you have clean copies of any documents, such as email messages or performance evaluations, you plan to show witnesses and ask them about.
- **Where you'll conduct interviews.** You want to respect the privacy of everyone involved and limit disruption—and gossip—in the

workplace. Choose a location away from the witnesses' regular workspace, and make sure it's private, with a locking door.

- **How to schedule interviews.** It's a good idea to set up employee interviews quickly and close together in time. This minimizes the potential for employees to gossip about the interviews, share information, or get overly anxious about being interviewed.

Interviewing Techniques

No matter whom you're interviewing—the reporting employee, the accused employee, or a witness—you must approach each interview as an opportunity to get the most information possible, while protecting the company's interests and maintaining your neutrality.

Start With the Facts

To the employees you interview, the facts might not be the most important part of the story. Employees could be focused on how the behavior or treatment feels, how it feels to be accused of misconduct, what effect the problem is having on their work or home life, or how others in the company might respond.

While this is understandable, you need to know what actually happened. While being respectful of the employee's emotions, you must still get the information you need. It's easy to get sidetracked if you don't focus on the fundamentals. Gather information like a reporter, by asking:

- **Who?** You need to know who committed the alleged behavior or action, who witnessed it, whom the employee told about it, and whether anyone else might have relevant information.
- **What?** Get the details about what happened. Don't settle for "He harassed me" or "I never said that." Find out exactly what was done or said, in what context.
- **When?** You need to figure out how long the behavior has been going on and when any incident or alleged incident occurred. Be as specific as possible. If the employee isn't sure, you might have to provide some reference points ("Was it in the morning or afternoon?" "Was it before or after we closed the Jones account?") to try to narrow things down.

- **Where?** The location of alleged events can help you figure out what really happened. For example, if the reporting employee says that she was harassed in the break room at lunchtime, there could be several witnesses to the incident. You can then explore what potential witnesses observed. If the activity occurred away from the workplace, you'll have to determine the company's responsibility for what went on. Make sure you find out where every alleged incident took place.
- **How?** Find out the means the accused employee used to instigate the harassment or discrimination—for example, through email, comments, or physical contact, or by altering the employee's work schedule, pay, or promotional opportunities.
- **Why?** You need to understand the context of the incident(s). Did the alleged violation occur suddenly or progress over time, such as joking that gradually became more and more offensive or the denial of a series of raises? You also need to know whether the employee believes the conduct was related to the employee's gender, race, or other protected characteristic, and the reasons for that belief.

 Common Questions

Q: *Our warehouse foreman is concerned that the night shift supervisor uses ethnic nicknames with his crew, a group of six guys, four of whom (plus the supervisor) are Latino. The examples he gave are in Spanish, but even translated, don't seem derogatory. Several of the crew members don't speak Spanish, and the foreman told me they just "blow it off because they don't know what he's saying anyway." No one has complained. How should I approach this? I don't want to put ideas in anyone's head.*

A: *You're right to investigate, but to avoid inciting anger or anxiety, you'll want to carefully word your inquiries. For example, you may ask the night shift employees, "Does anyone ever use nicknames in the warehouse?" If the answer is yes, you may follow up with questions about who does it, what terms are used, and how the employees feel about and respond to their use. These questions are likely to elicit some helpful answers, because you'll get confirmation that the alleged language was actually used, as well as get an idea about how employees feel about it.*

Keep your questions open-ended instead of asking questions that require only a "yes" or "no" answer. And avoid leading comments or questions, such as "You must have been so upset!" or "That wasn't really offensive, was it?" These questions give the employee the impression that there is a "right" answer. You're less likely to get the employee's honest perspective if you approach things this way. Another way to avoid getting a biased viewpoint is to simply wait for the witness to respond, rather than providing a response when a witness is slow to speak. Sometimes witnesses need to gather their thoughts, or they hope that they can avoid answering difficult questions by stalling for time.

In addition to these questions, ask everyone you interview if they have any physical evidence related to the underlying problem, such as memos, payroll documents, pictures, emails, notes, letters, voice mail, or text messages.

If the answers to your questions reveal new facts (and they often do), you might need to go back to earlier witnesses to ask more questions. You'll often have to go back to the reporting employee, because after interviewing others, you'll have a lot of new information to synthesize. It's a good idea to interview witnesses more than once as an investigation proceeds, so you can clear up (or nail down) inconsistencies and explore newly uncovered information.

 Common Questions

Q: *My company notified an employee on August 1 that it was eliminating her job. She complained to me of discrimination because just a few days before the notification, she'd told her manager she was pregnant. The manager told me they'd made the decision a couple weeks before that, and that he had an email to his VP, dated July 15, definitively backing this up. But another employee in the department told me that the pregnant employee had informally started telling people about her pregnancy as early as the beginning of July and that "everyone knew about it." I don't know what to believe. What do I do next?*

A: *You definitely have more work to do here, because you need to find out when the manager actually knew about the employee's pregnancy. Although the manager can show you that he made the decision before the employee told him directly that she was pregnant, you haven't said whether he denies knowing the employee was pregnant before she told him.*

To start, you'll need to go back to the employee and find out when she began telling others at work that she was pregnant, whom she told, and in what context. There's a big difference between, for example, telling one close friend in confidence and announcing her pregnancy at a team meeting. You'll also need to find out what the manager knew before July 15.

Only then can you explore whether the employee's pregnancy played any part in her separation from employment, which is the ultimate question to investigate.

Provide Information

Your investigation is more than an opportunity to elicit facts—it's also an opportunity for you to assure the employee that you're going to conduct the investigation in compliance with company policy. This instills employee confidence in the process and also protects the company legally. To make sure you communicate this important message, start by giving everyone you interview another copy of the company's policy prohibiting harassment and discrimination and urge them to read it again. This helps ensure that employees understand their rights and responsibilities and what to expect from the investigation. (For more information on what should be in the policy, see Chapter 3.)

Make clear to everyone you interview, especially the reporting employee, that retaliation is prohibited and should be reported to you immediately. Explain that the company doesn't want any employee penalized or treated badly for participating in the investigation. (You'll find information on preventing and responding to retaliation in Chapter 7.)

As you conclude each interview, discuss what will happen next. You don't have to provide any specifics; just let the employee know that you're going to investigate the complaint and that you'll follow company policy and legal requirements. Make sure the employee knows to contact you about any further violations or additional information.

Third Parties at the Interview

Sometimes, an employee being interviewed will want to bring a third party along. Whether you should allow this depends, in part, on whom the employee wants to bring.

- **Union representative.** Union members have a right to have a union representative present if the interview could result in discipline.
- **A lawyer.** You don't have to allow an attorney to be present, but you can and might want to if you think it will put the witness at ease and encourage open communication. But don't allow the attorney to take over the process or limit your inquiries—your purpose is to find the truth (without invading the employee's privacy), not present a case in court. If you're worried that the interview could digress into a legal attack, you can have the company's lawyer present too. Just recognize that this might make things feel more formal and undermine your fact finding.
- **A spouse, coworker, or friend.** It's usually not a good idea to allow a personal friend or support person to be present, especially if you're dealing with the accused employee. Employees sometimes feel ashamed about their behavior and might not want to reveal it in front of someone they know. In some cases (for example, if an employee is accused of sexual harassment and brings his wife to the interview), the third party might have a significant personal investment in the outcome of the investigation and could interfere with your questioning. Also, having an outsider at the interview unnecessarily compromises the privacy of the people being discussed.

CAUTION

Don't retaliate against employees for discussing discrimination or harassment issues. The law prohibits employers from barring employees from, or disciplining them for, discussing discrimination or harassment issues in connection with an investigation. Telling employees not to discuss the alleged harassment or discrimination with each other could get you in legal trouble. If you're worried about potential witnesses influencing each other's stories, try to schedule the interviews as close together as possible.

Separate the Reporting and Accused Employees

To reduce the risk of continuing problems and to show the reporting employee that you take the complaint seriously, you might want to separate the accused employee and the reporting employee as soon as you receive a complaint. Keeping the employees apart also makes it easier for you to conduct a thorough investigation, get each side's full perspective, and limit the potential for tension in the workplace. Given the pitched nature of harassment and discrimination allegations, separating the reporting and accused employees is generally a good idea if practical.

If an accused harasser is the victim's supervisor, you should definitely separate the two pending the investigation to prevent the possibility of further harassment. It's also appropriate to separate employees if you're worried about the potential for violence or confrontation, depending on the situation. For example, if a coworker has allegedly directed a racial epithet at the reporting employee, emotions might be running so high that they have to be separated.

Separating employees doesn't always mean complete isolation, however. That level of distance might not always be possible or practical, especially in a smaller workplace. But at the very least, you'll want to instruct the parties not to speak to each other about the allegations, investigate quickly to minimize the discomfort, and keep them as far apart as you can.

In addition to separating a supervisor accused of harassment from the victim, you should also remove the victim from that supervisor's line of authority and have the victim report to another supervisor. This action takes away the supervisor's opportunity to continue the alleged misconduct or engage in retaliation. You don't want a supervisor who's been accused of discrimination or harassment to be in a position to make any managerial decisions affecting the employee—about assignments, projects, discipline, raises, promotions, or layoffs, for example—until the allegations are resolved.

Common Questions

Q: *Recently, one of our salespeople, Glen, reported that a coworker, David, has made some "homophobic comments," like asking him to find a matching garment for a customer because he has good "color coordination skills." Glen thinks these comments are coded slurs about Glen's sexual orientation. He wants a full investigation, and he doesn't want to work the same shift as David. It's the holiday season (our busiest time of year), we're a small business and already stretched thin, and this is just impossible. I made sure that a supervisor was always present when they worked together and started to investigate, but midway through my investigation, Glen quit and has now filed a harassment charge with the state fair employment agency. Am I in trouble here?*

A: *You shouldn't be. You conducted an investigation in good faith and did all you could to separate the two without causing undue disruption to your operations. That's what the law requires of you. If it's truly not practical for you to separate the two entirely, the actions you took should be enough to protect the company.*

Of course, the degree of separation will also depend, in part, on the seriousness of the allegations. A physical assault is obviously much more serious than escalating joking between two friends, for example. In serious cases, you'll want to make sure the alleged harasser is far from the victim— perhaps even away from the workplace. The severity of the alleged conduct or the disruption to the workplace might call for placing the accused on paid leave. For example, if an employee accuses a coworker of sexual assault, you'll want to take the preventative step of keeping the accused employee away from the premises. If the company does not have an available place to move the accused employee, even temporarily, this might be the only logical solution.

But be careful: The law prohibits an employer from retaliating against an employee for complaining about harassment or discrimination. Transferring a reporting employee to a less desirable job or shift could be viewed as retaliatory, even if it's done to separate the accuser from the accused employee. For this reason, if a transfer is necessary, it is best to move the accused employee, even if you haven't determined whether the complaint is valid. Recognizing that separating employees puts employers in a difficult position, courts have upheld the approach of moving the accused employee pending an investigation.

Among the allegations of harassment that came to light in the midst of the #MeToo movement was the revelation that Hillary Clinton's "faith advisor" during her 2016 presidential campaign had allegedly repeatedly harassed a female member of the campaign staff. Upon learning of the allegations (during the campaign), Clinton's campaign manager urged her to fire the alleged harasser. Clinton, however, decided to transfer the female victim to a new job and keep the alleged harasser in his original position, with a pay cut and "counseling." A subsequent employer fired the alleged harasser for sexual harassment. Clinton faced widespread criticism for this decision. With best practices in mind, Clinton should have followed her campaign manager's advice, kept the victim in her original job, and ensured that the allegations were thoroughly investigated.

 Common Questions

Q: *A female assistant has accused the company CFO of grabbing her and fondling her breast in his office last night while the two were working late on an IPO scheduled to be announced next week. The CFO is the lead on the IPO, and the assistant has been working exclusively on it for months. I'm investigating her accusations and I know I should separate them, so I'm considering reassigning the assistant to another executive and another (probably lower-profile) project. The CFO really can't be taken off the IPO at this stage without harming its prospects for success. Is my plan okay?*

A: *Not necessarily. Reassigning the assistant to lower-profile work might be considered detrimental to her and her career, which could be considered retaliation. You don't say how many other executives your firm has in its financial group, so it's unclear whether the CFO really is indispensable to the IPO. If any other executive can step in and shepherd the IPO forward with the assistant's help, that's preferable. The CFO could advise his replacement outside the assistant's presence, if necessary, and could still be the "public face" of the firm for the IPO.*

Special Considerations When Interviewing the Accused Employee

When you speak to the accused employee, you have several obligations. You have to find out what really happened, so you can take action to protect the company and the reporting employee. You also have to act fairly toward the accused employee, however. Accusations aren't facts: If the accused employee believes that you've already made up your mind and aren't interested in the real story, you could be facing a legal challenge to any discipline you later decide to impose. That's why it's so important to remain neutral and calm when you conduct your interviews.

 Common Questions

Q: *A disabled dispatcher for our elevator maintenance company reported that a shift supervisor has started calling her "the Crip." She said he pretends he's joking, and he does use nicknames a lot when referring to other employees. After talking to the dispatcher, I called the supervisor in and asked him what the name Crip refers to. He stared at me, obviously angry, and said, "How should I know?" Then he said he wanted to talk to a lawyer before speaking with me any further on the subject. I'm not sure what to do next. Did I get off on the wrong track here?*

A: *You might have made a bit of a misstep because you opened your interview of the accused employee with, essentially, an accusation. The blunt question about the alleged slur immediately put him on the defensive, and he clammed up. Also, the way you worded your question gave him an out, because he could (and did) sidestep it. Try again with an open-ended, nonleading question, such as, "Do you ever call any of your coworkers by nicknames?"*

It's usually best to interview the accused employee after you've spoken to the reporting employee but before you interview other witnesses. The accused employee is more likely to feel the process is fair if it doesn't look like you're building an attack arsenal. You also have a better opportunity to assess the employee's unrehearsed response if the employee first learns of the problem from you—not from a witness you've already interviewed in conjunction with the investigation.

Naturally, an employee accused of harassment or discrimination might be guarded during the interview. Start by assuring the employee that your company will strive to keep the investigation as confidential as possible while making sure it is thorough and fair, and that you won't reveal information to anyone unless it's necessary. Also, make it clear that you haven't drawn any conclusions—that the purpose of the process is to get all the facts about what actually happened.

You'll have to provide enough information about the complaint so that the employee knows what you're asking about and can respond intelligently. For example, it's much more productive to ask, "What are the criteria you considered when deciding who should lead the Smith project?" than "Did you discriminate against Jane because of her gender?" You're looking for areas of agreement and disagreement between the reporting employee's and the accused employee's versions of events. In some cases, you might have concrete, documented actions to ask about, such as pay rates or promotion denials; in others, you might be dealing with complaints based on alleged statements, inferred intent, and general feelings. It will be your job to root out the details.

 Common Questions

Q: *After receiving a complaint of age discrimination from one of our employees who was recently demoted, I interviewed the accused manager. I explained, "You've been accused of making ageist statements." Right away, she got very defensive and told me that she'd joked about age with another female employee—not the employee who complained—who was "too sensitive about this stuff." Now that she's brought this up, should I speak with the other employee?*

A: *Yes. This is exactly why an investigation is so important: It can reveal facts you didn't know that can put the company at risk. Keep in mind that it's possible the other employee feels harassed too and just hasn't reported it to you. And if the accused manager doesn't even remember making any inappropriate statements to the reporting employee, that might be a sign that she really doesn't understand appropriate workplace behavior.*

As a side note, although you received a lot of important information that you wouldn't have if you hadn't started this investigation as you did, it's no surprise that your opening gambit made the employee defensive. To start with an accusation of bias, without any details or facts, generally leads the person you're interviewing to clam up or begin offering rationalizations, rather than answering questions fully. In this situation, the employee drew conclusions about what you meant by "ageist" statements and immediately started in on the justifications. Even though she revealed information you didn't already have, the tone of the interview was defensive. You could have avoided this by instead focusing on the who, what, when, where, and why facts at issue in the current complaint.

The employee might deny the allegations outright. Ask whether there are any documents or witnesses that could support the accused employee's version of events, then follow up to get that information.

Alternatively, the accused employee might attempt to justify, rationalize, or explain away the alleged conduct (for example, by saying "I was just joking around" or "He says the same things to me all the time"). You shouldn't argue with or cross-examine the employee. Just get the employee's side of the story, asking questions as necessary to get to the facts behind the employee's characterizations. For example, the employee who states, "He says the same things to me all the time," could then be asked to give examples, with information on when the incidents occurred, in what context, and who else was present. Then, you can follow up with additional interviews, if necessary.

CAUTION

Don't give a supervisor any special deference. As the investigator, you can't allow your impartiality to be compromised by a supervisor's position of authority or tenure with the company. If the accused employee is higher than you in the chain of command—and especially if you report to him or her—you might have to bring in an outside investigator, to make sure the investigation is viewed as fair. If you hire an outsider to investigate, you'll need to follow the rules set out in the Fair Credit Reporting Act, including providing certain information to the accused employee. (For more, see *The Essential Guide to Federal Employment Laws*, by Lisa Guerin and Sachi Barreiro (Nolo).)

Concluding Your Investigation

Once you have gathered all the facts you can, you have to decide what you think really happened, which can be difficult: You might have five different stories from five different witnesses, and you'll have to determine whose version makes the most sense. In some situations, the evidence could conflict so much that you aren't able to draw any firm conclusions about the underlying facts.

Understanding Your Goal

Your primary goal isn't to determine whether the law was violated—if worse comes to worst, a judge or jury decides that. But you can and should try to determine whether the accused employee violated your company's policy. You will want to base your disciplinary decision on the options and requirements laid out for you in that policy.

> CAUTION
> **If you're concerned that the law might have been violated, report it to company management.** Communicate this information to your boss, human resources, or company counsel. While your prompt disciplinary action might help your company avoid a lawsuit, you want to be fully prepared if one happens.

Again, your responsibility isn't to be the final arbiter of truth; your responsibility is to conduct a fair and impartial investigation and to reach a conclusion in good faith. As long as you do this, you are legally protected, even if your conclusion ultimately turns out to be wrong.

Reaching a Conclusion

After conducting a full investigation, you might conclude one of three things:
- **Company policy was violated.** If you find an employee has violated your company's policy, your course of action is clear: You must immediately take steps to stop the behavior and prevent future violations. You might have to discipline, train, or even fire the accused employee.

- **You can't determine whether company policy was violated.** Sometimes, the information you get will be too vague or contradicted by other evidence for you to determine whether the allegations are true. Don't succumb to the impulse to reach a conclusion just for the sake of finality. Above all, you're seeking the truth insofar as it can be determined.
- **The accusations are false or the behavior occurred, but didn't violate company policy.** If you determine the behavior didn't occur, don't punish the reporting employee unless you are certain the complaint was intentionally false—and you have evidence to prove it. Otherwise, you're inviting a retaliation claim.

It can be frustrating to conduct a careful, thorough investigation, only to find that you can't reach a conclusion. Many harassment and discrimination cases are "he said, she said"—that is, you'll have nothing more than the conflicting statements of the reporting employee and the accused employee. You're not required to take one employee's word as true in these situations, especially if no witnesses, documents, or other evidence supports either side. As long as you investigate fully and document your findings, you've done your job. If there are any further incidents, you can pull out your file and take a fresh look at the evidence.

Unless everyone you interviewed agreed on all the important facts, you will need to evaluate conflicting information. One way to do this is to develop a chart listing each significant fact, with columns to check for undisputed facts and disputed statements. In a third column, labeled "Contradictory Information," you can briefly note the person or document that contradicts the listed fact. You can scan this chart to determine which facts you can treat as true and which you'll have to evaluate to decide which version is more credible.

Sample Fact Chart			
Fact	Undisputed	Disputed	Contradictory Information
Joe Adams called Seth Regan "grandpa"		✓	Seth Regan interview 10/10/xx Joe Adams interview 10/15/xx

If facts are disputed, you need to evaluate the two (or more) conflicting versions and assess the credibility of each. Which is more likely, sounds more like the truth, makes more sense? Here are some things to consider:

- **Plausibility.** Start by considering whose version makes more sense. For example, let's say an employee complains that a pornographic picture was taped to her computer monitor when she arrived at work in the morning. Several witnesses, all of whom arrive at work early on a regular basis, report that they saw the accused employee in the complaining employee's office and that it was unusual for him to be at work so early. The accused employee says he was in the employee's office looking for a stapler, even though he has one on his desk, and that he just happened to arrive early that day. In this situation, the accused employee's account is not very plausible.

- **Specificity.** How much detail does each person provide? The more detailed the information, the more credible it is, in general. For example, one employee accuses another of making a racist comment in the company's parking lot. The reporting employee says, "I'm pretty sure it happened at around 3:00, because we were both there to meet the delivery truck on its afternoon stop. The truck was late, and Ned said something about how the driver was on 'CP time.' I didn't know what he meant; when I asked him, he said, 'You know, colored people time; you guys are always late.'" Ned says he doesn't remember whether he was in the parking lot that day, but that he "wouldn't" make a racist comment. In this situation, the reporting employee's story is a lot more specific, in ways that support his claim.

- **The source.** If witnesses are the source of conflicting information, what is the demeanor of each during their interviews? Do any of the witnesses have a possible motive for being other than totally honest? For example, a witness who just received a poor performance evaluation from a supervisor accused of wrongdoing might have a motive to make that supervisor look bad. Do the witnesses claim that they each personally observed the incident? Information about a firsthand observation is generally more credible than secondhand accounts.

If you've conducted the investigation and are having a tough time assessing the information you've gathered, have another manager or company HR professional take a look at it.

Common Questions

Q: *Hanif, who is Pakistani, told me that a coworker, Chuck, called him a "camel jockey" and draped a dust cloth over Hanif's head as if it were a head scarf. Hanif said that when he yanked the dust cloth off, he accidentally struck Chuck in the eye. Chuck did indeed have a black eye and said he got it when he and Hanif were "horsing around," but said it "wasn't a big deal." He denied making comments about Hanif's ancestry and said they were friends. No one witnessed these events, and I don't know who's telling the truth. Where do I go from here?*

A: *This is a textbook "he said/he said": Hanif says Chuck made an offensive statement, Chuck denies it, and there's no other account that will help you sort this out. Your first step here may be to go back to both employees for more information. For example, it's possible that Chuck honestly didn't believe the comment he made is about ancestry.*

If further exploration doesn't yield any new information, you should ask for help from an outside source. Have a human resources professional, your manager, or even company counsel review your investigatory file. With fresh eyes, they might help you see important details you didn't catch the first time around.

Once you've reached a conclusion, you must decide what action to take, if any. If you find that the accused employee has violated company policy, you'll want to impose a level of discipline consistent with the violation. Of course, the more serious or frequent the violations, the more serious the discipline should be in response.

Crafting a Solution

The best way to resolve a complaint depends on the facts of the underlying incident(s). Your goals in coming up with an appropriate resolution are to prevent and correct inappropriate behavior and to restore the workplace to a professional, collegial environment. Taking quick, effective action to address misconduct not only puts a stop to the immediate problem, but it also shows employees that the company takes their concerns seriously. It also shows potential wrongdoers that violating company policy will result in discipline. The more quickly and thoroughly you address employee complaints, the more readily the work atmosphere will improve for everyone.

CAUTION

Supervisor harassment requires special attention. As explained
in Chapter 2, the company faces a much higher liability risk when a supervisor
harasses a subordinate. Because of this risk, supervisor harassment calls for a
strong disciplinary response. In addition to taking away the supervisor's duty
to manage the reporting employee, you should consider whether that person
should be in a position of authority at all. Because of the liability risks—and a
supervisor's power to act for the company—you should allow a supervisor to
continue in a managerial role only if you are very confident that the supervisor
will behave appropriately going forward.

Communicating Your Findings

Once you've reached a conclusion, you must communicate the outcome to
the reporting and the accused employees. Your approach will depend on
whom you are talking to, as well as on the conclusion you reach.

Meeting With the Accused Employee

Your first meeting should be with the accused employee. Being accused of
harassment or discrimination is doubtlessly a very stressful event. The accused
employee should find out from you whether discipline will be involved, not
through the office grapevine. And, if you decide that discipline is appropriate,
you'll want to handle that before you talk to the reporting employee.

Be professional and respectful when meeting with the accused employee,
even if your investigation revealed serious misconduct. Focus on your duty
to enforce the company's policies and comply with the law. If you are
unsure what level of discipline is appropriate, get some guidance from
human resources or company decision makers first.

During the investigation, you should already have given the accused
employee an opportunity to respond to the allegations directly. You don't
have to reveal what particular witnesses said or all the reasons why you
reached the conclusions you did. If you will impose discipline, simply
explain that you conducted your investigation, you concluded, based on
all of the available evidence, that the accused employee violated company
policy, and you will have to impose disciplinary action.

TIP

A good faith investigation also protects you from defamation claims. Employees who feel they are wrongfully disciplined or terminated for harassment or discrimination might claim that you defamed them—that is, that you publicly spread negative information about them that wasn't true—or that their termination is wrongful or illegal. But as long as the employer has a reasonable belief, backed by a thorough investigation, that a violation occurred, courts have denied these claims.

Meeting With the Reporting Employee

When you meet with the reporting employee, you will need to walk a fine line. You must provide enough information to reassure the reporting employee that you took the complaint seriously, investigated it fully, and handled it effectively. At the same time, however, the reporting employee should not be privy to every detail of the investigation and the company's response. You must protect the confidentiality of the investigation and the privacy of the accused employee and any witnesses you interviewed.

To make sure the reporting employee understands your position, you might want to start the meeting off by stating that you aren't free to discuss all of the details your investigation uncovered or how the company decided to respond. Explain that, just as the reporting employee was entitled to confidentiality to the extent possible, so are the accused employee and any witnesses you spoke to.

Next, tell the reporting employee generally whom you talked to (for example, "I met individually with everyone who was at the meeting," or "I spoke to all of the employees you mentioned as possible witnesses to your conversation at lunch"), and whether your investigation turned up information that either supported or contradicted the reporting employee's complaint ("Four of the employees remembered hearing him make the statement you described to me"). Be careful not to reveal information you shouldn't, which can be especially tough if the employee asks questions about who said what. For example, if the employee asks,

"Who told you I raised my voice at the meeting?" you should tell the employee that you aren't free to reveal information like this, to protect the confidentiality of other employees.

Lessons From the Real World

Employer's honest, good faith belief that an employee engaged in sexual harassment defeats employee's wrongful termination claim.

Rollins Hudig Hall International, Inc., received an employee complaint that senior vice president Ralph Cotran had sexually harassed two female employees. Rollins conducted an extensive investigation, in which it interviewed more than 20 witnesses and obtained affidavits from the victims. Witnesses stated that Cotran had made obscene phone calls to female employees, exposed himself to them, and masturbated in front of them.

Rollins met with Cotran and reviewed the allegations with him. Cotran offered no explanations, but gave Rollins a list of additional witnesses to interview, which it did. One of the witnesses identified by Cotran said that she'd received a "strange" phone call at home from Cotran. Yet another told Rollins that Cotran had made obscene calls to her after a sexual relationship between them had ended. Based on all of this information, Rollins fired Cotran.

Cotran sued over his termination. After a trial in which Cotran offered evidence that he'd had consensual sexual relationships with the alleged victims, a jury found that Cotran had not engaged in sexual harassment and awarded him $1.7 million. Rollins appealed.

The California Supreme Court found that Rollins had good cause to terminate Cotran's employment. The company had an honest and reasonable belief that he'd committed sexual harassment based on its investigation, which had included an opportunity for Cotran to respond to the accusations. The court also ruled that the question in such a case is not whether the accused employee actually engaged in the alleged conduct, but whether the employer had an honest belief, based on an adequate investigation, that he had.

Cotran v. Rollins Hudig Hall International, Inc., 17 Cal.4th 93 (1998).

Lessons From the Real World

Separation doesn't have to be total.

Philip Feiner told coworker Melody Swenson that he dreamed of her, watched her "ass moving," and wanted to take her alone into a room and kiss her. Though Swenson rejected Feiner's advances, he grabbed her wrist and tried to pull her to him. Swenson yanked her hand back, screamed at him to stop, and reported the comments and incident to her supervisor. The supervisor informed Feiner that he had harassed Swenson, instructed him to cease, and temporarily transferred him away from Swenson's immediate work area, although the separation did not eliminate all contact between the two.

Swenson sued the employer, alleging that it failed to take prompt, temporary steps in response to her complaint. The appellate court disagreed and reversed the jury verdict in her favor. The court noted that the employer had moved quickly to separate the two and found that the separation was adequate, even though not total, because the employer did not have to "provide Swenson a Feiner-free workplace."

Swenson v. Potter, 271 F.3d 1184 (9th Cir. 2001).

You shouldn't give the reporting employee details about the discipline you will be imposing on the accused employee, if any. If the accused employee has been disciplined as a result of the investigation, you should say so, and tell the employee about any steps you've taken to prevent problems in the future. For example, if the employee complained of harassment by a supervisor, you can state that the supervisor has been disciplined and will no longer be responsible for managing the reporting employee. Let the reporting employee know that you appreciate his or her willingness to come forward, and encourage the employee to let you know immediately if there are any further problems or the employee faces any retaliation as a result of the complaint.

What to Say When Results Are Inconclusive

It's very hard to tell reporting employees that your results are inconclusive. They might feel they took a big risk in coming forward and feel hurt or angry that the company appears not to believe their claims. Make sure you don't compound the problem by denying it: Events might have occurred just as the reporting employee described, even if there wasn't evidence to support his or her claims.

When meeting with the reporting employee, make sure to:

- Thank the employee for coming forward.
- Explain that, after a full investigation, you were unable to substantiate the allegations.
- Make clear that you spoke with the accused employee and stressed the company's commitment to a workplace free of discrimination and harassment.
- Encourage the employee to come forward if there are any future incidents.

TIP

Follow up to make sure corrective action is effective. Calendar a date shortly down the road to check in on any progress or changes. Make sure the accused employee has complied with any training requirements or other instructions (for example, to leave the reporting employee alone). Talk to the reporting employee to find out if he or she has experienced any further problems or retaliation.

Closure Letters

One option for communicating your findings to the reporting and accused employees is to give each a "closure letter." In this letter, you tell the employees that you conducted a full investigation of the reported conduct and state the outcome, as described above.

Conclude with a statement that the company will proceed consistently with its policy, taking whatever action, if any, is called for under the circumstances. Reiterate that the employees should contact you if they have any questions or to report any further incidents.

Dos and Don'ts

Do:

- Take complaints seriously, and treat all employees involved with respect.
- Create a plan before you investigate.
- Ask who, what, where, when, how, and why questions to get details.
- Give every employee you interview a copy of the company's policy prohibiting discrimination and harassment.
- Separate the reporting employee and the accused employee as much as possible during the investigation.
- Take corrective action that complies with company policy and is reasonably calculated to stop the misconduct.
- Communicate your findings to the reporting employee and accused employee, without revealing unnecessary details.

Don't:

- Ask leading questions.
- Let your personal opinions cloud your objectivity.
- Reveal details about your investigation to people who don't need to know them.
- Hesitate to ask for management or human resources help when you're having trouble reaching a conclusion.
- Retaliate against employees for reporting or discussing sexual harassment or discrimination issues.

Documentation

As you take complaints and investigate claims of harassment and discrimination, you must document as you go. Good documentation is an essential component of a thorough investigation. It helps you keep track of dates, documents you reviewed, whom you spoke to, and what everyone said, so you can put everything together and draw a conclusion. Keeping good records also helps you recognize gaps in information you might need to explore further. And it allows other decision makers to take the information you gathered and draw logical conclusions from it, too. This is helpful if, for example, you are responsible for conducting the investigation, but not for deciding what action the company should take afterwards.

A good paper trail also gives you valuable legal protection. It shows that you are actively trying to resolve the problem and demonstrates the facts you had at your disposal as you reached your conclusions and decided what course of action to take. These facts ultimately justify your decisions, showing others that you have followed company policy and complied with the law.

If you are unable to reach a conclusion about what happened, your documentation will play a very important role in protecting the company. Your records will demonstrate areas where there were conflicting facts that prevented you from figuring out who was telling the truth, which demonstrates that you investigated in good faith. And, if further incidents involving the same people happen, the company can evaluate them in light of the history recorded in your documents.

The best documentation is complete, detailed, and factual. You shouldn't write down every stray thought that crosses your mind during the investigation; your thoughts, feelings, or inclinations about what happened don't belong in your documentation. At the same time, however, your records should include all of the facts you considered in reaching your conclusions and the source of those facts (for example, a witness statement or email). Be prepared for the worst-case scenario: If the company is ever sued, a clear record will help you recall what actually happened at the time and support the conclusions you reached. This chapter explains how to create documents that meet these objectives.

What Your Documentation Should Look Like

Your investigation file will contain different types of documents. Some of them were probably prepared for other purposes, but include information relevant to your investigation, such as emails, performance evaluations, personnel records, and so on. Others are documents you prepare during the investigation, such as notes from interviews and memos regarding your findings.

The first type of documents are historical and become part of the investigation file because they contain relevant information. The documents you create are a different story, however, as you are responsible for their content. All of these documents should serve as a useful, factual, and accurate representation of the information available at the time you conducted your investigation.

> **CAUTION**
> **Documents you create could be presented as evidence in court.** Unless you prepare the investigation and other documents for your company's attorneys or at their direction, the reporting employee can get copies of those documents after filing a lawsuit and perhaps even introduce them as evidence at trial. As long as you keep this possible audience in mind while drafting your documents, handing them over should help your company's case. The documents will show that you fulfilled your legal obligation to investigate the complaint and respond appropriately.

To create the most useful record of your work, make sure your documentation includes:

- **Dates.** Each document should include all relevant dates, including when it was created and when particular events described in the documents took place.
- **Source.** Your records should indicate where you learned particular facts or who gave you specific items, such as documents or photographs. This information might be obvious on the face of the document—for example, you can write your own name on interview notes—but if it's not, make sure there is some additional notation that reflects its origins.

- This notation is particularly important if other names appear on the document. For example, you might have a printout of an email containing a sexually explicit joke, sent by one employee to a group of coworkers. The document will probably show the names of the original sender and recipient, but it's also important to note where you got the printout: Did the sender give it to you? One of the listed recipients? Another employee to whom it was forwarded? Or did everyone deny the existence of the email until you had the IT department comb the archives and dig it out?

- **Full names.** Names might become important years later, when witnesses no longer work at the company and you get another complaint or are involved in a lawsuit. It's much easier to find witnesses if you know their full names.

- **Complete sentences.** Using full sentences makes it easy for anyone to read and understand your interview notes.

- **Facts.** Instead of drawing conclusions, explain the facts. For example, instead of saying an employee is upset, you might write, "When I asked her if she was upset by his question, she looked down and whispered, 'not really.' She then began to cry."

- **No legal conclusions.** Your job is not to determine whether behavior meets the legal definition of harassment or discrimination. In fact, putting a conclusion like that in your investigation file can do a lot of harm to your company in a lawsuit. Instead, you should decide whether the investigated conduct violates your company's policies; if you decide in the affirmative, that's the conclusion that should go in your records.

 Common Questions

Q: *I'm the head of human resources for my company. I received a complaint from a transgender male employee, Scott, that his supervisor, Loretta, told him to go after a sales target like a "typical alpha male." Scott said this happened when he was in a product update meeting with Loretta and his coworker, Adrienne.*

I interviewed Adrienne today and here are my notes: "Adrienne said she was in Scott's office when Loretta came in last Wednesday. I asked her if anything inappropriate happened in Scott's office at the time. She hesitated and then she said, no. I think she might not be credible because she could be protecting Loretta; I've heard they're friends outside of work. This leads me to conclude that Loretta probably did make a sexist or transgender slur about Scott." Have I documented all of this properly?

A: *Not even close. Your documentation (and your interview technique) have a number of flaws. First, you've drawn a conclusion rather than documenting the information you gathered. Your notes don't reflect that you even asked Adrienne if Loretta made the exact comment that Scott reported, but only that you asked if anything "inappropriate happened." You also don't indicate who told you that Loretta and Adrienne are friends outside of work or whether you asked Adrienne about that connection. Although this is a factor you may take into account when making your ultimate decisions, you have to nail it down—and decide how much weight to give it— before you can rely on it.*

What's more, the document is undated, the writer is unidentified, you don't give the full names of the individuals to whom you refer, it contains an unsupported opinion (that Adrienne might not be credible), and a conclusion that doesn't logically follow from the facts you've related. A follow-up interview, documented by more complete notes, is necessary here, to start.

What Documents You Should Have

The documents you gather will depend on what you are investigating. For example, if an employee complains that she was denied a promotion because of her gender, you'll need to collect personnel records, internal application documents, and other information on those who were considered for the position, in order to evaluate everyone's qualifications.

In addition to the documents you collect, you will create several types of documents during your investigation. Your company might call these documents by different names than the ones we use below. That's okay—there's no requirement that they take any particular form or have a specific title—as long as you're sure you're covering all the bases.

Summary of the Complaint

After interviewing the reporting employee, you should prepare a brief summary of the complaint. It should be a short, factual account of what the reporting employee told you.

Sample Complaint Summary

To: File

From: Leona Brown, Human Resources

Date: November 29, 20xx

Re: Tomiko Nishimura Complaint Summary

On November 29, 20xx, Tomiko Nishimura came into my office and she said that she believed her supervisor, Gordon Lewis, discriminated against her based on her race. Tomiko said that Gordon had terminated her employment that day and that no other non-Asian employees were terminated.

The purpose of a summary is simply to provide a context for the other documents. It needn't be a detailed recitation of the employee's complaint—and it shouldn't be, as that will be found in the notes of the interview of that employee and in the witness statement, if the employee signs one. Just make sure your summary is a brief statement of what the employee actually complained of, not your opinion of it.

Witness Statements

Although much of the information you collect will be your own notes or summary documents, you may also receive written statements directly from the witnesses you interview. A witness's signed, written statement is perhaps the best type of document—his or her account of what happened, without any interpretation by a third party.

Witnesses might not volunteer to provide written statements, but you can always ask them to do so. However, not all witness statements will be written as you might like. Witnesses might forget to include important facts—for instance, the date of an alleged incident or the first and last names of everyone present—and they might include their own thoughts or opinions, which usually aren't relevant. A raw witness statement can even distract from the actual facts the witness could convey. For example, a statement such as "Tomiko was being really rude," tells you how the witness felt about Tomiko's behavior, but doesn't give you any idea about what Tomiko actually said or did and in what context. A better statement might say something like, "Tomiko raised her voice, then turned and walked away before Gordon had a chance to answer."

To get the right information in and keep the rest out, it often makes sense for you to draft the witness statement based on the facts the witness tells you during any interviews, quoting the witness verbatim on key points. The witness can then review it for accuracy and, if in agreement with it, sign it. This way, you have an opportunity to make sure you understood the witness correctly and got all of the facts straight.

The witness might want to change something in your written statement. If you got something wrong, you should certainly change it to reflect the true facts. You can either correct the statement electronically before the witness signs it or cross out errors and write in your corrections on the original document. If the witness changes the story after the interview, however, you should have another conversation about it before getting a signed statement. Perhaps the witness is worried about retaliation or doesn't want to cause trouble. If the witness insists that the new version of events is the truth, you should allow the witness to sign a statement to that effect. However, you should draft a separate memo to the file describing the change; you might also need to do additional investigating to find out what's going on. Keep any draft statement that the witness marked up and note the date that you discussed it with the witness.

Common Questions

Q: *I interviewed an employee who said he saw an incident that formed the basis of a discrimination complaint another employee made against their manager. After the interview, I prepared a statement and asked the witness to sign it. He took it to review and returned it the next day with some changes. The new version essentially denies that he directly observed the incident, even though he told me during his interview that he had. What to do?*

A: *You need to have another conversation with the employee to find out the reason he changed his version of events. Tell the employee that the statement must accurately reflect what happened—that the company expects his honesty. Because he might feel apprehensive about making a statement that implicates his manager, you might want to also remind him that he can't be retaliated against for assisting in the investigation.*

If the witness continues to insist that the revised version of events is accurate, keep the altered statement in the file and document the discrepancy. If you find other evidence that supports the complaining employee's version of events, you want to be able to show why you gave less credence to this witness's "new and improved" statement.

Don't argue with a witness who changes the "facts." Just ask about the change and make a note of the discussion and the changed version of events. And don't speculate in your notes about why you think the witness changed his or her story.

 Common Questions

Q: *I received the following written, signed statement from a witness I interviewed in connection with a sexual harassment complaint: "On January 5, 2020, I was in the lunchroom when Rebecca Cranston and Jorge Lopez came in. Rebecca bent over to get her lunch bag out of the refrigerator and Jorge said, 'nice view.' This was a disgusting comment. Rebecca stood up quickly and told Jorge, 'I'm sick of your jokes.' Then she left the room. She seemed really upset. Signed Lucas Owens, January 7, 2020." This is a good piece of evidence, isn't it?*

A: *It's not quite good enough because it's missing some key information, and it contains some unnecessary and unhelpful material. The statement doesn't explain how the witness knew that Rebecca was upset. That is, it should present the facts that led to this opinion instead of just the opinion (for example, she was frowning and stormed off). It also doesn't indicate whether anyone else was present, which is an important fact, nor does it reveal why Lucas felt that Jorge's statement was disgusting (in other words, if it's because Jorge was clearly looking at Rebecca's posterior when he said it, the statement should relate that fact).*

Interview Notes

As you conduct your interviews, you should take notes of the important facts. Start with the basics: the date, the witness's full name, and your name. Keep in mind that you might not work at the company forever—at some point in the future, the company might need to review the notes and will want to know all of these details.

The notes themselves should record the important questions you asked in the interview, how the witness responded, and any other information that was volunteered or seemed relevant. These notes are for you and the company—not for the witness. If you see a discrepancy in something the witness said, for example, you should note it here for follow-up questions.

Use a consistent format for your documentation from witness to witness and from investigation to investigation. This practice will help you make sure you include all of the necessary elements. Your company may have a standard form for this purpose; if not, you can write a simple memo to the file (see "Sample Interview Notes," below).

When possible, include direct quotes from the witness. Don't speculate about what witnesses mean or why they're saying it. If you want to record a witness's demeanor, focus on observable facts (such as, "She raised her voice when she said this," instead of "She was angry"). It might also make sense to document the next steps you plan to take to follow up on the information obtained.

Sample Interview Notes

To: File
From: Leona Brown, Human Resources
Date: November 30, 20xx
Re: Interview with Marnie Farrell

On January 7, 20xx, I met with Marnie Farrell to discuss an alleged incident between Rebecca Cranston and Jorge Lopez. According to Rebecca, Marnie was in the lunchroom on January 5, when the incident occurred (see memo to file, January 5, 20xx).

I asked Marnie if she was in the lunchroom on January 5 with Rebecca and Jorge. She said that she was. She told me that Lucas Owens and Bob Stevens were also there, but no one else was present.

I asked her if she saw Rebecca open the refrigerator and heard Jorge make a comment. She said, "I saw her open the door, and I heard him say something but I don't know what because I was on my cellphone." When I asked her what happened after Jorge made the comment, Marnie said, "Rebecca slammed the refrigerator door and left the room. Jorge said, 'I'm just kidding; don't be mad,' but Rebecca didn't say anything, she just left."

Based on this interview, I will follow up and interview Bob Stevens and re-interview Lucas Owens.

This sample interview note contains all the necessary elements: the date of the interview; the full names of the interviewer, the interviewee, and all involved parties; a sufficiently detailed recitation of the substance of the interview; and no speculation.

Take notes as you're conducting each interview. It can be hard to get down every relevant fact and remain engaged in the interview, so you might find yourself taking shorter notes with abbreviations and codes only you can read. That's fine as long as you later translate them into full, coherent notes that others will be able to read and understand. It's best to do this immediately after each interview, when everything is still fresh in your mind. And make sure that if you quote the witness, the quote is accurate.

CAUTION

Use an intake form to interview the reporting employee. The form will give you a standard format for receiving complaints, thus ensuring you ask for all of the relevant information. This practice will help you conduct your investigation and make it less likely that you'll need to go back to the reporting employee for more details. You can find a sample intake form online at Nolo's companion page for this book. See Appendix B for details.

Create a Timeline

It's important to establish the chronological order of events relating to a complaint. As you get each employee's account of what happened, note when the events they describe occurred (or when the employee says they occurred). Rarely do all relevant events occur on the same day. Instead, often a history or pattern of behavior or previous statements or acts exists that seems more relevant once a problem has escalated.

A detailed timeline of events will help you keep all the events and the witnesses' stories straight. You can create one after speaking to the reporting employee and add information as you speak to other employees.

Sample Timeline

To:	File
From:	Lane Crawford
Date:	May 12, 20xx
Re:	Working timeline, Gray/Howard investigation

March 23, 20xx	Date of alleged incident between Marie Gray and Roger Howard (see memo to file, April 22)
April 2	Marie's performance evaluation meeting with Roger
April 18	Marie received performance appraisal from Roger; refused to sign
April 22	Marie reports alleged harassment to me

This sample timeline is helpful because it gives the dates and the events in a clear, chronological fashion. You might have to rework the timeline frequently as you gather more information that either changes the dates or order of events (for example, if you discover the performance meeting actually occurred on April 3, and Marie just got the date wrong) or that adds new events (for example, if Lane learned during a later interview that Marie had closed a major deal between the March 23 incident and her April 18 receipt of the performance appraisal).

If witnesses differ on their recollection of when an event occurred, put all of the dates in the timeline with a notation identifying who reported it, making clear that the chronology is in dispute. For example, if Marie and Roger insist that the performance evaluation meeting took place on different days, your timeline might say: "April 2: Marie claims she and Roger had a meeting to discuss her performance evaluation; Roger disputes (see email from Roger Howard, May 13, 20xx). April 5: Roger claims he and Marie met to discuss her performance evaluation; Marie disputes (see notes from interview of Marie Gray, April 22, 20xx)." If you later receive information that definitively places an event on a particular date, note that on the timeline, too, with reference to the new information and its source.

Keep your timeline brief and to the point. Remember, you might have to use it as evidence and turn it over to the other side if a legal dispute arises later over the investigation, the events leading to it, or the company's response. Short entries will also help you make the best use of the timeline. Its purpose is to allow you to see the sequence of events and their relationship to each other, which will be easier if you keep your notes brief. Include only as much information as you need to trigger your memory, such as "alleged incident in kitchen" or "Ellen notified of promotion decision." The details of each event can be included elsewhere in your notes.

Physical Evidence

If you have photographs, cartoons, letters, emails, or other items that are implicated in the reported incident, you should keep a copy in your file, along with a note that explains when, how, and from whom you received the item(s). If the originals are later destroyed or lost, a record of what you were considering when you evaluated the case will still exist.

Sample Evidence Note

On September 18, 20xx, I made a photocopy of a cartoon hanging on Mark Stuart's cubicle wall that Jeffrey Townsend had complained about (see Townsend complaint, 9/18/xx). The copy of the cartoon is attached to this note. I also instructed Mark to take the original cartoon home, at least until the investigation of Jeffrey's complaint is concluded.

At times, you might need to describe physical evidence that can't be copied (such as online videos). Keep these notes in the investigation file and be sure to note the date and location when you examined the evidence. When possible, copy a link, URL, or take a screenshot of online or digital evidence.

Many companies have security software to track (and capture) employee Internet activity on company computers. If your company uses such software, it's possible to copy screenshots, Internet searches, keystrokes, or other data that could be relevant to an employee complaint. For example, if an employee reports that a coworker had pornographic material visible on his or her work computer screen, it might be possible to verify that the accused employee visited websites displaying offensive material, along with the dates and times of those site visits. And, of course, security cameras might provide evidence of certain incidents or behaviors (such as unwelcome touching in the company parking lot).

 CAUTION

Advise employees of company monitoring in your handbook. Although employees have a limited right to privacy with respect to their conduct in the workplace, state laws differ about the degree of privacy they retain. Having a written policy informing employees that your company monitors their electronic communications and computer activity reduces employee expectations of privacy, which will help your company avoid legal problems. Disclosure is also in your company's interests: Fewer employees are likely to stray in cyberspace or use your company's email system to send inappropriate messages if they know that they might get caught.

Policy Distribution Log

During your investigation, keep a log of everyone to whom you've given a copy of the company's antiharassment and antidiscrimination policy. (Hint: Every employee you speak to during the course of your investigation should be on the list.) Be sure that you also put a signed form acknowledging receipt of the company policy in each employee's personnel file. The policy distribution log can be simple, with each employee's name and the date you gave him or her the policy, as well as a check box indicating that the employee returned a signed acknowledgment form with the date it was returned (see Appendix B for a sample form). If you haven't received the acknowledgment form within a few days, make sure to follow up.

Sample Policy Distribution Log

Policy Distribution Log—Jansen/Doyle Investigation, October 15, 20xx			
Employee Name	Date Policy Received	Acknowledgment Received?	Date Acknowledgment Received
Scott Jansen	10/15/xx	✓	10/15/xx
Lorenzo Doyle	10/15/xx		
Adrienne Prather	10/15/xx	✓	10/16/xx

The Final Report

At the end of your investigation, you should write a summary report that puts your findings together. You'll take the information you've collected from all of the sources and assemble it in one place, along with the conclusions you drew from all of the facts. You might want to have a superior or human resources representative review the document, to make sure it includes all of the necessary information and supports your ultimate conclusion.

Sample Final Report

To: File
From: Nellie Ray
Date: July 30, 20xx
Re: Eli Dolan complaint

This report summarizes my investigation of Eli Dolan's complaint of discrimination by his supervisor, Katherine Ross.

    On July 23, Eli reported that he had been denied a promotion to a position that recently opened up in his department and said he believed his supervisor, Katherine, selected someone else instead because of his ancestry. Eli is Israeli. Eli did not allege that Katherine had ever made any statements about his ancestry; he stated, "I just have a feeling it is because I am Israeli." I asked Eli if there were any other witnesses who might have relevant information, and he stated that there were not. I also asked Eli if there were any other documents or information he would like me to consider, and he said no. (See Intake Form, July 23, 20xx.)

    I reviewed Eli's personnel file, which contained his performance reviews and his application for the promotion. Each review rated Eli as "meets expectations." I met with Katherine on July 25 and asked her why Eli was not selected for the promotion. (See memo to file, July 25, 20xx.) Katherine said that she chose another candidate, Simone Cameron, because Simone is better qualified. She provided me with a copy of the job description. When I asked Katherine to list Simone's superior qualifications, she cited Simone's greater experience in the field, the fact that she held a similar position in her last job for several years, and that she has an advanced degree. Katherine also said that Eli doesn't have an advanced degree, nor has he held a similar position. Katherine said she would definitely consider Eli for promotion in the future and wouldn't hesitate to select him if he is the most qualified candidate, but he was not in this case. I asked Katherine if she was aware of Eli's ethnicity prior to making the promotion selection. She said she was. Katherine said that Eli's ancestry did not affect her decision in any way. I asked Katherine if any witnesses might have additional relevant information, and she stated no.

    After meeting with Katherine, I reviewed Simone's application and confirmed the information Katherine gave me. Simone did have the education and experience requirements listed on the job posting, while Eli did not.

    Based on the above information, I've concluded that no violation of company policy occurred. I will meet with Eli to communicate the results of my investigation.

Discipline Report

If you decide to discipline the accused employee or anyone else based on your investigation, a brief report that discipline was imposed on that basis should also go in the complaint and investigation file. A copy should also go in the accused employee's personnel file, so that supervisors and managers will respond appropriately if the employee engages in similar violations in the future. The report should also state what discipline was imposed. It isn't necessary to include the reporting employee or victim's name in the discipline report. If there are conditions imposed on the accused employee or requirements that he or she must complete, list those, along with any due dates, and include a space to check once they have been satisfied or completed.

Sample Discipline Report

To: File
From: Alison Bruger
Date: March, 20xx

As a result of my conclusion that Marcus Green violated company policy during the holiday party (see Marcus Green Investigation Final Report, March 10, 20xx), Marcus must:

☐ complete a three-day suspension without pay from March 20 through March 23; and

☐ attend a harassment webinar on April 5.

Document Management

Preparing and collecting good records of the investigation doesn't do you much good if you can't find the documents you need, when you need them. And, if other managers or company lawyers need to review the documents, the papers need to be easy to locate and navigate. Here are some tips for creating an organized, coherent file on a complaint, the investigation, and any resulting disciplinary action or other company response.

How to Manage Documents

Keep all documents relating to a complaint and investigation in one file, separate from other employee files. This practice helps protect confidentiality because the documents won't be accessible to people who shouldn't see them. It also helps prevent retaliatory behavior because information that shouldn't affect other employment decisions won't be available to those making the decisions.

Within the file, organize the documents logically. The most common method is chronological order, with your investigatory notes first and leading up to your final report and disciplinary report, if applicable. If a witness refers to an item of physical evidence, such as a letter, cartoon, or email, attach a copy of that item to the interview notes for easy reference.

If the investigation turns up evidence that might deteriorate over time, such as handwritten notes or photographs, make backup copies of that evidence for the file. Likewise, if the personal property of an employee or anyone else is possible evidence in the matter and you cannot take the item itself, make a copy or take a photograph of it. You might also need a photograph of physical evidence that can't be copied (such as graffiti on a worksite wall). Keep the photocopies and photographs in the file along with a note that includes your name and the date and location on which you examined the item.

Where to Keep Documents

Keep the complaint and investigation documents in a secure and private place that employees and others without a need to know can't access, such as a locked file cabinet. Some evidence, investigation notes, and reports may also be maintained in an electronic format. If so, be sure to protect them by saving them to a secure file that others can't open, perhaps with password protection. And, if electronic documents as well as hard-copy documents exist, make sure they cross-reference each other.

Although it's essential to maintain these documents in a secure place, don't hide them. You might have trouble remembering where you put them, and others could need to look at them in the future. One way to make sure that documents don't get lost is to share their location and any password with at least one other manager.

How Long to Keep Documents

Your company should keep the documents relating to a harassment or discrimination complaint and investigation for as long as it typically keeps financial and other sensitive documents. The EEOC requires employers to retain records related to potential violations for the period of the statute of limitations on the potential legal claim (at least one year after the incident) or until a matter filed with the agency is finally disposed of (via verdict, court order, or settlement), whichever is later. States may have their own retention requirements.

To be safe from a legal perspective, keep the complaint and investigation files and documents for at least five years. If the employees involved still work for you, you might want to extend this time period. This practice could be helpful if the investigation documents become relevant later—if, for example, more allegations are raised against the accused employee.

 Lessons From the Real World

Statements from other employees about prior discrimination supported later employee's claim.

After United Cerebral Palsy/Spastic Children's Foundation fired Dewandra Johnson, she filed a pregnancy discrimination lawsuit. The organization asked the court to dismiss the case. Johnson submitted statements by former employees detailing pregnancy discrimination they had themselves experienced or witnessed against other employees by United Cerebral Palsy.

The court rejected United Cerebral Palsy's motion, allowing Johnson's pregnancy discrimination case to go to trial. The declarations of the other employees, along with other evidence, persuaded the court that Johnson was entitled to a trial of her claims.

Johnson v. United Cerebral Palsy/Spastic Children's Found., 173 Cal.App.4th 740 (2009).

To the extent that prior employees have complained about a similar type of discrimination in the past, your company will be in a better position to address such violations and defend itself if it has maintained good records showing that it addressed those prior issues as they arose.

Dos and Don'ts

Do:

- Include vital details in your documentation, including full names, dates, and other essential facts.
- Prepare witness statements, and ask witnesses to review and sign them.
- Keep any draft statements that witnesses have marked up.
- Photocopy or photograph physical evidence to preserve a record of it.
- Protect the confidentiality of the complaint and investigations file.
- Organize documents in a logical fashion.

Don't:

- Insert personal opinions, impressions, or reactions into your documentation.
- Allow a witness to change his or her version of events without asking about the reasons for the change.
- Neglect to revise your timeline as your investigation proceeds.
- Draw legal conclusions.
- Inadvertently prevent others with a need to know from accessing your investigative files.

After the Investigation

Once you've finished investigating a discrimination or harassment complaint, documented all of your findings, and taken (or recommended) any necessary disciplinary action, you might think your job is done. However, some additional challenges could be left to deal with, even after your investigation file is closed. A complaint can lead to a host of related problems, from office gossip to allegations of retaliation to new complaints by other employees.

Part of your job might be managing the additional challenges a complaint can bring to the workplace. The way you handle these issues can go a long way toward maintaining a positive work environment that's free of harassment and discrimination and helping you limit the company's liability in the event that an employee files a lawsuit.

This chapter explains how to:

- deal with the aftermath of a complaint
- handle new complaints as they arise
- avoid retaliation claims, and
- keep the company informed of your efforts.

Dealing With the Aftermath of a Complaint

Rarely will a complaint of harassment or discrimination completely escape the notice of other employees. Despite your best attempts to keep your investigation confidential, rumors often fly. Part of your job will be keeping these rumors in check. If you don't, employees might decide for themselves what's happened and why, regardless of the facts. They might misunderstand the company's role because they don't know what you've done to investigate and resolve the problem. And, all that time employees spend speculating, gossiping, or worrying about what happened and what it means is time they're not spending on work.

The solution isn't to publicize every detail of your investigation, however. You still have to keep the investigation and underlying issues confidential to protect the process and encourage employees to continue to come forward with complaints. Revealing things like who complained, what an accused employee was alleged to have done, or what discipline was imposed can also lead to legal problems if the employees involved believe that your comments have harmed their reputations. Your job is to provide enough information to assure employees that the situation has been handled appropriately, without giving too much away.

Controlling Gossip

One of the most common side effects of a workplace harassment or discrimination claim is an increase in office gossip. Even if all of the witnesses respect your requests for confidentiality, it's natural for coworkers to be curious if they see others heading to your office to be interviewed or learn that the accused employee has been put on paid leave, reassigned to another department, or even fired.

When dealing with the office rumor mill, your goal is to stop the gossip and redirect employees' attention back to their jobs. As soon as you learn that employees are spreading rumors about the complaint or the investigation, you should do what you can to limit or stop it. A good first step is to reiterate your company's policy on handling complaints. Take gossiping employees aside individually. If they were involved in your investigation in some way (for example, as witnesses), remind them that the process must be kept confidential. Use the opportunity to tell employees again that they should immediately come to you if they have concerns about new incidents or retaliation. Also ask supervisory staff to report gossip and rumors to you.

For employees who weren't involved in the investigation, you'll need to be a bit more circumspect. You might start by saying something more general, such as: "I've heard that you have some concerns about the company's antiharassment policy and investigations procedure. Do you have any questions, or would you like to discuss anything?" This tactic can give you the opportunity to squelch speculation about a complaint, even if you're not able to provide detailed information about what really happened.

If an employee wants to know the details of a specific situation, tell the employee that the company takes violations of company policy very seriously.

Anytime the company receives a complaint, it investigates immediately, as required by company policy. Explain that the company also respects the privacy of its employees and doesn't reveal information about investigations to those without a need to know. This means that you can't reveal any details of a particular complaint. Ask that the employee respect colleagues' privacy, too.

Sometimes, the gossip about a complaint might itself violate company policy against harassment or discrimination. For example, employees gossiping about a sexual harassment complaint might speculate in graphic detail about harassing conduct or joke inappropriately about the nature of the complaint. When you hear about situations like these, you need to intervene. In addition to responding as you ordinarily would when employees make inappropriate comments, tell the employees that they need to do their part to help maintain a collegial, professional environment. Emphasize that gossiping thwarts that goal and can itself violate company policy.

 Common Questions

Q: *A few months ago an employee complained that a coworker made a derogatory comment based on a racial stereotype. The accused employee admitted making the comment and apologized. In compliance with our company policy, he received a written warning and went to a diversity training class. The reporting employee was informed of the outcome and registered no further complaints. Now, though, another manager has told me that she's heard employee rumors that the accused employee was a "racist" and the company swept it under the rug. What do I do?*

A: *Following your company's policy was the right thing to do, and under the circumstances, it was reasonable to deal with a single discrete incident as you did— and to keep it confidential. But now you have more work to do. If the problem of employee gossip is too widespread to address it with individual employees, send out an email or memo with the company's antiharassment and antidiscrimination policies attached. You should also reiterate that employees are to bring any concerns about past or present discrimination to you promptly. Explain that you expect anyone who has further questions to discuss them with you privately—not with each other on company time.*

Handling Additional Complaints

When one employee comes forward with a complaint of harassment or discrimination, it might give other employees the courage or confidence to report incidents themselves. While this might seem like a bad thing, at least it gives you an opportunity to address systemic problems before they lead to legal liability. Multiple complaints should make you question whether there is an organizational problem that you need to correct before it gets worse.

When you are faced with additional complaints following an investigation, you should look for:

- **A pattern among the incidents.** A pattern—lots of discrimination complaints coming from a single department, repeated reports of inappropriate jokes being sent on company email, and so forth—is a red flag that a fundamental change might be needed. It could suggest that there's a common misconception about appropriate behavior within the organization, or that a supervisor or manager is failing to intervene or prevent discriminatory or harassing behavior. Understanding these patterns can help you make simple changes that have widespread effect. For example, if you receive several reports that employees are viewing pornographic images on their computers, drafting or reiterating a company policy on appropriate use of its computer equipment—perhaps along with installing software that blocks access to inappropriate sites—could solve the problem.
- **A breakdown in the reporting structure.** Sometimes, receiving several complaints at once indicates that previous violations weren't being reported or investigated correctly. For example, you might find that supervisors were dealing with complaints informally because it's less complicated, or because they didn't know they were supposed to report problems elsewhere.
- **A repeat offender.** You might have several complaints against the same person. If your separate investigations of each of the complaints reveal them to be true, your disciplinary response should take all of the events into account. In this situation, terminating the offender's employment could be necessary.

A systemic problem is going to require more work. You'll have to delve into the reasons for the repeat problems. You might need to circle back and interview people you talked to in the course of your previous investigations. You might also need to look for gaps in your company policy or discuss misunderstandings about the policy with the employees you talk to.

At the same time, your duty as a fact-finding investigator requires you to consider each complaint anew. Don't draw conclusions without taking a good, hard look at the facts in each case.

TIP

Don't protect a high-powered harasser. Among the revelations of the #MeToo movement is that different victims made multiple allegations of harassment against high-powered harassers, but management and boards of directors protected the alleged harassers and paid hush money to the victims to silence them. Some of these companies are now facing legal repercussions as a result. Regardless of the role an alleged harasser plays in a company or the amount of business the harasser brings in, best practices require a full investigation and effective response to every allegation of harassment. It might be intimidating to confront the issue of harassment or discrimination by a high-level employee. But employees, company owners, and the public at large are counting on you to do your job.

CAUTION

Make sure you report repeat patterns up the chain of command. A serious systemic flaw increases the potential for repeat problems and creates more legal exposure. Be sure company executives understand the problem and are ready to close the gap. If you discover a number of past incidents that have gone unreported or a major problem in one area of the company, this might be a good time to consider bringing in an employment lawyer to help you figure out how best to handle the situation.

If the problems you uncover stem from a single source, you'll have to figure out what to do about it. If your company policy has a weakness that results in supervisors not reporting incidents, you might need to rewrite the policy to make reporting requirements more explicit and retrain supervisors. If you see a pattern of poor behavior, it could mean that employees don't realize they've stepped over the line, either because they don't understand appropriate workplace conduct or because their managers are letting them get away with it. In either situation, training, possible policy revisions, and consistent enforcement of the company's rules will help you get a handle on the problem.

If you're not sure how to resolve the problem, ask for help. Bring your concerns to your manager or to company officers and work together to formulate a plan that will turn things around.

TIP

Responding to a pattern of complaints protects your company. Judges and juries can be extremely unsympathetic to a company that has allowed problems to continue unchecked, especially when a repeat offender is involved. Once you learn of systemic issues, you must take action to stop them— and your response should take into account the full scope of the problem. Your action will help you stay out of court because you'll put a stop to the behavior going forward. And, if you do face a lawsuit, you'll be able to show that you did all you could to end the misconduct as soon as you learned about it.

 Common Questions

Q: *We've recently had five harassment complaints in one department (way more than any other department), all against different employees. The complaints are all based on inappropriate comments or emails. I've investigated the complaints and found that all of them raise valid concerns. The responsible employees have been disciplined as company policy requires, but I'm wondering whether I should do more. I'm suspicious that something else is going on here, but I'm not sure what. What should I be looking for?*

A: *A collection of five complaints from one department is certainly troubling, but you don't really have enough information here to explain what's going on. You want to look for anything the company might be doing to communicate that the behavior is okay: Do the employees understand the rules? Start by speaking with the department supervisor. Has the supervisor received any complaints? If so, and you didn't know about them, it could be an indication that the problems have escalated precisely because nothing was ever done to deal with complaints in the first place. As a result, employees might have begun to feel the inappropriate behavior was accepted or condoned by the company. Correct that problem by giving supervisors a refresher in the company complaint policy.*

Look for patterns of behavior, as well. Are employees sending personal emails at work when they shouldn't be? If so, do they have any reason to believe that behavior is acceptable—for example, is the department supervisor aware of it, but either doing nothing to stop it or even participating? The whole department might need some training on what's permissible and what isn't.

Communicating the Results of Your Investigation

Usually, you will not need to tell employees that you've received, investigated, and resolved a complaint. And, to maintain confidentiality, you ordinarily shouldn't reveal this type of information. But sometimes— for example, if you fire someone after a high-profile incident—you should address the decision publicly. After all, the unexplained "disappearance" of a coworker or supervisor can be disruptive and stressful for employees. If a number of employees knew about the incident, they might also be concerned about whether the company is doing all it can to prevent similar incidents in the future.

But this doesn't mean you should reveal all the facts. In most cases, it's best simply to explain that you conducted a thorough, unbiased investigation in accordance with company policy and came to a conclusion based on that investigation. Reiterate that the company is committed to a workplace free of harassment and discrimination, and suggest that employees with questions or concerns come to you privately. In most cases, you needn't (and shouldn't) even mention names. If an employee has been terminated, however, you should say that the person no longer works for the company. Employees will notice that the person is gone, and there's no point denying the obvious. Just don't give out any details or state the conclusions of your investigation. It's fine to say "John is no longer working here," but not to say, "We fired John after concluding that he discriminated against Andrea."

CAUTION

If physical safety is at issue, don't be so discreet. If you fire an employee because of a physical assault or threatened assault, you should tell employees that the attacker is barred from the workplace and that they should inform you immediately of any threats to safety. In such a case, it is more important to protect your employees' safety than the privacy of the accused individual. As long as you conducted an investigation and concluded that the threat was real, you should be on safe legal ground. You might also want to contact law enforcement authorities.

Common Questions

Q: *We recently conducted an investigation of a male project manager who was accused by a subordinate of assigning jobs based on racial preferences. We couldn't substantiate the allegations. The project manager shares responsibility with another project manager, who heard about the incident and is demanding to know what's going on. She says that team members are asking her about it. How much should I tell her?*

A: *Not much, because she doesn't have any real need to know. Instead, explain to her—and encourage her to explain to employees—that the company was looking into an employee's concerns involving that manager and that those concerns have been resolved. Tell her that the issue is confidential. If employees want to discuss this further, they can come to you. And if she has specific concerns, she should be encouraged to raise them with you as well.*

Retaliation

Federal law and the laws of most states bar employers from retaliating against an employee who reports harassment or discrimination, or who participates or assists in an investigation, complaint, or lawsuit. These laws protect not only an employee who files a complaint, but also any witnesses you interview and any employee who opposes harassment or discrimination. Protection against retaliation ensures that other employees will not be deterred from reporting harassment and discrimination and that employees will participate fully in company efforts to investigate and remedy problems.

Lessons From the Real World

Witnesses who provide information during an internal investigation are protected from retaliation.

During an investigation into rumors of sexual harassment by a supervisor, a human resources officer for the Metropolitan Government of Nashville asked Vicky Crawford, a 30-year Metro employee, if she'd ever witnessed any inappropriate behavior. Crawford said she had and then recounted several harassing acts by the supervisor toward her. Nashville fired Crawford and two others who had reported harassment, but didn't discipline the supervisor. Crawford filed a retaliation lawsuit.

Nashville argued that, because Crawford didn't file a complaint herself but instead reported the violations only in response to questioning, she wasn't protected from retaliation. The Supreme Court disagreed. It held that an employee "opposes" harassment by answering an employer's question, just as if she had reported the same information on her own initiative. To find otherwise would compromise the company's ability to investigate complaints and discourage employee participation in those investigations.

Crawford v. Metro. Gov't. of Nashville, 129 S.Ct. 846 (2009).

Despite these legal protections, retaliation still occurs. It can take the form of any action that has a negative impact on the employee, if that action is taken because of the employee's complaint or participation. While terminations or demotions are obvious adverse actions, transfers, reassignments, shift changes, pay changes, and benefits changes can be, too. In some cases, retaliation can even include actions taken outside of the work environment, such as a negative job reference or an unfounded criminal or civil charge against the employee.

Lessons From the Real World

Employer retaliated against employee who filed EEOC charge by firing her fiancé.

Miriam Regalado and her fiancé, Eric Thompson, worked for North American Stainless. In February 2003, Regalado filed a sex discrimination charge against North American Stainless with the EEOC. Three weeks later, North American Stainless fired Thompson. Thompson sued the company for retaliation under Title VII. North American Stainless got the case dismissed by the trial court, arguing that Title VII did not give Thompson the right to sue for retaliation based on Regalado's protected activity of filing her EEOC charge.

The U.S. Supreme Court disagreed and held that Thompson could proceed to trial on retaliation under Title VII. The Court explained that, because an employer's termination of the fiancé of an employee who filed an EEOC charge could discourage other employees from filing charges, it was retaliation under the law.

Thompson v. North American Stainless, 562 U.S. 170, 131 S.Ct. 863 (2011).

If managers, supervisors, or company officers are aware of actions by coworkers that interfere with an employee's job, but fail to step in and stop the behavior, that might also be retaliation attributable to the employer. An employer that permits a reporting employee's peers to negatively affect his or her job is condoning that behavior.

Even though you must be conscious of negative reactions, not every adverse incident following a complaint will meet the legal definition of retaliation. The negative act must be significant enough to dissuade a reasonable employee from reporting or supporting a harassment or discrimination charge. As the Supreme Court puts it, "petty slights or minor annoyances" don't count.

Lessons From the Real World

Any action that might deter a reasonable employee from reporting harassment or discrimination can be retaliation.

Burlington Northern & Santa Fe Railway Co. hired Sheila White as a "track laborer" and assigned her to a forklift operator position. White reported that her supervisor, Bill Joiner, made inappropriate, sex-based remarks to her. Burlington suspended Joiner for ten days and sent him to a sexual harassment training session. At the same time, Burlington also reassigned White to track labor duties, ostensibly because some of her coworkers had complained that the forklift position should go to a "more senior man." Although these duties were within White's job description and didn't affect her pay, they were more arduous, dirtier, and less desirable than her previous assignment.

White filed a lawsuit claiming that Burlington's reassignment of duties was retaliatory. The Supreme Court agreed, even though the reassignment didn't affect her pay or job level. The Court reasoned that the risk of being assigned to a less-desirable job could deter a reasonable employee from complaining about harassment.

Burlington Northern & Santa Fe Ry. v. White, 548 U.S. 53 (2006).

Preventing Retaliation

You can, and should, do all you can to prevent retaliation. Retaliation compromises your company's efforts to eradicate harassment and discrimination and allows problems to continue unresolved. It can also lead to significant legal exposure. The fundamental unfairness of punishing someone for coming forward to report mistreatment seems to resonate strongly with judges and juries, who are willing to award large damages in these cases.

Here are some steps you can take to help prevent retaliation:

- **Tell employees retaliation is prohibited.** Redistribute the company's written policy when you meet with or interview employees involved in an investigation. Encourage employees to report alleged retaliation.
- **Keep complaints confidential.** The fewer employees who know about the alleged complaint—particularly managers, supervisors, and those in positions of authority—the fewer opportunities there are for anyone to retaliate against the reporting employee or others involved in the investigation.
- **Take care when disciplining an employee involved in a complaint.** You are still permitted to discipline an employee for behavior unrelated to the complaint and should follow company policies consistently. But you should have very good proof to support what you're doing.

 Common Questions

Q: *We were finalizing paperwork to terminate an employee for poor performance when she came in and complained that her boss was discriminating against her. We investigated but didn't find anything that suggested he'd violated company policy. We want to go through with the termination, but are concerned about her claiming retaliation. Are we safe?*

A: *It sounds like it, but you'll want to be very careful. You must have solid evidence that your decision is based on her performance, not on her complaint. Your best evidence would be documentation of clear communications to the employee, prior to her making the complaint, that her performance was poor, and that you'd warned her of the likely consequences if it didn't improve. If you have other contemporaneous documents—for example, communications between her supervisor and human resources, discussing the plan to terminate employment prior to the complaint—those documents would also be helpful. To make sure you've dotted every "i" and crossed every "t," consider having your attorney review your evidence before proceeding with the termination.*

Also, keep in mind that as long as she made her complaint in good faith, it doesn't ultimately matter that the complaint didn't pan out. You are still prohibited from retaliating against her. Even if you suspect she made the complaint to put you in this exact position—hesitant to discipline for a valid reason for fear of a retaliation complaint—you should not discipline her for it unless you can prove her complaint was made with this improper motive.

Finally, be aware that even if you do everything exactly right, there's no guarantee that the employee won't try to bring a lawsuit against you. Although you'll be in a good position to defend yourself, terminating employment right after receiving a complaint tends to make fair employment practices agencies and courts a little suspicious. Be prepared to defend the company's position, even if it's just.

Responding to Retaliation

Even the best efforts to prevent retaliation sometimes fail. If you learn that any employee involved in a harassment or discrimination charge or investigation might have been retaliated against, you must respond promptly to correct it. Your goal should be to investigate the alleged retaliation just as thoroughly as the underlying complaint. While you're conducting the investigation, make sure the alleged retaliation stops. And, if your investigation reveals a violation of the company's antiretaliation policy, you need to restore the employee to the position he or she was in before the retaliatory conduct occurred. For example, if the employee was put on a less desirable shift, you should move him or her back to the preferred shift.

 Common Questions

Q: *An employee complained six months ago that a coworker was harassing her. We found a violation of company policy, for which the coworker was disciplined. The employee who filed the original complaint recently told me that the harasser's friends at work are making her work life miserable. They barely acknowledge her and invite everyone in the department, except her, out to happy hour on Friday nights. If what she says is true, is that retaliation?*

A: *It depends on the situation. Social snubbing isn't retaliation. However, it's not an open and shut case. If the department supervisor uses happy hour as an opportunity to discuss how to staff projects, for example, the employee might be at a serious professional disadvantage by not being part of the discussion. Though there's no civility code, it's important that the employee's job opportunities aren't affected by the snub.*

Also, you need to make sure that this truly is personal behavior—friends of the accused coworker acting out of friendship—rather than behavior by the company. If the department supervisor condones or approves the behavior, you need to step in. For example, if the coworker's friend talks over the employee in a department meeting, saying "No one wants to listen to a snitch," and the manager doesn't stop it, a larger problem exists. In that situation, it starts to look like the company is allowing the employee to be intimidated for making a complaint, which could well lead other employees to decide not to come forward with concerns.

Getting Others Involved

As the person receiving or responding to a complaint, you play a major role beyond your job as investigative fact finder: You are the liaison between the reporting employee, the accused employee, and the company. You might have to report to company officers or directors about what's going on in the workforce, because these situations—and the way you handle them—can significantly affect employee morale, impact head count and staffing, and can create potential legal liability for the company. If you don't have the ultimate authority to make decisions and take disciplinary action, someone else might need to take the information you gather and decide what to do with it.

TIP

The company needs to track patterns, too. Companies need to keep information about harassment and discrimination complaints in one place. Doing this helps identify patterns of behavior that need correction and makes it easier to find the information on past complaints, if necessary.

Keep Management Informed

No one likes to be the bearer of bad news, and a complaint of harassment or discrimination is certainly that. But the company—in the form of its officers, directors, or top management—needs to know what's going on, especially if the situation could lead to larger problems down the road.

Once you realize that the problem underlying a complaint is serious, bring in senior management. Don't wait until a problem has spiraled out of control. While you probably won't need to report every complaint you receive, you will want to notify higher ups when your investigation suggests that inappropriate behavior might have occurred.

You don't have to provide a thorough description of every last detail, and you don't need to draft a separate written report (beyond your documentation of the investigation, described in Chapter 6). Just be prepared to succinctly explain the root of the problem and to confirm that you've followed company policy in conducting your investigation. If you need help in deciding how to handle the problem, be sure to ask for it.

Investigating an Executive

Complaints can be lodged against anyone in the company, including high-ranking company executives or managers. In those cases, how do you avoid the awkwardness of handling a complaint against a member of upper management and reporting on it to his or her peers?

The best solution is to hire an outside investigator. An outside investigator won't face the same pressures you might to support a popular executive or find fault with an unpopular one. An outside investigator won't be intimidated by the hierarchical disparity, either. Employees are more likely to see an outsider as truly neutral and, therefore, more likely to view the process and its outcome as fair.

For serious complaints, you might need to inform management of the problem when it first surfaces, then provide updates as you progress through the investigation. If you are pressed for a conclusion before you're prepared to give one, tell them that your investigation is continuing, or that the result is inconclusive. A hasty decision that's made before you know all the facts or one that's ultimately not supported by the investigation doesn't serve anyone's interests.

 Common Questions

Q: *I am investigating a harassment charge against one of the partners in the law firm where I'm the HR manager. The other partners are nervous about having this partner continue to supervise less senior attorneys, and they're really pushing me to tell them what I've found, but I haven't finished my investigation yet. How much information should I give?*

A: *Just tell them that your investigation is ongoing, and that you can't draw any conclusions yet. You could find new information that will affect your conclusion and right now, your primary goal is still to act as fact finder. You'll lose credibility if you suddenly flip-flop midway. Moreover, you take the risk that your initial impressions will circle back to the partner in question. This could compromise the credibility of your investigation if, for example, the partner puts pressure on witnesses to shore up his version of events.*

Instead, explain why you're not ready to draw any conclusions yet. Emphasize the need to be fair and accurate: It's more important than being speedy.

Of course, you could have avoided this difficulty altogether if you'd hired an outside investigator. In situations involving an accused employee at the very top of the company ladder, it's almost always a better idea to bring in an outsider—it avoids the politicking you find yourself caught in right now.

Hiring a Lawyer

Although you'll probably be able to handle most complaints on your own or with the help of an outside investigator (discussed above), some instances call for getting a lawyer involved. If your company has an in-house employment attorney, it should be easy to ask questions or get legal input when you need it. Otherwise, consult an attorney knowledgeable about employment laws in your state.

CAUTION

You can hire a lawyer as an investigator, but don't plan on having the lawyer represent you in a lawsuit. It isn't uncommon for companies to hire employment lawyers to conduct investigations. Just keep in mind that if you do this, you'll need to hire a different lawyer to represent the company if sued. That's because you have to be able to disclose the results of your investigation in court to show that the company tried to resolve the problem. It's undesirable to have your lawyer take the stand to testify about this, so plan on hiring someone different for each role.

It usually makes sense to bring in an attorney if:

- **An employee has filed a charge with the EEOC or state fair employment practices agency.** If that's the case, your obligation will extend beyond conducting an investigation—you will have to respond to the employee's charge. Because this might be the first step toward a lawsuit, you need to make sure your response protects the company's interests. You might even be able to stop the charge from proceeding further with the right response. Agency charges are covered in Chapter 8.
- **The complaint is of physical assault or a serious threat of physical harm.** If you're concerned that employee safety could be at stake, you might want to pursue legal remedies to keep an accused employee off the premises and away from other employees. A lawyer can help you do this, quickly.

- **The accused employee is a supervisory employee and you find that a violation of company policy has occurred.** The company's responsibility for supervisory misconduct is significantly greater than for lower-level employee misconduct. A lawyer will help you protect the company as much as possible if a complaint against a supervisor turns out to be true.
- **The investigation was botched.** If the complaint and investigation process has been compromised in some way, an attorney can offer a legal perspective on how best to correct mistakes.

Dos and Don'ts

Do:

- Step in immediately to quash rumors and gossip about a complaint, an investigation, or a disciplinary action taken.
- Examine systemic reasons for frequent or repeated complaints.
- Briefly explain the outcome of your investigation to employees who need to know.
- Separately and quickly investigate retaliation complaints.
- Keep company officers, directors, or other senior management apprised of serious problems and important developments.

Don't:

- Give details of the outcome to employees who are not directly involved in the complaint and investigation.
- Retaliate against an employee for making a complaint or participating in an investigation.
- Fail to keep management fully informed of the risks and possible liabilities in the course of an investigation.

CHAPTER

8

Dealing With Government Agencies

E very employer hopes to resolve employment disputes internally, and the strategies provided in earlier chapters will help you achieve that goal. In rare situations, however, an employee might take a complaint outside the company. Perhaps an employee wasn't satisfied with the company's investigation or how it decided to resolve a problem. Or, the employee might not have made an internal complaint at all, having chosen instead to go straight to a government agency or a lawyer for help.

Typically, your first indication that an employee has made a complaint outside the company comes in the mail, in the form of a notice that the employee (or, more often, former employee) has filed a harassment or discrimination complaint with a federal or state fair employment agency. Receiving a formal complaint can certainly be unnerving, and for good reason: It might mean that a government agency will investigate your company's handling of the situation, or even that the employee plans to file a lawsuit against your company. Once you understand how the process works, however, you'll see that you can take steps throughout to protect your company.

Once an employee gets a government agency involved, you'll have deadlines to meet and documents to prepare. Your company will have to respond to, and cooperate and communicate with, the agency. This chapter covers the agency's role in receiving, processing, and resolving complaints, so you know what to expect. It explains what you can do to make sure the process goes as smoothly as possible, including how to work collaboratively with a lawyer representing your company in agency proceedings. Although you might feel some anxiety after receiving an agency complaint, the information in this chapter will guide you through the process.

 SEE AN EXPERT

If your company receives an agency complaint, consult with a lawyer. This chapter provides an overview of the agency process, but you shouldn't respond to an employee's complaint without some expert advice. An agency complaint is often the precursor to a lawsuit, and the statements and arguments you make now might limit your company's options later. To best represent and protect your company, you should consult with a lawyer as soon as you receive an agency complaint. Even if you decide to write your own response and handle settlement discussions on your own, a lawyer can review your strategies and documents to make sure you're putting the company's best foot forward. A lawyer can also help you decide whether your company should try to settle the case—and for how much—or take its chances in court.

The Role of Fair Employment Agencies

Claims of workplace harassment and discrimination are handled differently than most other legal disputes. Usually, people who believe they were harmed by someone else's illegal conduct can go straight to court and file a lawsuit. When employees claim they've been harassed or discriminated against by their employers, however, they can't just file a lawsuit. Instead, they must first report their complaints to the Equal Employment Opportunity Commission (EEOC) or a state fair employment practices agency (FEPA).

What is the point of this requirement? These agencies were created to help look into and address violations of Title VII and laws prohibiting discrimination. Because they are devoted exclusively to workplace harassment and discrimination, the agencies can assess and handle these claims more effectively than courts that hear all types of cases. The administrative process is designed to:

- **Identify claims that don't qualify.** The legal concepts of harassment and discrimination are a bit complicated and can easily be misunderstood by employees. By bringing their complaints to the EEOC or a FEPA, employees can gain a better understanding of what constitutes harassment or discrimination from a legal perspective—and what they'll have to prove to win a lawsuit. When employees get a better sense of their rights under the law from the agencies, they are more likely to abandon claims that don't meet the legal requirements and pursue only those that are well founded.
- **Focus resources on the most serious violations.** The complaint system enables the agencies to identify and pursue more serious violations of employee rights. Generally, agencies are more interested in cases

involving a number of employees, extremely egregious behavior, or issues that are an enforcement priority. (For example, if a state governor ran on a platform of protecting low-wage workers, that state's FEPA might be especially interested in pursuing cases involving such employees.) If an agency wishes, it can prosecute complaints itself by filing its own lawsuit against the employer on the employee's behalf.

- **Resolve small problems before they get to court.** The EEOC or FEPA complaint puts the employer on notice that a problem exists and gives the employer and the employee an opportunity to resolve the problem before it goes any further. As explained below, agencies provide opportunities for mediation and informal settlement discussions, which can help the parties come up with a workable solution on their own. In 2020, the EEOC reported that it resolved about 70% of cases through mediation.

The Equal Employment Opportunity Commission (EEOC)

The EEOC is the federal agency charged with enforcement of federal laws prohibiting harassment and discrimination. It receives and processes complaints alleging violations of Title VII, the Equal Pay Act, the Americans with Disabilities Act, the Age Discrimination in Employment Act, and the Genetic Information Nondiscrimination Act. An employee who believes your company has violated one of these laws can bring a complaint to the EEOC. But if federal law doesn't apply—for example, if your company is too small to be covered by these laws or the employee alleges that you are discriminating based on marital status, which isn't prohibited by federal law (but may be by state law)—the EEOC won't accept the complaint.

Every state has EEOC field offices. If the EEOC accepts a complaint from one of your company's employees or former employees, the field office in your company's region will contact you, as discussed below.

State Fair Employment Practices Agencies (FEPAs)

Most states also have FEPAs that receive and process complaints alleging violations of a state's own laws prohibiting harassment and discrimination.

Like the EEOC, the state FEPA contacts employers after an employee or former employee files a complaint. The process followed by state FEPAs is usually similar to that of the EEOC, but every state is a bit different. An experienced employment attorney can explain how your state agency operates. Differences might include the deadlines for responding to the complaint, the extent of the agency's investigation or conciliation efforts, or the actions the agency is legally authorized to take once it completes its investigation.

Often, an employee who brings a complaint believes that the employer has violated both state and federal law—because, for example, both prohibit discrimination based on gender. In that case, the employee is typically required to bring a complaint to either the EEOC or the FEPA, not both. The agency receiving the complaint will file a duplicate complaint with the other agency, but only one agency (usually, the one that received the complaint) will process and investigate it. As an employer, this means you may be contacted by either the EEOC or a state FEPA regarding a complaint, but you will typically have to deal with only one agency.

State Agencies That Enforce Fair Employment Laws

To find a list of state fair employment practices agencies and EEOC offices, go to www.nolo.com/legal-encyclopedia/fepa.html.

The Complaint Process

An employee may file a complaint with the EEOC or a FEPA in person, online, or by telephone. The agency must first decide whether to accept the complaint at all; it might not if, for example, the employee is complaining of something that isn't prohibited or the complaint has some other basic problem. If the agency accepts the complaint, it will follow a series of steps similar to those described below. Remember, if the complaint is filed with your state FEPA, the process might work a little bit differently.

The Employee's Complaint

If the EEOC or FEPA accepts a complaint against your company, it will notify your company in writing. As noted above, the agencies won't accept complaints that are not legally valid. If an agency rejects a complaint, it will typically send the employee a notice (called a "right to sue" letter), stating that the employee has met the requirement of first bringing claims to the agency for resolution and now has the right to file a lawsuit. (Lawsuits are discussed in Chapter 9.)

 Common Questions

Q: *We recently investigated an internal complaint of racial harassment and ended up firing the accused employee. We determined that he had teased several Chinese American employees about their accents and made fun of their appearance, even after they told him to stop. Now, the harasser has filed a lawsuit against our company! Doesn't he have to file an agency complaint first?*

A: *Not unless he's claiming that your company discriminated against him or harassed him. Sometimes, employees who are fired for committing harassment or discrimination make this type of claim, contending that they were disciplined more harshly than other employees based on a protected characteristic. For example, let's say your company received a complaint that two supervisors—one white and one Latino—were engaging in sexual harassment. If your company gives a written warning to the white supervisor and fires the Latino supervisor, the fired employee might claim that your company discriminated in meting out the discipline.*

If you're not facing that type of situation, the fired employee might be bringing claims of wrongful termination, breach of contract, or defamation, none of which have to be brought to an agency before the employee can file a lawsuit. Only claims of harassment and discrimination must be taken to an agency first.

Incidentally, some employees who claim to have been discriminated against or harassed bypass the agency, too, sometimes because they miss the deadline for bringing an agency complaint. If they sue for violation of the laws prohibiting harassment and discrimination, your company can move to dismiss their claims because they should have been raised with the agency first. (See Chapter 9 for more on dismissing claims from a lawsuit.) However, the employee may choose to forgo these claims altogether and bring a lawsuit for infliction of emotional distress or assault, for example. These other legal claims don't have to be filed with an agency before the employee may file a lawsuit, even if they arise from alleged harassment or discrimination.

A copy of the complaint will be sent to your company, along with instructions from the agency explaining how your company should respond (including the deadline for responding and the form your response should take). The claim will include only basic information: the name and address of the employee and employer; the basis of the complaint (for example, that the company discriminated against the employee on the basis of race); and a brief description of the allegations that support it.

The purpose of the claim is to tell you what the employee contends; it isn't an indication that the agency has adopted the employee's version of events. You'll have the opportunity to give the company's version in your response to the complaint.

The Company's Response

After receiving a complaint, the company gets the opportunity to answer the employee's allegations. Your written response is important: It sets out the facts supporting your company's side of the story.

 CAUTION

Your company can be held to the statements in its written response. After the agency concludes its investigation, the complaining employee can obtain a copy of the agency file, including the company's written response. The complaining employee can argue in court that the company's statements to a government agency are binding or that any change in the employer's story shows that the explanation isn't credible. An employer's inconsistency in explaining its employment actions can be used as evidence that a discriminatory motive might be at work. Because your company's response can carry such legal weight, you might want to work with a lawyer, even if it's just to review the response you've drafted yourself.

You will have a limited amount of time, usually 30 days, to prepare your company's response and get it back to the agency. You should immediately pull together and review all of the materials from any investigation your company already conducted. If your company didn't investigate, either because the employee never complained internally or for some other reason, you should do so right away. The agency complaint will provide basic facts alleged and, frequently, will also identify some of the people allegedly involved in the matter, such as employees who might have committed or witnessed misconduct. Of course, you will want to speak to them if you haven't already, or follow up with them if the complaint includes new allegations.

Your response should address each of the employee's allegations in a separate paragraph. The purpose of your response is to use the facts available to you to show that the employee's claim isn't valid. Start with any dispute about the complainant's status, for example, if the person claims to be an employee but is actually an independent contractor. Then, address the employee's legal claims, which will be identified on the complaint form by category of discrimination. The employee will have checked a box or written a description of the type of discrimination claimed, such as age or sex. Beneath the identified categories of discrimination is a brief statement explaining the claims. Your response should address each claim by providing any facts that refute the employee's facts—that is, facts that contradict or undermine what the employee says.

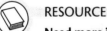 **RESOURCE**

Need more information on who qualifies as an independent contractor? Because the protections of Title VII typically extend only to employees, proving that a claimant is an independent contractor can be a successful defense to an agency claim. For an entire chapter dedicated to independent contractors, see *The Employer's Legal Handbook*, by Fred S. Steingold (Nolo).

Sample Format for Company Response to Agency Complaint

The Parties

[Identify your company. Briefly describe its business. Give the number of employees in the location where the complaining employee worked.]

Example: ABC Interiors is a furniture showroom in Cincinnati, Ohio, with 18 employees.

[Identify the complaining employee and his or her job (or the job applied for). Note any issues with the employee's status (for example, that he or she was actually an independent contractor).]

Example: Jeremy Baker is a CPA with whom ABC contracted to provide accounting services for a few weeks each quarter. Jeremy Baker was not an employee of ABC. He worked out of his own office elsewhere in town, he uses his own materials and equipment, and he performed his work without supervision.

The Company's Response to the Allegations

[Addressing each allegation in a separate paragraph, state the facts that support your company's decisions or actions. State the company's lawful reason for taking the challenged action. Note the number of employees in the complaining employee's protected category who are still with the company (for example, how many employees are over age 40, if the employee complains that he was fired because of his age). If the employee made an internal complaint, provide information on your investigation and findings. If the employee didn't make an internal complaint, make note of that fact.]

Example: ABC elected not to contract with Jeremy Baker last fall because of budgetary constraints. ABC assigned its accounting duties to the CFO, Margaret Ware, and her assistant, Jonas Young, both of whom were already employed by ABC. Mr. Baker's age was not a factor in ABC's decision not to contract with him. At present, ABC has seven employees age 40 or older.

Company Policy

[Summarize and attach a copy of the company's antiharassment and antidiscrimination policy, including the investigation procedure. Firmly state that the company always abides by its policy of zero tolerance of harassment or discrimination.]

Example: As noted in the attached ABC Personnel Policy, ABC does not engage in, nor does it tolerate, discrimination based on age or any other protected status.

Agency complaint forms can be quite terse and lack specifics. If you are not sure what something in the complaint means or you need clarification to do a thorough investigation, contact the agency in writing to request additional information. Be as specific about what you need as possible (for example, "the complaint we received does not indicate what decisions the employee believes were made for discriminatory reasons" or "the complaint we received does not state who allegedly harassed the complaining employee"). The agency will then ask the complaining employee to supply more information. Once the agency receives that information, it will summarize the additional information in a letter to your company.

If you need more information, also ask for more time to respond to the complaint. Agencies typically will give employers additional time to respond to a complaint upon request. Ask sooner rather than later, however, so it doesn't look like you're just stalling. Confirm the new deadline in a letter to the agency.

 Common Questions

Q: *I just received an EEOC complaint of disability discrimination filed by a former employee. The complaint alleges that the employee has a disability and was denied accommodation, but no one involved in the complaint knew about the disability or recalls being approached for a reasonable accommodation. How do I respond?*

A: *Make a list of the information you will need to prepare a formal response. For example, it sounds like you'll need to know more about the employee's disability, when he alleges that he requested accommodation, whom he alleges that he asked to provide the accommodation, and what accommodation he alleges that he requested. Send a letter to the agency, asking it to provide this additional material. In your letter, ask for more time to respond once the employee supplies the information you need. The agency will probably give you more time; if so, confirm the extension and your new deadline in writing.*

TIP

Your questions may alert the agency to weaknesses in the employee's complaint. In the example above, an employee is claiming denial of accommodation but never told the company about his disability. If you ask the agency to get more information about the employee's alleged request for an accommodation, and the employee can't come up with the goods, the agency may dismiss the complaint or issue a finding that it lacks sufficient support. Had you not requested more information, the agency probably wouldn't know that the employee's complaint lacked merit.

A good way to prepare to draft a response to an agency complaint is to create a fact sheet that lists each of the allegations in the complaint and, in a separate column, lists facts that the company believes respond to each, along with a note of the source of the fact. Keep your fact sheet brief and, well, factual. As explained in Chapter 6, the documents you create may well become evidence in any resulting lawsuit, unless you prepare them for, or at the request of, a lawyer (and you don't show them to any outside parties). Editorializing or noting issues that could be a problem for your company might come back to haunt you.

Sample Fact Sheet

Response to Dave Koi's agency complaint

Allegation	Response
1. Koi has a disability	Unknown to company (Human Resources, Supervisor)
2. Koi requested accommodation	No record of any request (Supervisor, Human Resources; personnel file)
3. Company refused accommodation	No request made (See 2)
4. Koi was fired because of disability	Koi laid off in reorganization, along with 22 other employees; decisions based on seniority. (Reorganization memo from Human Resources to Koi, dated 2/23/20; Supervisor; selection committee (Todd Jones, Selena Ilosa, Mara Kwan))

Use this information to write out your narrative response, devoting a separate paragraph to each allegation. (This part of the response is sometimes also called a "position statement" or "statement of position.") If you are working with an attorney (for the reasons stated above, a good idea), the attorney will probably write the statement for you, based on the information you provide, or review and revise the statement you draft. If the attorney writes the statement, make sure to read it over to verify that it is accurate.

The EEOC doesn't provide employers with a standard form for their responses, nor does it require you to follow a particular format. However, your state FEPA may have a specific form or require your response to meet certain requirements. If the complaint you receive doesn't indicate what your response should look like, contact the state agency to find out whether you need to follow any rules.

Agency Actions

Once your company submits its written response, the agency has a number of options. It may decide to take one or more of the following steps:

- **Conduct an investigation.** The agency will typically investigate the claim unless the employee has asked the agency to close the case. (As explained below, an employee might do this to file a lawsuit right away, without waiting for the agency to take action.) An agency will not investigate if the complaint is invalid on its face. In this situation, the agency typically doesn't accept the complaint in the first place, so your company might never even find out about it.
- **Offer to mediate or settle.** If either or both parties express an interest in mediating or settling the dispute, the EEOC or FEPA may facilitate this through its own mediation process.
- **Issue a "right to sue" letter.** The most frequent response is for the EEOC or FEPA to issue a letter to the employee, called a "right to sue" letter, which explains that the employee has the right to bring his or her lawsuit in court. As noted above, the employee has to file with the agency before bringing a lawsuit, and the right to sue letter

shows that the employee has met this requirement. The issuance of a right to sue letter doesn't necessarily mean that the agency believes the complaint is valid. The agency can also issue this letter after its investigation, if it doesn't find a violation has occurred. And, if the EEOC doesn't complete its investigation within 180 days from the complaint, it must issue this letter to the employee upon request.

- **File an agency lawsuit.** If a violation might affect more than just the complaining employee (because the employer is large, the illegal practice is widespread, or grounds for a class action exist), the agency itself may file a lawsuit on behalf of the employee(s). This is a rare occurrence, but it can happen if the agency believes that the case has merit and will have a large impact.

The agency can also dismiss the complaint at any point in the process if it determines that further investigation wouldn't result in a finding that the law was violated. (As noted, it might even reject a complaint upon filing if, during the agency's initial interview, the complaining employee fails to provide sufficient evidence to support the allegations.) When an agency dismisses a complaint in this manner, it isn't necessarily the end of the road for the employee. Instead, the employee gets a right to sue letter, giving the employee the right to take the case to court. The complaining employee usually has 90 days to file suit after receiving a right to sue letter from the EEOC, although that time may be extended if the employee also has state law claims. States have their own time limits, which are usually longer.

Preparing for an Agency Investigation

If the EEOC or FEPA decides to investigate an employee complaint, it will contact your company and ask for more information. Usually, this contact will come in the form of a written request after your company submits its written response. The agency likely will want to interview employees who might have information about the allegations. It will also request copies of company documents and possibly even visit the worksite where the violation allegedly occurred. The agency will arrange interviews, document reviews, and onsite visits with your cooperation, to limit disruption.

Interviews are usually conducted by telephone. The agency often sets up a telephone conference with the person to be interviewed. Typically, no one else is included in these phone interviews. Neither the complaining employee nor his or her attorney attends employee interviews, onsite visits, or document reviews.

Once you get a list of the employees whom the agency wants to interview, you should meet with each employee individually. During this meeting, explain that the EEOC (or FEPA) has received a complaint of harassment or discrimination against the company and that the employee has been identified as someone who might have information related to the allegations. Tell the employee to answer the agency's questions truthfully and that the employee will not suffer any repercussions for speaking to the agency. Explain that the interview is a normal part of the agency's procedures after receiving a complaint. You should also set a date and time for the interview, which you can pass along to the agency.

You might want to ask the employee if he or she has any information about the allegations other than what he or she provided during the company's investigation of the employee's internal complaint (if any information was provided previously). If so, ask the employee to share it with you so that you can look into the matter, in compliance with the company investigation policy.

If you are working with an attorney, he or she will help you prepare employees for their interviews, respond to the agency's requests for more information, and participate in its investigation. Your company has a legal duty to cooperate with the agency, but there's no reason not to do so in a way that puts your company in the best light—and protects your company's interests, if the dispute ends up in a courtroom. You might have questions about what documents you should make available, what information you should provide to the company's investigators, how to investigate a complaint internally while the agency's investigation is ongoing, and so on. Whether your company chooses to have an attorney represent it in dealing with the agency or simply consults with an attorney for behind-the-scenes advice, that relationship will be extremely valuable once you have EEOC or FEPA employees in your workplace.

⟨?⟩ Common Questions

Q: *The EEOC contacted me to set up phone interviews with three of our salespeople. These employees travel a great deal, especially during this season, so it's hard to schedule the interviews. I offered to have each employee witness write a brief summary about the complaining employee's charges, but the EEOC investigator nixed that idea. Do we have to schedule these interviews? What if we refuse?*

A: *Bad idea. If you refuse, the EEOC will note that you did so and will likely find in the employee's favor because of lack of evidence from your company to refute the claims. A finding like this is not binding in court, but it's still important. It could embolden the employee and make it harder for your company to informally resolve the matter. The finding may also be presented as evidence in court if the employee sues.*

At the conclusion of the investigation, the agency will make a finding. Among the options are:

- **The evidence doesn't establish that a legal violation occurred.** If this is the case, the agency will notify the parties in writing, close the case, and give the complaining employee a right to sue letter.
- **The evidence establishes that a legal violation occurred.** In this situation, the agency will explain the finding in writing. The agency may then offer mediation or suggest terms for resolving the complaint. If the employer doesn't want to participate or the parties can't informally settle the dispute, the agency may decide to file a lawsuit on the employee's behalf. If not, it will issue the complaining employee a right to sue letter.
- **The evidence is inconclusive.** If the finding is inconclusive, the agency will inform the parties in writing and issue a right to sue letter.

The agency's findings are not binding in court if the employee later files a lawsuit. The judge or jury will look at the evidence and decide whether or not the law was violated. However, the agency's finding is still important: A finding in the employer's favor might discourage an employee from pursuing a lawsuit (and discourage attorneys from taking the employee's case). A finding in the employee's favor might encourage the employee to sue, or make it harder for the employer to resolve the matter informally, because the employee will believe he or she has a strong case. And, the finding may be introduced in court if the employee does sue.

 Common Questions

Q: *I received a notice that the EEOC's investigation of an employee's age discrimination complaint didn't support the employee's allegations. Our lawyer said that we might not be in the clear, because the employee can still file a lawsuit. If there's no evidence of discrimination, how can he sue us?*

A: *An EEOC finding isn't like a verdict by a jury or a decision by a judge after a trial. An agency investigation is aimed at finding out whether the allegations justify filing a lawsuit. The process identifies cases that may be hard to prove or don't meet minimum legal standards, gives the parties an opportunity to settle before getting into the expensive process of a lawsuit, and helps employees and employers get a more realistic sense of the strength of their cases.*

However, the agency's investigation doesn't have the legal effect of a trial. No matter what the agency finds, the employee is free to go forward. Even an employee who has a lousy case can file a lawsuit, although the case may be thrown out relatively early in the process if it's really groundless.

If the employee does decide to file a lawsuit and you have a full trial, both you and the employee will probably present a lot more evidence than was brought forth in the agency investigation. But take heart—the fact that the employee couldn't establish a violation at that point is good news for you because it suggests the employee might not have the strongest case going forward, either. That means not only that your company might succeed in having the lawsuit dismissed early on, but also that the employee might have trouble finding a lawyer to take the case in the first place.

After the agency concludes its process, each side can request a copy of the agency's closed file on the matter. The file will contain correspondence with the parties, notes from witness interviews, and other materials related to the complaint and investigation. This information can be useful if the employee later files a lawsuit. You should request a copy of the agency file whenever an employee makes a complaint against your company. The information in it can be useful whether or not the employee ultimately files a lawsuit. It might alert you to gaps in your company's policies or practices or to ways that you can deal with the agency more effectively, if you ever find yourself in this position again.

Mediation

Rather than pursuing an investigation—or after doing so—the agency might offer you the opportunity to mediate the dispute. Mediation occurs only if both the complaining employee and the employer agree to it. If the agency hasn't yet investigated, it will put its investigation on hold while the mediation proceeds.

The Mediation Process

Mediation is an informal process aimed at reaching a settlement of the complaint through negotiations guided by a neutral third party trained to help parties resolve their disputes. The mediator doesn't make a decision in the case, but instead tries to help the parties come up with a solution that will work for everyone.

The discussions, offers, counteroffers, and everything else that occurs during mediation are confidential. So neither party can use things brought up at the mediation if the case moves forward. If mediation is unsuccessful and the parties don't reach a settlement, the agency can resume its investigation. If a complaint is successfully mediated and settled, neither party may bring the matter to court unless the terms of the settlement are not honored.

If both parties are interested in mediation, the agency will send them a list of potential mediators. The parties can choose a name from this list or agree on another mediator. A potential mediator may be unacceptable for a variety of reasons, such as a conflict of interest (say, because the mediator previously represented one of the parties). Once both sides agree on a mediator, the mediation is scheduled for a date everyone can attend.

Before the mediation, the mediator may ask the parties to provide a brief written statement of the facts and arguments supporting each side's position. If your company has retained a lawyer, the lawyer will prepare the statement. Your company's statement should refer to the evidence that supports its position, but you don't have to present every piece of evidence to the mediator. It might make sense to include a particularly strong piece of evidence with your company's statement, but don't inundate the mediator with material. And, if you don't want the mediator to share the evidence with the other side, say so explicitly in writing and by marking the statement or evidence "for mediator's eyes only."

 Common Questions

Q: *Our company is going to use the state human rights agency's mediation program to try to resolve a harassment complaint by a former employee. The company president stressed that when I attend this meeting, I am not to admit any liability. I'm a little nervous about how to follow his wishes or if I even can. What do you think?*

A: *You should be able to satisfy the president's demand, but you might not resolve your disagreement with the employee. The purpose of mediation is for the parties to reach an agreement about how to handle the dispute. Nothing about mediation requires the company to admit any wrongdoing. The company's position isn't uncommon: A nonadmission of wrongdoing statement is frequently demanded by companies in settlement agreements.*

Recognize, however, that sometimes employees are emotionally attached to their claims. They might feel an admission of guilt is fundamental to resolving the issue. If that's the case, and the company won't budge, you might find your attempts to mediate unsuccessful. If this becomes a problem during the mediation, you can always call the president to see if his position changes when the company has a chance to resolve the dispute. One point of leverage might be to suggest to the president that the company offer the employee more money in settlement in exchange for not admitting wrongdoing.

Also, you might be able to negotiate for something less than an admission that's still valuable to the employee, such as a written apology, a positive job reference, removing certain materials from the employee's file (such as a poor job evaluation), and so on. In this way, you can acknowledge, in a roundabout way, that mistakes were made, without actually coming right out and admitting wrongdoing.

Attending Mediation

Even though mediation is fairly informal, especially compared to a trial, it can still be intimidating to attend as the company representative. If you're in this position, the attorney representing the company should accompany you, to help you weigh the strength of the employee's legal case and decide whether it makes sense to resolve it quickly. (For more on getting ready for the mediation, see "Preparing for Mediation," below.)

The mediation itself will probably take place in a conference room or several conference rooms, most likely at the offices of the EEOC or FEPA. You, the lawyer representing the company, the employee, and the employee's lawyer (if the employee hired one) will all sit at a table with the mediator, who will describe the process and may ask each side if it wants to make an opening statement. Your attorney will usually make the statement, although the attorney might ask you to speak about certain factual or other matters (which you'll cover in preparation meetings ahead of time, discussed further below). The statement is an opportunity for each side to make its case directly to the other party.

After each side makes its statement, the mediator often puts the parties in separate rooms. The mediator then goes between the rooms, talking to each side about its position and trying to find a way to address both parties' concerns. The mediator will communicate each side's offers and demands to the other side. You and the attorney representing the company will have time alone to discuss each offer made by the employee and how you wish to respond on the company's behalf. The proposed terms may include payment, requirements to conduct training, or even an apology—very few things are beyond consideration, though each party may have some "sticking points" on which it refuses to budge. The mediator will try to help you work through these, too.

If you have settlement authority (meaning you can approve a settlement agreement on the company's behalf without anyone else's approval), you can resolve the dispute as long as you and the employee agree. If you don't have settlement authority, your company will have to make someone who has such authority, such as a company officer, available during the mediation, either in person or by telephone. You will have the opportunity to consult that person about any offers and other settlement terms.

If the mediation isn't successful and you can't agree on a resolution, the agency will pick up where it left off. If it has not yet investigated, it can proceed with its investigation. If it has already investigated, it can give the employee a right to sue letter.

If the mediation is successful, either the mediator or one or both of the lawyers will write up the agreed resolution. Usually, some back and forth will happen between the parties on the document's exact wording, with each side proposing changes, additions, or deletions. Once you come up with a final written settlement agreement, the employee and a company representative will sign it. The agency complaint will then be dismissed pursuant to the terms of the agreement.

Your Role in Dealing With Investigative Agencies

It can be stressful to act as the liaison between your company and the agency. You'll want to accurately represent the company's position and fully protect its interests, while also cooperating with the agency and trying to get the complaint resolved. Here are some tips that will make your job a bit easier.

Prepare for the Worst

No matter what direction an employee's complaint takes, it pays to be prepared. Whether you're responding to a complaint, attending a mediation, or responding to inquiries in an investigation, the more organized you are, the better prepared you will be to present the company's perspective. And, if you work with an attorney at any stage of the process, having everything in order will make it easier for you to hand the case off—and potentially less expensive, because the attorney won't have to spend billable hours digging for additional information or putting it into an organized format.

Your responsibilities start when you first receive a complaint and respond to it. You will need to:

- **Get your files in order.** Chapter 6 described some of the important documents your files should contain. Make sure you have those handy, in an organized way. If other people in the company have important documents you need—for instance, if the employee's direct supervisor received and documented the initial complaint—make sure you also have those.

- **Review the files carefully.** Once you review the complaining employee's personnel file and any files related to complaints the employee made under the company policy, including the investigation file, you'll be in a position to prepare for attorney meetings, plan the company's response, and cooperate in the agency investigation.

- **Create or update your chronology.** Chapter 6 explained the importance of creating a chronology of the incidents raised in the complaint. If you haven't already done so, create one now. If you have one, you might need to update it to include new or different information raised in the agency proceedings.

TIP

Documents created for company attorneys are privileged. If you create a chronology or another document to assist company attorneys or at their direction, the document is protected by the attorney–client privilege; it doesn't have to be disclosed to the complaining employee, the employee's lawyer, or anyone else. On the other hand, handing over documents to the company attorney doesn't convert them into privileged documents. For example, if you create a chronology for your own purposes, then later hire a lawyer to represent the company in dealing with the EEOC, your chronology doesn't become privileged simply because you give it to the lawyer. If, however, the attorney asked you to write out a list of steps you took in responding to an employee's complaint, that document would be privileged.

- **Use your chronology to outline your company's position.** The more complete a portrait of events you can paint, using the facts that you have evidence for, the more clearly you will be able to put forth your best arguments. But definitely don't sugarcoat bad facts or try to hide negative incidents; your attorney can only help you respond to issues the attorney knows about. And, any misstatement of facts will make your company (and you) look bad if and when the chronology is introduced into evidence at trial.

- **Prepare for attorney meetings.** Preparing for attorney meetings ahead of time can save a lot of time (and money, if the attorney bills by the hour). Make sure you understand the purpose of each meeting. Then, prepare written questions you have about the process, points you feel are important (for example, that the employee never complained of harassment), and lists of witnesses and documents. Give the attorney the fact sheet you've prepared and a copy of your chronology.
- **Organize your questions and information for the agency.** As explained above, get more information if you need it to respond to the complaint. Ask questions to alert the agency to areas of weakness in the employee's complaint. Have a list of such questions and of information supporting the company's position ready when you contact the agency to request more information.
- **Get your marching orders.** Discuss the complaint and the allegations with your manager and company officers, so that you know the company's position and strategy for responding to the complaint. Find out what the company expects of you and wants to achieve during any mediation. Take detailed notes of these discussions to bring with you to meetings with company lawyers and to the mediation.
- **Be a model of calm professionalism.** An agency complaint is no cause for panic, so proceed methodically and coolly. This will reassure your superiors that you have things under control. It will also assuage the natural anxiety of any employee witnesses who may be contacted during the agency investigation.

Assisting the Company's Attorney

As we've discussed, your company should seek the advice of a knowledgeable employment attorney if it receives an agency complaint of harassment or discrimination. If you are the liaison between the company and its counsel, you'll have to be well organized and communicative. Share the investigation file with the attorney, as well as any thoughts, concerns, or theories you have about what's going on, based on your knowledge of the workplace and the employees involved. Remember, in most cases, the attorney will not have had the same access to the workplace that you have had—the attorney will depend on you to share the company culture, practices, and attitudes, in addition to the facts of the actual case.

Your private discussions with the attorney are confidential and protected by the attorney–client privilege. So neither of you will be required to disclose what you talked about in court. This confidentiality is important because it gives you the opportunity to speak freely without worrying that it will somehow work against you. However, you can destroy this protection if you reveal your discussions to others, so keep things private. Your lawyer can explain how the attorney–client privilege works if you have any questions.

As explained above, you should make sure you've read and understood the investigation file before you meet with the attorney. Also, be prepared to give the attorney copies of all documents that might be relevant to the complaining employee's allegations, including employee statements, investigation notes, physical evidence, and any pertinent personnel documents. Find out if you need to schedule meetings between the attorney and any witnesses or other employees. If so, try to schedule all of them for the same day, which is most efficient for both you and the attorney, and will help keep costs down because it will minimize the time that the attorney spends traveling or waiting around.

Cooperating With Agency Investigators

An agency investigator serves a very different function than your company's attorney. While the attorney is trying to protect your company, the agency investigator is interested only in determining whether the employee's claims are valid. You must cooperate with the investigation, but you should always keep in mind that the agency investigator is not "on your side." Your communications with the agency investigator are definitely not privileged, and whatever you or other company representatives say to the investigator will become part of the agency's file on the case. So your statements will be available to the complaining employee after the agency closes the matter and may be used against you in a lawsuit.

Maintain your composure and professionalism in dealing with the agency and its investigators. You might feel the company has been unjustly accused of wrongdoing, but that's not something to discuss with agency representatives. Instead, focus on presenting the facts that will ultimately prove that your company did the right thing. Your calm, businesslike response to the complaint and the investigation will reassure employees and lessen the impact that the investigation has on the workplace.

 Common Questions

Q: *We're dealing with an EEOC charge of race discrimination that is likely to progress to a lawsuit. I'd like the EEOC to see our impeccable record: We have a very diverse workforce, regularly donate to organizations promoting diversity and equality, and we have had almost no complaints of any kind in our ten years in operation. Would it be a good idea to prepare a presentation for the EEOC to promote this?*

A: *While your own attorney might find this information helpful, you should present it to the EEOC only if it's relevant to the specific issues raised in the complaint. The EEOC will be looking for information that responds directly to the employee's allegations. If the charge alleges that the company makes a regular practice of discrimination or that discrimination is tolerated, information about the corporate culture would be directly relevant to the charge and should be provided to the EEOC. Otherwise, it is likely not relevant at this stage. Talk it over with your attorney. And keep in mind that, although this type of information might not be useful during the EEOC investigation, it could be very helpful in a lawsuit or settlement discussion with the employee should you get to either stage.*

You should do what you can to cooperate with the investigation. However, don't provide information or documents without first discussing it with your company's lawyer, who can tell you what information must be provided to the agency and what information should be kept confidential (for example, because it is protected by attorney–client privilege) or is simply not relevant. Show agency representatives that you are cooperating in good faith by returning calls promptly, showing them courtesy and respect, helping coordinate necessary interviews, and providing relevant documents approved by your attorney.

Preparing for Mediation

If you are going to attend mediation as a company representative, you'll need to prepare ahead of time, likely with the help of the company's attorney. You'll probably meet at least once, when the attorney will explain the mediation process and talk about the relative strengths and weaknesses of the employee's claims. Be prepared to ask the attorney any questions about the mediation and your role in it, including when, if at all, you'll be expected to speak directly to the mediator. Also ask what documents or other materials the attorney wants you to bring to the mediation.

Talk to the appropriate company officers or managers to determine what the company's position is and what it expects of you at the mediation. As explained above, you (or another company representative whom you can reach during the mediation) must have authority to settle the dispute, so make sure you know the details of what your company wants. For example, the company might want a provision in the settlement agreement stating that the complaining employee will not apply for a job with the company in the future. Make detailed notes of this information to bring to the mediation, as it's easy to forget even key points and instructions in the heat of the negotiations.

Common Questions

Q: *I've been selected to be the company representative at the EEOC mediation of a pregnancy discrimination complaint by an employee. In the EEOC complaint, the employee falsely accused me of making inappropriate statements about her pregnancy and participating in her termination. I'm outraged to be maligned in this way, and I'm ready to let her have it. How should I prepare?*

A: *It's normal to have a strong emotional response to the allegations against you, but you need to rethink your plan. The purpose of the mediation is to try and reach an agreement with the employee, not to get revenge or personal vindication. It is important to maintain your composure and professionalism at the mediation.*

The best thing you can do is put together all the details ahead of time that show what really happened. When faced with these facts and supporting evidence, the employee will have a hard time proving her claims. This should enhance your company's bargaining position at the mediation.

Nonetheless, you can't focus on the employee admitting she is wrong. If you really don't think you can look past this and work on getting the best solution for the company, discuss it with your management and the company's lawyer. You might not be the best person to attend on the company's behalf.

Preventing Retaliation

As unpleasant as it is to receive a harassment or discrimination complaint from an agency, it's even worse to later receive a retaliation complaint based on the way the initial complaint was handled. When a current employee files an agency complaint, it can make things awkward in the workplace. However, you must make sure it doesn't result in retaliatory actions against the employee. (For a refresher on what constitutes retaliation, revisit Chapter 7.)

Retaliation against employees who participate as witnesses in an agency process is also prohibited. When you meet with employees identified as possible witnesses by the agency complaint or in connection with the agency investigation, tell them that they should be cooperative and professional during interviews with the agency. Reiterate that the company will not retaliate, and will not tolerate any retaliation, against them for participating in the agency process.

Dos and Don'ts

Do:

- Contact the EEOC or FEPA if you need more information to respond to the complaint.
- Make sure files and documents relating to the complaining employee and any internal complaints are in order.
- Maintain a calm, professional demeanor after receiving an agency complaint and throughout the agency process.
- Urge employees to be cooperative and professional if contacted during the agency investigation, and reassure them that there will be no retaliation.

Don't:

- Hesitate to conduct an investigation of the allegations in the agency charge, if you haven't already done so.
- Let emotion govern your response to the agency complaint or interfere with your role in the agency process.

Lawsuits

A stranger comes into the office and asks for you by name. You greet her as she smiles and hands you a legal-sized envelope, saying, "You've been served." In the envelope is a complaint, along with other official paperwork, formally initiating a harassment or discrimination lawsuit against your company. Your stomach drops to the floor.

Getting hit with a lawsuit is every manager's worst nightmare. And while you might not be the one to whom the papers are actually handed (unless you are sued personally, as discussed below), you probably will be involved in defending the company, which might include the way you handled the employee's concerns from the start.

Of course, facing a lawsuit is a scary proposition. It can be even more anxiety provoking when the allegations include harassment or discrimination. Accusations like these might imply, or flat out state, that your company and its managers (perhaps including you) are racist, sexist, or prejudiced. The work you do to help with the lawsuit—and any work you did to address the employee's internal complaint—might come under intense scrutiny. You might have to prepare documents to hand over or use as exhibits in court, face harsh questions from the employee's attorney, or even take the stand and testify in front of a jury.

The best way to prepare yourself is to understand the process and the role you will play. This chapter will unravel the mystery of litigation. It explains how lawsuits actually work, how cases are settled out of court, and how to work effectively with the company's lawyer to get the best result for the company. This chapter also covers the worst-case scenario: what to expect if you are sued, personally, by an employee.

Although you might be worried about what's to come, remember that you won't be alone or unarmed. Your company's lawyer will take charge of the process, handling the legal filings and deadlines and working with you to present the company's facts in the best possible light. And, if you've followed the advice in earlier chapters, the hard work you've already done to prevent harassment and discrimination, investigate claims, resolve problems, and deal with agency investigations will serve you well now. You'll have the documents and other evidence you need to show the judge and jury that your company handled the employee's situation appropriately.

TIP

Don't panic—it's a process. When an employee files a lawsuit, you might feel an immediate sense of panic. Take a deep breath. Though things might feel urgent, the process of litigation involves a series of steps that take place over a long period of time. Of course, you should notify your lawyer as soon as you're aware that a lawsuit has been filed and forward any court documents to him or her immediately. That way, your lawyer can calendar the deadline for your response, ask you to gather relevant documents, and set up a meeting with you to discuss the case.

Why Employees Sue

Before considering the mechanics of an employment lawsuit, it helps to think about *why* you've arrived where you are. In other words, what does the employee want from the lawsuit and what is the employee likely to receive if he or she wins?

The Employee's Goals

Of course, employees may have a number of different motivations for suing. For many employees, a lawsuit is a last resort after efforts to resolve the problem within the company have gone nowhere. An employee might be frustrated with the company's failure to remedy an ongoing harassment problem or might finally decide to sue after seeing yet another promotion go to a younger employee. Other employees could just want a simple apology. They might believe that they were treated unfairly and might be unable to move forward in their lives until they get some closure. At times, an employee might be motivated by money or a desire for revenge or vindication.

Understanding an employee's motivations, and the possible outcomes in court, might help you come up with a way to resolve the problem before heading down the protracted, expensive path to a trial. In the long term, a settlement is less expensive, time-consuming, and stressful than trial.

Common Questions

Q: *My company has been sued by a former employee who lost his job in a layoff last year. We laid off 15 employees, all deemed by their managers to be the most expendable. Now, he claims that he was included in the layoff because of his national origin (he's originally from China). The employee says that his manager had made negative statements about activities by the Chinese government, which proves that the manager included him in the layoff for discriminatory reasons. I don't know what the manager said, but it seems to me that criticizing a country's government isn't discrimination. I also know that this employee had consistently poor performance reviews. The company wants to settle his claims, but I think we should fight it out in court. Why should we pay this guy when we didn't do anything wrong?*

A: *Cases settle for lots of reasons, not all related to the strength of the other side's case. Even if no evidence of discrimination exists, the company might sensibly decide to pay some money to make the problem go away. After all, every day the case goes on, your company is paying attorneys' fees and spending time dealing with the employee's claims. Settling the case puts an end to these ongoing costs, as well as the uncertainty over how the lawsuit will progress.*

Other times, a company wants to settle a case to avoid having to reveal unpleasant facts in discovery and in court. For example, even if this particular fellow doesn't have a good case, the way the company handled the layoffs might have some problems. Or, the company might have some reason why it doesn't want to have to reveal its current financial situation, which often comes out when the company's defense is that cost-cutting measures were necessary. Or there might be more to this case than meets the eye. Although the employee received poor performance reviews, those reviews were written by someone accused of discrimination. Perhaps other employees have complained, or some other evidence of discrimination exists that the company believes could tip the scales in the employee's favor.

Monetary Remedies

An employee who files a harassment or discrimination lawsuit might be seeking several different solutions. In most cases, the employee's complaint will ask for money damages to compensate for harm the employee suffered as a result of the alleged harassment or discrimination. For example, if the employee felt forced to quit because working conditions were intolerable (called "constructive discharge," as discussed in Chapter 2) and was unemployed for several months before accepting a job at lower pay, the employee might seek payment for the months of unemployment and the difference between his or her former and current salary. Or, an employee who began meeting with a therapist and taking antidepressants after being subjected to extreme harassment might seek reimbursement for these medical bills, as well as some compensation for pain and suffering (the emotional upset caused by the harassment).

Nonmonetary Remedies

While an employee usually requests money in a lawsuit, that might not be all the employee is seeking, or even what the employee cares most about. Most of us are very emotionally connected to our jobs. Employees considering litigation often feel that they were treated unfairly and want it set right. Here are some of the nonmonetary things an employee might hope to get from filing a lawsuit:

- **An opportunity to be heard.** Particularly if the employee's problem wasn't properly or fully investigated the first time, or if the employee didn't feel the investigation was fair, the employee might want the company to hear his or her side of the story and how he or she was harmed.
- **An apology.** Sometimes, an employee who feels wronged needs to hear the wrongdoer take responsibility and express some remorse. The employee might want an apology from the alleged harasser, the investigator, or even the company as a whole.

- **Reinstatement.** Frequently, employees don't want their jobs to end even after they've experienced workplace discrimination or harassment. They might want to go back to the way things were before the harassing or discriminatory conduct occurred. An employee who's been fired unfairly or forced to quit might want nothing more than getting the job back.
- **A promotion, transfer, or job change.** An employee might feel entitled to a previously denied promotion or might want a transfer to a different shift, position, or department. Such a change might make the workplace more tolerable for the employee, particularly if the problem was caused by a supervisor or coworker.
- **Reasonable accommodation.** As discussed in Chapter 1, failing to accommodate an employee's disability might be a violation of the ADA or state disability discrimination laws. An employee may seek a court order requiring the employer to provide reasonable accommodation, so the employee can return to work.
- **Company-wide action.** If the employee believes that he or she is one of a group of employees that has been treated unfairly, the employee might want the company to change the way it does business. For example, the employee might want the company to require diversity training, revise its promotion policies, or drop a discriminatory job requirement (such as a strength requirement for a job that doesn't involve much heavy lifting).

The employee's true objectives might not be obvious in the documents filed in the lawsuit. You might learn what else drives the employee during the litigation process, as you explore the possibility of settling the case out of court, discussed later in this chapter. While the company will ultimately decide whether to settle the case, having a sense of the employee's underlying motivations will help you come up with creative ways to formulate a settlement offer.

Common Questions

Q: *My company just got hit with a discrimination lawsuit filed by a former employee who's alleging six causes of action and seeking punitive damages. At our lawyer's suggestion, we held a meeting with the former employee and his lawyer to see if there was any way to resolve this quickly. At the meeting, the former employee looked right at me and said that he wanted the company to apologize to him for the shoddy treatment he suffered under his former boss (who, admittedly, is a difficult, demanding manager). I met privately with our lawyer, who urged me to offer an apology on behalf of the company. I'm suspicious and reluctant to walk into some kind of trap. Should I be wary?*

A: *Probably not, as long as you consider your words carefully. Apologizing to the former employee for having to work under a difficult boss is no admission of illegal conduct and might go a long way toward addressing at least some of the issues that led him to file the lawsuit. And, it shows a willingness to negotiate. Your lawyer can then turn to the former employee and ask for the same in return, in the form of dropping some or all of the claims or making some other sort of settlement offer.*

How Lawsuits Work

A lawsuit is made up of many different (and seemingly unrelated) steps, most of them occurring before the actual trial. Long stretches can occur when you have little or no involvement in the case, while the attorney (or attorneys) representing the company take care of many legal maneuvers without your input. Then, you'll have some times when you have to devote your full attention to the case, helping the attorney get the details and facts straight, providing documents and information, and preparing to testify. Often, your company's legal team will be working on very short deadlines, so you might need to act quickly and under pressure.

> **CAUTION**
> **You'll have a lot more to do if you've been sued personally.** Of course, if you are a defendant in the lawsuit, you will have more responsibilities and concerns. See "If You Are Sued Personally," below, for more information.

By understanding how civil lawsuits generally wind their way through the courts, you'll know what to expect and how to prepare for what's coming (and why everything seems to take so long). This section explains the typical steps in a lawsuit, from start to finish. The specifics of this process might differ somewhat from case to case and court to court, but the general stages of a lawsuit are similar everywhere.

One advantage to facing a harassment or discrimination lawsuit is that you'll usually have some advance warning—not only of the lawsuit itself, but also of the arguments the employee will make. As explained in Chapter 8, an employee who wants to file a discrimination or harassment lawsuit must first file a complaint with an agency, which will notify your company. You might even have had an opportunity to respond to the employee's claims and present evidence in an agency investigation. Although not all cases that go through the administrative process wind up in court, you can be fairly certain that an employee who goes to the trouble of filing an administrative complaint is planning on following through with a lawsuit if the issue isn't resolved.

> **CAUTION**
> **This process will work differently if the company and employee have agreed to arbitrate.** If that's the case, you can find out more in "Arbitration," below.

The Employee Files a Complaint

After following the procedure required by the EEOC or your state's fair employment practices agency, the employee, former employee, or applicant can begin a lawsuit by filing a document called a complaint. (The person who files the complaint is called the plaintiff.) The complaint will include a list of the plaintiff's causes of action—the allegedly illegal behavior the plaintiff believes the employer is responsible for (such as sexual harassment or race discrimination). The complaint will also include some basic facts that support each cause of action (in a sexual harassment case, for example, the complaint might state that a coworker created a hostile work environment by posting offensive cartoons). It also explains what the plaintiff is seeking, usually in general terms by referring to different categories of money damages, like lost pay and punitive damages. Complaints frequently don't specify the precise amount of money the plaintiff is seeking in damages.

The plaintiff serves the complaint on the employer (the defendant in the lawsuit), usually by having it hand-delivered by a neutral third party. Once that happens, the defendant has a set period of time to respond to the lawsuit, by filing a document with the court and serving it on the plaintiff.

 Common Questions

Q: *We just got served with a complaint filed by a former employee who claims she was fired for reporting sexual harassment. She did make an internal complaint that her manager had touched her inappropriately, but our investigation was inconclusive. The manager denied touching her and no witnesses to the incident, so we moved him to a different department. A few months later, we discovered that she had been falsifying her time records for a few years, and we fired her for that. Now, she's filed a complaint that includes half a dozen causes of action, all based on the same incident! She's claiming sexual harassment, assault, wrongful termination, retaliation, defamation, and even breach of contract. Why does her complaint have so many different legal claims?*

A: *It's fairly common for a complaint to include a handful of different claims based on the same underlying incidents. Many reasons can explain why employees include a variety of legal claims when filing a lawsuit, some of them strategic and others having to do with damages. For example, an assault claim can be brought only against another person, not against the company. So this claim may have been included in order to name the manager as a defendant in the lawsuit, for the reasons explained in "If You Are Sued Personally," below.*

You don't mention whether she's alleging harassment and retaliation in violation of federal or state law. If she's suing under federal law, there's a cap on the total amount of punitive and compensatory damages she can be awarded if she wins the case. The cap ranges from $50,000 to $300,000, depending on the size of the company. Because of this limit, employees suing under federal law often include "tort" claims: claims for personal injury brought under state law, to which these caps don't apply. This might explain the defamation cause of action: Defamation is a common personal injury claim brought by plaintiffs in employment cases, often alleging that the reasons the employer gave for firing the plaintiff were false and damaged the plaintiff's reputation and prospects for getting a new job.

Although the plaintiff has to prove different things to win each claim, the same fact might decide one or more causes of action. For example, if your company can prove that it fired the plaintiff for a valid reason, that's a defense to most of her claims, which succeed only if she shouldn't have been fired. Similarly, if she can show that she was really fired in retaliation for making her sexual harassment claim, your company is likely to lose several times over.

The Company Responds

A defendant can respond to a complaint in several different ways. (Remember, the process may vary slightly, depending on where the lawsuit is filed.) How to respond will be a strategic decision made by the attorney representing the company, but you might need to provide some information to help with that decision.

Bear in mind that the company will have only a limited amount of time, often as few as 30 days, to file its response. If the company has not already hired a lawyer, it must do so immediately. If the company has hired an attorney, you need to contact the lawyer right away to make sure the lawyer knows that the complaint has been filed.

With the help of its attorneys, your company will respond to the complaint by filing one of the following documents:

- **An answer.** In this document, the company responds to each allegation in the plaintiff's complaint, either by admitting or denying them.

- **A motion to dismiss.** A motion is a request that the judge take a particular action in the case. A motion to dismiss, sometimes also called a "demurrer," is a request that the court reject the plaintiff's complaint because, even if all of the allegations were true, the plaintiff wouldn't be entitled to relief. In other words, even if everything the plaintiff claims actually happened, it wouldn't break the law.
- **A motion to strike.** A motion to strike is similar to a motion to dismiss, but it applies only to certain causes of action. For example, if the complaint's discrimination claim is legally sufficient but the harassment claim is not, the defendant might file a motion to strike just the harassment claim.
- **A motion to compel arbitration.** This motion may be filed by a defendant if the plaintiff previously agreed to arbitrate his or her claims. For example, if your company requires employees to sign an agreement to arbitrate any claims that arise out of the employment relationship, your lawyer may file this motion to ask the court to force the plaintiff into arbitration and out of court.

Your lawyer will advise your company of its options and handle the necessary paperwork. If the company decides to file an answer, the case will then proceed to discovery, as described below. However, if the company files a motion to dismiss or a motion to strike, a series of interim legal steps will happen, with attorneys for both sides filing documents and perhaps appearing in court to argue before the judge. For example, if your company files a motion to dismiss, the plaintiff will have the opportunity to explain why the complaint is legally sufficient and should not be dismissed. Eventually, usually after a hearing, a judge will decide whether the motion should be granted. If it is, the plaintiff may be given an opportunity to fix the problem by filing an amended complaint. You then start the same process over: The plaintiff files and serves the amended complaint, and the defendant can either answer or move to dismiss or strike. If the judge denies the motion, the company will probably have to file an answer.

This initial stage of the lawsuit won't require a lot of your time, because it's almost exclusively based on the words in the complaint and the legal standards that govern them. This gives you an opportunity to start organizing your files and documents in preparation for discovery, which, as explained, can be very time-consuming.

 Common Questions

Q: *Our company is defending a sexual harassment lawsuit, and the attorney just sent me the answer he's planning to file. I can't understand most of it, but it looks like he's denying every single fact in the complaint, including stuff that's obviously true. What's the point of this?*

A: *It's true that some attorneys can go a little overboard with the gamesmanship. But denying a fact in a complaint doesn't necessarily mean you're saying it didn't happen; instead, you're saying that the plaintiff is going to have to prove it. And there are often very good reasons for denying "facts" that appear to be true, typically because a legal argument is buried in the way the fact is stated.*

For example, the complaint in your case might say "John supervised Jane." Even if this appears to be correct, admitting it implies that John qualifies as a supervisor, for whose sexual harassment the company is automatically liable, under federal or state law. Similarly, admitting a fact like "XYZ is a parent corporation of ABC" could concede that XYZ should be liable for any damages award against ABC—or even that all of the employees of XYZ should be counted when calculating the size of the company. As mentioned previously, the company's employee count determines whether the laws prohibiting discrimination and harassment apply and what cap on damages applies, among other things. At this point in the lawsuit, it's often best to deny all of the allegations and keep your legal options open.

Discovery

If the complaint isn't resolved once the legal wranglings of the first stage are completed—a process that can take weeks or months—the case moves forward. The next step is for the parties to exchange relevant information and evidence through a process called discovery.

It might seem counterintuitive to share evidence with your opponent in the lawsuit, but the law requires you to exchange relevant information, documents, and other evidence. Each of you needs information that will be in the hands of the other, and the law is interested in getting at the truth. For example, if the plaintiff claims a coworker sent sexually suggestive emails to his or her personal email address, you'll want to see those emails, and you might have to rely on the plaintiff to provide them. Exchanging evidence also encourages settlement: Once each side has a good idea of the evidence the other side will present, it's easier for everyone to assess the strength of their arguments and their likelihood of success.

Practically speaking, the employer usually has a lot more relevant information than the plaintiff does. Like any business, your company probably keeps records throughout the employment relationship as a matter of course. For example, you might have a full personnel file, including signed documents, performance evaluations, disciplinary notices, information on compensation, and other material related to the plaintiff's employment. You'll have even more records if the employee filed an internal complaint. It's very likely that you'll be asked to gather paperwork and other information—copies of emails, voice mails, photographs, and so on—by the attorney representing the company. You might also be able to help the attorney figure out what evidence to request from the plaintiff, identify which employees might serve as witnesses, and so on.

The parties exchange this information through a variety of methods, including:

- **Interrogatories.** "Interrogatories" are written questions that each side asks about information related to the lawsuit, requiring written answers signed under oath. For example, an employer often asks the plaintiff to describe all of the damages the plaintiff claims to have suffered, list every incident of alleged harassment that occurred, or provide the names of all witnesses to any of the allegedly illegal behavior. Usually, the total number of questions each party can ask the other is limited by law.

- **Demands for document production.** These are written requests for documents, often including electronic documents and data, as well as any photographs, cartoons, emails, correspondence, diaries, and other types of written or recorded materials. For example, the plaintiff might ask your company to provide all records relating to your investigation of the plaintiff's internal complaint, or all documents relating to a particular promotion or layoff decision.
- **Requests for admissions.** In some cases, either party may ask the other to admit certain facts, so the party doesn't have to prove those facts in the lawsuit. For example, the plaintiff might ask the company to admit that it employed the plaintiff (rather than hiring the plaintiff as an independent contractor), so the plaintiff won't have to prove this fact at trial.
- **Physical inspection.** Either party may request to physically examine a location or piece of evidence that can't be handed over. For example, the plaintiff might request an opportunity to physically inspect and photograph the worksite to show that the plaintiff's work station was not modified in response to the plaintiff's request for a reasonable accommodation.
- **Physical or psychological examination.** If the plaintiff claims to have suffered emotional distress as a result of discrimination or harassment, your company may want to ask that the plaintiff be examined by a psychiatric expert. The expert's role is to determine the validity and extent of the claimed distress.
- **Depositions.** In almost every lawsuit, each side wants to question people who may have relevant information. This usually happens through a process called a deposition, in which a witness answers questions under oath and a court reporter transcribes the testimony. If you investigated an internal complaint made by the plaintiff or played any other role in the events underlying the lawsuit, you may have your deposition taken in the case. You'll find more information in "Trial Testimony," below.

- **Subpoenas.** This is a court order that is served on a person, demanding that he or she show up to testify at deposition or trial, produce documents, or both. In most courts, a subpoena is used to require testimony or documents from someone who isn't a party to a lawsuit. For example, if the employee alleges that he or she earns less at a new job after being fired for discriminatory reasons, your company may want to issue a subpoena to obtain payroll records from the plaintiff's current employer.

 Common Questions

Q: *I used to supervise an employee who was fired for poor performance, after plenty of warnings, coaching, and formal discipline. Now, he's filed a lawsuit claiming that he was really fired because of his race. His lawyer has filed a document request asking me to hand over my day planner. Our company lawyer explained that the lawyer probably wants to see any notes I made about the employee in the calendar, the dates of performance evaluations and meetings, etc. I guess I can see why the employee wants this, but the problem is that I use the same calendar for personal stuff, too. Does this employee really have the right to see all of my dates, doctors' appointments, and reminders about my kid's school conferences?*

A: *No, the employee doesn't have the right to see your personal information, but he does have a right to see everything on the calendar that might pertain to his claims against the company. This problem—documents that include both relevant and irrelevant information—comes up fairly often in employment lawsuits.*

The solution is to separate what's relevant and hand it over. First, the parties have to agree on what will be produced and what won't. If they can't agree, they'll have to file motions and fight it out in court, so the judge can issue an order explaining what information has to be provided. Then, someone—probably your company's attorney—will go through a copy of your calendar, blocking out (or as the lawyers say, "redacting") everything the plaintiff isn't entitled to see. The lawyer will then make a copy of the final product and give it to the plaintiff's attorney.

Unsurprisingly, discovery doesn't always go smoothly. Discovery works on a sort of honor system: It's largely up to each party to ask only for relevant information and to provide all relevant documents and information in response to discovery requests. Often, the parties don't agree on where the boundaries of relevance lie. For example, the plaintiff might ask for a record of all employee complaints against an employer, but the employer could feel that some aren't relevant to the lawsuit, that it would take an unreasonable amount of time to compile that much information (especially in a large company), or that some information in the complaints must be kept confidential to protect employee privacy. The parties might also need clarification of discovery requests. For example, if a question isn't clear, the answering party might have to ask for more information. If the parties can't work these issues out on their own, they might have to file motions requesting a judge to decide for them, sometimes followed by oral arguments. Again, this can take weeks or months.

 Common Questions

Q: *My company is in the middle of a lawsuit filed by an unsuccessful job applicant who says we rejected her based on her age. During the interview process, the hiring supervisor sent me an email in which he referred to the applicant as a "cougar" (meaning an attractive, older woman). The supervisor meant it as a compliment and it was really just an off-hand remark—we didn't hire her because we found a candidate with much better qualifications. I deleted the email without responding. Now our attorney has asked me to gather all of the documents, including emails, related to the applicant, so we can respond to her document request. Our attorney doesn't know about the supervisor's email to me. Do I have to get a copy to the lawyer or can I pretend it never happened?*

A: *You'd better find it and turn it over to your lawyer. It may well come to light because the sender reveals it during his deposition, because you're forced to talk about it when you are asked about communications regarding the applicant under oath, or because someone else who saw or received a copy spills the beans.*

Not only will failing to produce the email make it seem like you were hiding something, it might be illegal in your state or result in a court order that could damage your company's defense. It won't seem like an offhand remark if it looks

*like you tried to bury it because you were worried about its content. And, keep in
mind, even if no one at your company reveals the email, the plaintiff's lawyer will
probably want all emails and other electronic documents related to the applicant.
Technologies are readily available that the lawyer can, and will, use to make sure
everything is turned over.*

The lawyers will be heavily involved in the discovery process as they
try to work out these details. You should expect to be quite busy, too.
The lawyers representing the company will want to talk to you about the
information and documents you have that might need to be handed over.
You should take these requests seriously and err on the side of providing
more information rather than less. It is not your responsibility to decide
whether the plaintiff gets the information—your company's attorneys will
evaluate the evidence and decide whether it must be disclosed under the law.
They'd much rather have you provide too much than too little, so they're
not surprised by evidence they didn't know about later in the proceedings.

You might also have to help gather information from others, often by
setting up meetings between the company attorney and employees who
might have information about the allegations in the lawsuit. Even if you
already interviewed these people (for example, in your original investigation
of the incidents underlying the complaint), the attorney will no doubt want
to interview them again. You will want to make sure they have a private
place to conduct these discussions, such as a conference room.

You might be asked to sit in on meetings between the attorney and these
potential witnesses. Just keep in mind that the purpose of the meetings is
to allow the attorney to ask questions. If you think the attorney should ask
about a particular incident or fact, discuss it privately with the attorney. You
should not plan on offering your thoughts or opinions unless the attorney
asks you to. Otherwise, it might look like you are telling the witness how
to testify, which could undermine your own credibility, as well as that of
the witness. Tell every employee the attorney interviews that the company's
policy prohibiting retaliation extends to employees who testify or provide
information in connection with a harassment or discrimination lawsuit,
and ask them to come to you if they feel that they've suffered any negative
consequences as a result of their participation in the case.

Pretrial Preparation

Once all the evidence is gathered and the discovery phase is finished (usually a specified number of days before the trial date), the company attorneys will begin preparing for trial in earnest. The attorneys will have to organize all of the physical evidence (such as documents) and witness testimony (from deposition transcripts and witness interviews). It usually also means a lot of meetings with company employees and, especially, with supervisors, managers, and human resource representatives who were involved in the incidents alleged in the complaint. The attorneys will also have to write their opening and closing arguments, prepare to select a jury (if there will be one), get ready to argue about what evidence should be admitted and kept out at trial, and handle dozens of other details.

During the weeks just before the trial begins, you, the attorneys, and anyone else present from the company will discuss how the attorneys plan to defend the company at trial. For example, the attorneys will tell you the names of the witnesses they intend to call and the order in which they intend to call them, the exhibits they'll introduce and in what form (for example, some may be electronically scanned or blown up to poster size), and the overall anticipated trial schedule. Your feedback will be important as these decisions are made. And, you might have to prepare to testify yourself.

As a result, this is a phase in which you might have to devote a lot of time and energy to the lawsuit. Plan ahead: Ask the company's lawyer to tell you the trial date as soon as it is set, so you can put it on your calendar and make time in the weeks leading up to (and during) the trial to assist when requested.

TIP

Prepare a litigation calendar and reminder system for yourself. Ask the attorney to notify you of all hearings, depositions, and other important litigation dates that might require your assistance. Create a reminder system to alert you days or weeks in advance of critical dates (like depositions or the trial date) so you'll have time to prepare. (A sample litigation calendar can be found later in this chapter.)

A lot can happen in the pretrial stage. For instance, it isn't uncommon for the parties to settle the lawsuit just before trial. Each side will finally have all of the information that's relevant to the case, which may enable everyone to take a fresh look at the dispute and come up with a resolution. Once the discovery dust settles, the relative strengths and weaknesses of each side will be clearer, which often makes it easier for everyone to agree on a settlement figure.

Additionally, more court hearings might take place as the parties try to use the legal process to end or limit the case before trial. One common way for parties to do this is through a summary judgment motion. Summary judgment motions are very frequently filed by employers in harassment and discrimination lawsuits. Such motions are filed once all the evidence has been gathered and the parties and court can better see whether there is enough evidence to support the employee's claims. If all of the plaintiff's evidence, even if true, still doesn't add up to a valid legal claim, the defendant can try to have the whole case (or particularly weak causes of action) dismissed on summary judgment. Plaintiffs also occasionally file motions for summary judgment, in which they argue that the defendant's evidence fails to refute, or even supports, the plaintiff's claims. However, courts are not quick to grant summary judgment motions, at least not ones that would dismiss the entire case. In general, most cases raise some question of fact that should be heard by a jury at trial.

 Common Questions

Q: *Our company's lawyer wants to file a motion for summary judgment. We've asked her to give us a rough idea of the hours it will take, and her estimate seems astronomical! Is a motion for summary judgment really that time-consuming—and if so, is it worth the cost to file one?*

A: *Summary judgment motions eat up a lot of attorney time. To prepare a motion, the attorneys have to comb through all of the evidence—the documents, deposition transcripts, and so on—to show that the plaintiff doesn't have enough support for his or her claims. The attorney has to prepare a fairly long written legal* *argument, along with a separate document that lays out all of the facts supporting the argument, with citations to the exact place in the records where the fact can be found. Basically, it's your company's case on paper citing all the supporting evidence and making arguments for your case, and identifying the weaknesses in the plaintiff's evidence and arguments.*

Whether a summary judgment is worth the cost depends on the strength of your company's arguments. If your company wins the motion, the plaintiff's case could be over. Even if your company wins only on certain claims, you could knock the legs out from under the case. For example, if your attorney gets all of the claims for personal injuries thrown out, the claims that remain for trial might offer only limited damages, and the plaintiff might be much more interested in settling the case. Talk to your company's lawyer about the likelihood of success on the motion. If the lawyer feels good about his or her prospects, it could well be worth the hefty price tag.

Trial

If the case doesn't settle by the time discovery is complete, the next step is a trial. The trial is when the parties tell their stories, present their evidence, and argue their cases, either to a judge or jury. All the hard work you've done to help your company's attorney gather evidence will be put to use here, as you get ready to go to court. No doubt you'll continue to work with the attorney at this point, helping to iron out details or gather evidence to present in the courtroom.

The plaintiff has what's called the "burden of proof," which means that it's up to the plaintiff to show that the wrongs alleged actually occurred; your company doesn't have to prove the opposite. Theoretically, the company could win the case without presenting any evidence or calling any witnesses, if the judge or jury thought that the plaintiff didn't prove that harassment or discrimination took place.

Of course, it doesn't work that way in reality. Your company didn't hire a lawyer just to fill a chair at the trial. Instead, the company's lawyer will work hard to show that the company didn't violate the law. In a harassment case, this typically means showing that the incidents didn't occur or weren't as bad as the plaintiff claims, or that, even if they did occur, the company shouldn't be held liable. In a discrimination case, the company typically seeks to prove that it had legitimate, nondiscriminatory reasons for the actions the plaintiff is complaining about (for example, failing to hire or promote, or terminating employment).

The company will offer its own evidence to undermine the plaintiff's case. For example, if the plaintiff claims that the company failed to accommodate his or her disability, the company might offer evidence showing either that the plaintiff doesn't have a disability or that he or she failed to inform anyone at the company about it. The company may also defend itself by proving that the employee was fired (or suffered another negative job action) for a reason that doesn't violate the law—for example, that a plaintiff who claims to have been fired because of his or her gender was actually fired for ongoing performance problems, which the company documented along the way.

A harassment or discrimination case may be tried before either a jury or a judge. Plaintiffs typically prefer a jury trial if they have the option: Most jurors are employees rather than employers and are likely to sympathize with the plaintiff. In a jury trial, the judge presides over the case, rules on legal motions and objections (for example, that certain evidence shouldn't be admitted), and instructs the jury about the relevant legal principles. Once all the evidence has been presented, the jury goes into a private room, sorts through all of the facts, and applies the legal principles provided by the judge in order to reach a verdict.

Sometimes, a judge decides the case without a jury. This means that the judge weighs all of the evidence and enters a verdict. In a trial before a judge sitting without a jury (sometimes called a "bench trial"), much depends on the leanings and predispositions of the judge who hears the case. Although judges are supposed to be impartial, any employment lawyer practicing in your area will have an opinion as to which local judges are considered to favor plaintiffs or defendants in employment cases.

Before any evidence is presented at trial, several other preliminary steps will happen. For example, the parties, with the judge's oversight, will select a jury. And the parties will have to notify each other of the evidence they plan to put forth. In some cases, when one party objects to the other's evidence, it may file a motion to exclude it. Motions like these can delay the trial by days or weeks.

Once the trial is underway, it can last anywhere from a few hours to a few weeks. (Trials in employment cases rarely go longer than this, although there are occasional exceptions.) At trial, the plaintiff will usually present evidence first, and the defendant will have the opportunity to cross-examine the witnesses that the plaintiff calls. You may be present for some or all of the trial. To prepare, you might be assisting the company's attorney by gathering relevant information or documents to ask each witness about. The company might have its own witnesses to put on the stand, too. In fact, one of your important functions might be to serve as a witness, as explained below.

Alternatives to Litigation

After hearing about the arduous process of getting through a civil lawsuit, you'll probably be relieved to hear that most legal disputes don't end in a trial with a jury verdict. Instead, most cases are resolved before a full trial through settlement negotiations, mediation, or arbitration.

Settlement

A "settlement" is simply a private agreement between the parties that resolves a dispute. The parties (or more likely, their attorneys) often discuss settlement at various points after the lawsuit is filed. Even if earlier settlement discussions don't go anywhere, it's not uncommon for cases to settle "on the courthouse steps," on the eve of trial. Many cases settle via mediation, which we discuss in Chapter 8 and further below.

Sometimes, the court is involved in settlement efforts. For example, many judicial systems require the parties to attend a settlement conference, often with a different judge or a private lawyer in attendance to try to facilitate the negotiations. More often, parties work out a settlement agreement on their own.

In a harassment or discrimination case, a settlement usually involves the defendant paying some money in exchange for the plaintiff dropping the lawsuit and giving up the right to ever bring it again. In addition to— or instead of—money, the defendant might agree to take certain actions, such as promoting the employee, reinstating the employee to his or her former position, providing company-wide antiharassment training, and so on. The defendant might also want the plaintiff to do some things, such as agreeing not to reveal the terms of the settlement, not to disparage the company, or not to apply for a job at the company in the future.

Because settlements are relatively common, the company's attorney will probably raise the possibility with you before trial. This can happen at any stage in the lawsuit, and it might happen more than once if the first effort to settle fails. Cases can even settle after a jury verdict, to avoid spending time and resources on an appeal.

TIP

Consider settling early on with a severance agreement. If you get the impression that a current employee is considering filing a lawsuit for harassment or discrimination (because the employee made an internal complaint, for example), it might be wise to offer a severance package or other settlement to the employee to nip it in the bud. Not only can this save your company large amounts in legal expenses, but it can also build goodwill by showing that your company is willing to step up, address the situation promptly, and offer fair compensation to the employee. And, it will mean avoiding the prospect of a lawsuit that drains your company's time and resources. However, be sure to consult with your company's lawyer beforehand—you'll want to have the employee sign an effective release, preventing the employee from suing the company for the acts in question in the future.

Mediation

Private mediation of a lawsuit is quite similar to mediation of an agency complaint, described in Chapter 8, with a couple of differences, however. One significant difference is that mediation during litigation will be conducted by a private mediator whom the parties select, rather than by one from a list proposed by the EEOC or FEPA. And, private mediation costs money, while mediations offered by an agency are usually free. Mediators, like arbitrators, are paid by the hour or day, and their fees can run to hundreds of dollars per hour.

Another difference is that the pressure to resolve a court case at mediation is higher than it is to resolve an agency complaint, both because a good deal of money is invested in the private mediation process and because the risks of failure to settle (that is, having to go to trial and possibly lose) are high for all concerned. Because of this private mediation can be more effective than an agency mediation.

Arbitration

In an arbitration, the parties agree to have their dispute decided by one or more impartial arbitrator. Unlike a mediator, who tries to help the parties reach their own solution, an arbitrator decides the case much like a judge. And the parties must abide by the arbitrator's decision, unless they agree ahead of time that they will have the right to challenge the decision in court.

Arbitration is a private proceeding. Unlike a courtroom, where taxpayer dollars fund the costs of the courtroom and judges', clerks', and bailiffs' time, an arbitration proceeding is funded by the parties (typically an hourly or daily fee). The parties and their attorneys present their evidence to the arbitrator, much as they would at trial. No jury is present at an arbitration hearing, and the proceedings are a bit less formal. For example, the parties might sit around a conference table rather than standing to make arguments, and the usual rules about what evidence a party can present and how don't apply. Company representatives may be present at the arbitration, and witnesses give testimony under oath.

The less formal process makes the arbitration hearing shorter than a trial would be, so arbitration offers the benefit of speed. Unless the parties agree otherwise, the arbitrator's decision typically can't be challenged or appealed (unlike a court judgment or trial verdict). So the dispute is decided, once and for all, quite a bit sooner than if it had been tried in court. The arbitrator's decision can be enforced by a court, however, if either party refuses to abide by it.

Most significantly, arbitration is not a public hearing of a case. No members of the public may be present without the consent of the parties to the arbitration. And, no public record of findings and decisions exists that may be relied on, or even reviewed, by anyone other than the parties.

 Common Questions

Q: *Our company requires new hires to sign arbitration agreements, stating that they must bring any legal claims against the company in an arbitration proceeding, not a lawsuit. An employee we fired has sued us anyway, and our company's lawyer says we have to file a motion to force the plaintiff to arbitrate the claims instead. Between the costs of filing and arguing this motion and the costs of arbitration, wouldn't we be better off just letting the plaintiff have her day in court?*

A: *Probably not. Arbitration offers companies a number of advantages over litigation. Arbitration is much faster than legal proceedings, and often pretrial procedures—such as discovery and motions—are limited. Also, arbitrators tend to be less swayed by emotional arguments (and less likely to make huge damages awards) than a jury would be, which often works in a company's favor in employment cases. All in all, arbitration is probably going to save your company money in the long run (which is undoubtedly why your company required employees to sign arbitration agreements in the first place). Keep in mind, though, that unlike a trial verdict, your company won't have the option to appeal the arbitration decision. Arbitration decisions are truly final and binding.*

In several decisions over the past couple of decades, the U.S. Supreme Court has upheld arbitration agreements between employers and employees. As a result, employers are increasingly making such agreements part of their new hire paperwork. In general, employers are free to require employees to sign arbitration agreements as a condition of employment, although California enacted a law in 2021 restricting such conditions of employment (the law is being challenged in court). Another trend, also in response to Supreme Court rulings, is for employers to include a class action waiver in the arbitration agreement. This means that employees must arbitrate their claims against the company separately, rather than grouping their claims together.

While arbitration is greatly favored by employers, employee advocates have raised several concerns about arbitration, including:

- When employers condition employment upon signing an arbitration agreement, employees often have no choice but to sign if they want to get or keep the job.
- Arbitrations are private while lawsuits are held in open court, which means that employees (and the public) don't know if an employer has been charged with similar conduct in the past.
- There is no requirement of a written record (called a "transcript") of arbitrations.
- Parties to an arbitration have no right to appeal the arbitrator's decision.
- Arbitrators are often industry insiders or lawyers drawn from firms that represent employers.
- Arbitration decisions do not create precedent and are unknown to anyone but the parties and the arbitrators, which creates less incentive for employers to stop discriminatory practices.

Despite these concerns, however, the clear trend is that more employers are requiring employees to sign arbitration agreements, and more courts are upholding these agreements.

SEE AN EXPERT

In May 2018, the U.S. Supreme Court held that employers can use arbitration agreements to bar employees from joining together to legally challenge workplace practices. Arbitration law is dynamic and the subject of court decisions (and some new laws, as in California, referenced above) every year. And, some state courts have issued decisions affecting the enforceability of arbitration agreements in those states. Check with an experienced employment lawyer for the status of the law wherever you do business.

Your Role in a Lawsuit

As you read about the stages of litigation and all the different ways employee complaints can be resolved, you might feel overwhelmed. But don't worry: Your company's attorney will be there to walk you through these different stages, explaining the process as you go.

Although you can offer assistance in plenty of ways as the trial proceeds, the attorney will be responsible for the bulk of the work: making arguments to the judge, preparing paperwork for court, interviewing witnesses, and so on. Your two main roles during a harassment or discrimination lawsuit are:

- to act as the liaison between the company and its attorneys, and
- to be an effective witness on behalf of the company, showing publicly that it met its legal obligations to prevent and correct harassment and discrimination.

Being an Effective Liaison

As explained above, the company's lawyer will need your help getting ready to defend the company in the lawsuit. Although the attorney knows the law, you know the facts: what actually happened, who was involved, and how the company handled it. You might also know the personalities of the various employees involved, including the plaintiff. And, you know the company's record-keeping procedures. All of this knowledge means you have an important role to play in assisting the company's lawyer.

When you first meet with the attorney after the lawsuit has been filed, remember that the attorney might not know much about the underlying events, especially if the attorney wasn't involved in making the company's case to the EEOC or state fair employment practices agency. So you must be prepared to fill in the details. If you did the investigation and prepared the materials discussed in Chapters 5 and 6, this shouldn't be hard to do. You can summarize the plaintiff's history with the company, the plaintiff's complaint, how you investigated, and what your investigation revealed. Show the lawyer all of the documents and files that the company has concerning the plaintiff. While you might have to search for some of this anew, a lot of it will probably be material you compiled in the course of your investigation.

TIP

Don't forget to check and assemble emails and other electronic documents that might be relevant. Your company's attorney will need to see any documents, including electronic documents, that might relate to the lawsuit. These can include emails, company intranet messages and posts, company electronic bulletin board or blog posts (including those administered by outside vendors), and the like. Be sure to check all systems and sites used by your company and its employees for relevant material.

The attorney might ask you to prepare a brief, chronological narrative of events (similar to the timeline described in Chapter 6), which the attorney can use to quickly understand and organize the facts of the case. A list of pertinent documents is also tremendously useful. List each document and give the title or a brief description, the date it was prepared, the author, the recipient, and its location (for example, in a personnel file, database, or investigation file). List the documents in a logical order. Chronological order is a good method, but sometimes grouping documents chronologically within categories (for example, "personnel documents," "investigation documents," or "medical documents") is more sensible, especially if many documents were created in a short span of time. Remember to err on the side of providing too much information. Leave it to the attorneys to decide what is relevant.

Common Questions

Q: *Seven female mechanics who used to work for us have sued our company for sex discrimination in a single lawsuit. They each worked for us for a different amount of time, held a variety of positions, and complain about different supervisors and coworkers in the lawsuit. Three of them worked in the same shop, but the others worked at two of our other shops in town. Their records are located in different places, as are the witnesses they name. Our lawyer wants me to get all the relevant information to her about these plaintiffs. I don't know how to put it together in a way that will make sense for her. Ideas?*

A: *First, get all of their personnel files. Do a separate chronology of the work history for each plaintiff. Include the events they each allege and note whether each event is disputed by the company or not. Then, create a document index for each plaintiff.*

In a complex case like this, consider making a chart or another diagram that indicates any overlap in their work histories or allegations (for example, that certain plaintiffs worked at the same time, in the same position, or for the same supervisor), as well as any evidence that's common to two or more of the plaintiffs. Try to get a "big picture" view and fill in the details in a way that makes clear what is verified (or undisputed by your company) and what is disputed.

One of the first things your company's attorney will consider is whether to try to divide up the case—to force each plaintiff to bring her own lawsuit, rather than bringing all of the claims together. A divide and conquer strategy can be effective for a company because it requires much more attorney work for the plaintiffs, who might each need a separate lawyer. And, when separated, the damages and fees each case would generate might not be high enough to attract a good plaintiff's attorney. What's more, your company might have an easier time at trial answering the claims of one plaintiff, rather than a group of plaintiffs all making similar allegations. To convince the court to separate the lawsuits, your company's attorney will have to show that the claims are sufficiently different that they shouldn't be tried together. This is where your overlapping chronology comes in: The attorney can use it to determine how much the cases intersect and how likely a court would be to divide them.

If you prepare the chronology and document index specifically for the attorneys to review and use to defend the company, those documents will be protected by the attorney–client privilege. That means you do not have to give them to the plaintiff, even if they are requested during discovery. This should encourage you to list every document and fact, good or bad, without having to fear that the plaintiff will see it and use it against you. With the chronology of events and the document index in hand, the company's lawyers can then ask you for particular items they wish to review or employees they wish to interview.

Sample Document Index

Document	Date	Author	Recipient	Location
Offer letter	2/10/18	Jay Wilkerson	Todd Jackson	Personnel file
1st warning	8/21/19	Jay Wilkerson	Todd Jackson	Personnel file
Employee complaint	11/15/19	Todd Jackson	Bob Marshall	Investigation file

As liaison, you might also be involved in things like scheduling meetings between attorneys and potential witnesses, document reviews (when the plaintiff's attorney may be on site to review relevant documents) or other physical inspections, and employee depositions. As explained above, it's a good idea to keep a litigation calendar: a separate calendar you keep just for the lawsuit, but with crucial dates entered into your regular office calendar. One reason to have a separate litigation calendar is that you can take a quick look at the whole schedule of dates and plan ahead. Often, you'll need days or weeks of lead time to meet a particular lawsuit deadline. For example, if you are helping answer interrogatories in discovery, it will take you some time to gather the necessary information, give it to the company's attorney, then review the attorney's final draft of the company's responses. So you'll have to get started at least a few weeks before the interrogatory responses are actually due.

By regularly reviewing the litigation calendar, you can note in your daily planner the dates when you'll need to start preparing for particular litigation events. This reminder system will help you plan ahead for periods of intense lawsuit work. That way, you won't be surprised on a Monday morning to find out that you have to show up at a deposition the next day. For a blank copy of the litigation calendar, see Appendix B.

Sample Litigation Calendar

Plaintiff's name: __Todd Jackson__

Event	Event Date	Reminder Date	Participants	Location	Reminder Sent? (Yes/No)
Doc. Production Date	05/07/20	04/20/20	Bob Marshall	Office	yes
Deposition Prep. Mtg.	06/15/20	05/25/20	Jay Wilkerson	Lewis Graham office, 950 Main Street	yes
Deposition	06/25/20	06/21/20	Jay Wilkerson	950 Main Street	yes

In this sample, you would enter the dates on your daily planner, too. The reminder for Jay Wilkerson's deposition preparation meeting with attorneys will alert you, if you are the company liaison, to remind Jay about the meeting and make any other arrangements necessary (like setting up an office or conference room for the meeting or gathering documents that the attorneys have asked to see).

Ask the attorney to notify you of upcoming court dates and to keep you in the loop if anything changes (a fairly common occurrence). Don't hesitate to check in with the attorney every couple of weeks to find out if anything new has come up that you should be aware of. The company is the attorney's client, and you represent the company, so don't be shy about asking for information. Most attorneys are happy to provide it, although they might occasionally need a gentle reminder.

Being an Effective Witness

In addition to being a liaison, you might have another important role: You might be a witness in the litigation itself. If you were involved in taking the complaint, investigating it, or managing the employee, the employee's attorney will almost certainly want to hear your version of events. And, your company's attorney might also want you to testify, to present the company's side of the story.

For many people, the thought of testifying in a courtroom under oath can be intimidating or scary. After all, testifying as a witness is different from simply being interviewed, say, by your employer's attorneys. When you testify, you take an oath to tell the truth, and you are questioned (usually by the plaintiff's attorney) either in court or in a conference room with several people present. What you say is transcribed by a court reporter, sometimes along with a video or audio recording.

Fortunately, it's highly unlikely that you'll be thrown into the fray without any preparation. The attorney for the company will meet with you ahead of time to discuss the purpose of the questioning, answer any questions you might have, and explain how to handle yourself.

Still, even with that kind of preparation or training, it's a good idea to understand a few basic principles that will help you do your best as an effective witness on the company's behalf. Whether you are answering questions in a pretrial deposition or on the stand during trial, follow these tips to put your best foot forward:

- **Listen very carefully.** In a normal conversation, we often know (or think we know) what other people are going to ask or say before they finish speaking. But don't make this assumption when giving testimony. Your testimony will be accurate only if you know exactly what is being asked. And, if you don't allow the questioner to finish the question, you might end up giving an answer to a different question entirely— one that the questioner might not have thought to ask!
- **Ask for clarification.** If you're not sure what you're being asked, don't speculate. Politely ask the attorney to rephrase or clarify the question. Don't answer until you're sure you understand, even if you feel like the attorney is frustrated. The important thing is to be accurate.

- **Answer only what is asked.** Especially if you are answering questions from the plaintiff's attorney, you don't want to volunteer information. You have a duty to answer the questions asked, but don't blurt out everything you know. The best way to make sure your testimony is accurate and helpful to the company is to provide only the information requested, and nothing more. When your company's attorney questions you, he or she will make sure you have an opportunity to provide all of the information necessary to help your company make its case.

 Common Questions

Q: *I just had my deposition taken in a harassment lawsuit filed by a former employee. The employee's attorney asked me if I'd ever seen the employee's supervisor touch the employee. I answered that he never touched her in an inappropriate way and that he is a very professional person. I thought this would be helpful, but the attorney for the company spoke to me about it afterward and said I needed to only answer what was asked. What did I do wrong?*

A: *You were trying to be helpful, but providing extra information could be damaging. The employee's lawyer only asked if you'd ever seen the supervisor touch the employee. That calls for a "yes" or "no" answer, which is the only answer to give. Even though you wanted to give more of what you felt was helpful information, doing so can be dangerous. Many times, witnesses give the opposing party a whole new area of questioning. For example, here you concluded that the supervisor's touching had never been "inappropriate" and suggested that his "professional" behavior means he wouldn't do anything he shouldn't. This might lead the employee's attorney to ask about other touching (that is, touching that isn't "inappropriate") that you might have witnessed. Or, it could lead the attorney to explore whether your investigation was biased—that is, whether you let your personal opinion of the supervisor cloud your professional judgment about his actions. In the future, stick to the questions you are asked.*

- **Don't explain if "yes," "no," or "I don't know" answers the question.** The urge to explain is a strong one. However, keep in mind that, if a question calls for a yes or no answer, that is all you should provide. Again, providing too much information can harm you by opening new areas for questioning or ambiguity.
- **Keep emotions in check.** It's common for a lawyer to try to rattle a witness. This tactic is used for a variety of reasons, including making the witness appear defensive and less credible or provoking the witness to blurt out more information than he or she otherwise would. Even if you feel insulted, offended, or angry, don't show it. And, don't let it cloud your ability to listen closely and answer only what is asked. If you start to get upset, take a deep breath and refocus on the exact words of the question. You can even ask to take a break if you need a few minutes to compose yourself.
- **Always tell the truth, no matter how painful.** You might be asked to give information that you believe will hurt your company, your coworkers, or yourself. As hard as it may be to do, you must tell the truth when testifying. You are under oath and lying is perjury, which is a crime in most jurisdictions. Also, if the other side learns that you have lied under oath, it will destroy your credibility, causing the judge or jury to doubt the reliability of all of your testimony, even testimony that was truthful.
- **Be consistent.** If you contradict an earlier statement, be prepared to explain the discrepancy. Otherwise, the plaintiff's attorney will ask you the type of question no witness wants to answer: "Were you lying then, or are you lying now?"

Common Questions

Q: *An employee has filed a discrimination lawsuit. My problem is that the employee did come to me and mentioned that he felt unfairly treated by his supervisor. After he described the situation, I could see that it was probably just a misunderstanding. I told him I'd talk to his supervisor, but I got buried in other work and forgot. Our lawyer said that the employee filed an agency complaint and requested an* *immediate right to sue letter, so the lawsuit was the first we heard of his claims. I'm afraid that if I have to testify and tell the truth about dropping the ball, it will hurt my company. And, the employee doesn't really know whether or not I looked into his situation. I'd like to just answer that I investigated and found no evidence of discrimination. Is that okay?*

A: *Not even close to okay. You would be lying under oath and could face penalties for perjury if you're caught. And, you probably would be caught because, even though the employee doesn't know what you did or didn't do, other people do. You can safely bet that the employee's attorney is going to scour the evidence for information about your "investigation." Unless you're planning to create false documentation and coach other employees to lie for you, the attorney isn't going to find anything that supports your story. That would not only not help your employer, it would make the company look worse.*

Talk to the company's lawyer about your concerns beforehand and let him or her figure out how to deal with the fall-out after you tell the truth during your testimony. Attorneys anticipate these problems and have ways to deal with them, but only if you don't compound the problem by lying.

The different situations in which you might be testifying under oath are: at arbitration, in a deposition, and at trial. As explained above, a deposition occurs during the discovery phase, when you are asked questions outside the courtroom, usually by the plaintiff's attorney. The deposition testimony is transcribed and can then be used as evidence in pretrial motions and in some cases, at the trial. You might also testify at the trial itself. Because these situations are a little different, you should prepare for each of them a little differently.

Deposition Testimony

A "deposition" is a question-and-answer session outside of court, usually in a conference room at the offices of the lawyer who's taking the deposition. In spite of the relatively informal setting, deposition testimony is given under oath, has the same effect as testimony in court, and can be used at trial (often by the other side's attorney reading the testimony aloud to show that the witness has changed his or her story).

It's very important that you are well prepared for your deposition. You want to make sure that you don't say anything that will conflict with statements you've made in the past or will make in the future at trial.

TIP

Ask the attorney representing the company for any materials you can review about general deposition procedure. Some law firms have videos or other informative products for witnesses to review before a deposition. You can also check out *Nolo's Deposition Handbook,* by Paul Bergman and Albert Moore. Keep in mind, though, that the plaintiff's lawyer can demand to see anything you reviewed in preparation for a deposition.

You won't be alone during the deposition; the attorney representing the company will be with you. The attorney will meet with you beforehand as well, to help you prepare. You'll cover the most important topics that are likely to come up during the deposition, so the attorney can hear how you plan to answer and explain or explore the effects of that answer—for example, to prepare you for more intense questioning by the plaintiff's attorney on a specific issue.

At the deposition itself, you will probably sit at a table with the company's attorney sitting next to you. (If you are being sued individually, as explained below, it might be your own attorney sitting next to you.) Across the table will be the employee's attorney, who will ask you questions; the employee might be there as well. A court reporter also will be at the table, taking down everything you say, and someone might be present with a video camera too. Don't get distracted by the crowd or the recording equipment; just focus on the questions themselves.

If you follow the tips described above, you will do the best you can to represent the company. And don't worry—the attorney for the company won't just be sitting there. The attorney will be making sure that the questions asked are proper. In some cases, the attorney might object to certain questions before you answer. This is a clue to wait before answering. When an attorney objects in court, the judge can immediately rule on, or decide, the objection—that is, whether the question is proper (and therefore, you have to answer it) or not. For example, a judge may decide that you don't have to answer a question because it isn't relevant. Because the judge isn't present to make these rulings at a deposition, however, the attorney must register the objection on the record (that is, the court reporter must write it down). It is important that you give the attorney an opportunity to do this after each question is asked, because it might affect the company's right to have the evidence excluded at trial.

In some cases, the company's attorney will instruct you not to answer particular questions. Very heated exchanges can occur between the lawyers for each side during a deposition. The attorneys might raise their voices or disagree about something you don't understand. Don't worry about this. Just stay focused on answering the questions asked of you, unless otherwise directed by the company's attorney. If you start to get upset and feel it's interfering with your testimony, ask for a break between questions. Then you can step out and cool off, or talk to the company's attorney about what's happening.

Although the company's attorney will go over the entire process with you ahead of time, it's a good idea for you to prepare and review relevant documents before that, so you can ask any questions you have and assuage your fears or concerns about the process. Write down the issues you'd like to discuss with the attorney before the deposition. Although you might have the opportunity to talk privately during the deposition, you might be too confused or flustered to remember what you wanted to ask. And if you leave the room for private consultation, the plaintiff's attorney might try to prevent you from doing so and suggest that it looks like you're getting coached by the company's lawyer, which can hurt your credibility.

CAUTION

Don't reveal privileged communications at deposition. As a representative of the company, your communications with the company's attorney about the case are protected by the attorney–client privilege. This means you shouldn't talk about these private discussions at your deposition. If you have any concerns about these communications, discuss them with the company's attorney ahead of time, and don't answer a question on the subject unless you're certain you're not disclosing something confidential.

As mentioned above, a court reporter will be taking down everything that's said at the deposition, in shorthand. A few days or weeks after the deposition, the court reporter will provide the attorneys for each party with a written copy of the transcript of the deposition: a full record of all of the questions, answers, objections, arguments, and discussions on the record. (Any whispered discussion between you and the company's attorney, or conversations you have outside the deposition room, aren't recorded.)

The company's attorney will probably ask you to review the written transcript of your deposition to make sure all of your answers are accurate. You can make changes to your deposition testimony, but if you do, the plaintiff's attorney can comment on the changes at trial. The attorney might try to make it look like you were not completely truthful, either at the deposition or in your changes to the transcript. However, if any errors are in the recorded answers or the court reporter made a mistake, be sure to point them out to the company's attorney so he or she can take care of them.

Trial Testimony

Thanks to TV and movies, as virtually everyone knows, when you testify at trial, you do so on the witness stand beside the judge and in front of the jury. Like deposition testimony, trial testimony is given under oath and recorded by a court reporter. However, the much more formal courtroom setting, the judge's oversight role, and the interruptions of objections, argument, and rulings by the judge can make the procedure more anxiety provoking than a deposition. And you can't correct the record of your trial testimony or take breaks to compose yourself. For these reasons, preparation is even more important for trial testimony.

 Common Questions

Q: *I investigated an employee's discrimination complaint, and now the employee has sued. I have to give a deposition and probably testify at trial, and I'm terrified. I've never been comfortable with public speaking, and now I'm going to be cross-examined in front of a judge and jury! Every time I think about it, I start to panic. What can I do?*

A: *First off, realize that you're not alone. Most people are afraid of speaking in front of others, and having to testify at trial provokes anxiety even in the most fearless among us. Tell the company's attorney about your fears and ask for help. One option is to have the attorney videotape you during a couple of practice sessions, so you can see how you sound and what you can do to improve. The more confident you are about how well you're going to do, the more comfortable you'll be.*

If you're a party to the lawsuit or are the designated company representative, you will be at trial every day, sitting beside your attorney. If you're simply called as a witness, you'll probably be at trial only on the day when you testify, although you might still play a very active behind-the-scenes role in assisting the company's lawyers, as discussed above.

The company's attorneys will prepare you to testify in court, often by pretending to be the plaintiff's attorney and asking the questions you are likely to face. The attorneys will also review with you any documents that you're likely to be asked about. They'll go over how you should present yourself and how to listen carefully not only to the questioner but also to the judge. And, they'll tell you to stop answering and listen if either attorney makes an objection, being sure to wait until both attorneys and the judge have finished speaking. When objections are made at trial, the judge will usually signal when you can answer the question.

A courtroom is a lot like a stage—and when you're in the witness box, you're the lead actor! All eyes are on you. This can be extremely unnerving, so it's important to get as comfortable as you can with the idea of answering questions in public. Again, ask the company's lawyers for suggestions, resources, or to set up a mock deposition. Some people even find that watching movies with trial scenes is helpful.

TIP

Sit in on a trial. If at all possible, go to your local courthouse sometime before you have to testify and sit in the audience of a trial during witness cross-examination. It doesn't matter what type of case you observe; the idea is to get more comfortable with the setting and the roles of the witness and other trial participants.

Your prior deposition testimony might come into play during trial. The plaintiff's attorney will ask you a lot of the same questions and pounce on any deviation in your trial testimony from your deposition testimony. So, it's important to review the written transcript of your deposition as you prepare to testify at trial. The attorney may read aloud certain passages of the transcript and ask you to explain any contradictions. Of course, if your deposition was videotaped, instead of reading the transcript, the attorney will replay the video of the particular question and answer that he or she wants to highlight. This can be excruciating (few of us enjoy seeing our images on screen!), but focus on the question and answer and the attorney's follow-up question, and you'll get through the awkward moment just fine.

As with deposition testimony and other stages of litigation, the company's attorney will guide you through the process and prepare you for your role. If you have questions or feel unprepared, be sure to ask for help.

If You Are Sued Personally

A plaintiff may name you individually as a defendant in his or her lawsuit. This might happen if the plaintiff alleges that you personally harassed him or her or that you engaged in other conduct for which you can be sued individually (for example, that you defamed the plaintiff by lying to prospective employers about the reasons why he was fired).

As distressing as it is to be called as a witness in a case against your employer, it's considerably more troubling to be named as a defendant to a harassment or discrimination lawsuit along with your employer. Not only are you being personally accused of misconduct, but your personal assets might also be at risk if the plaintiff wins. This means you have a lot at stake, and you will have to work even harder to make sure you're prepared. But don't panic. As explained below, you will be represented by a lawyer—in most cases, either the same lawyer who represents the company or your own lawyer who is paid by the company.

Your Lawyer

If you are named as a defendant in a lawsuit, the first order of business is to make sure you have a lawyer. If the company has also been sued (as is almost always the case), the company's attorney will often represent you too, at least at the outset. The attorney will explain that he or she can represent you both as long as there is no conflict of interest between you and the employer. A conflict of interest means that your interests are sufficiently different—and opposed—that the lawyer cannot represent you both at the same time.

You will likely have the option of either agreeing to the dual representation (with the understanding that the attorney will notify you if a conflict arises) or hiring your own lawyer. Many individual supervisors and managers choose joint representation, probably because the company will often foot the entire bill for the attorneys' fees.

If you go this route, however, problems might arise if you and the company develop opposing interests. This might come to light during the course of the lawsuit. For example, if the company comes to believe that that you actually harassed an employee, it might no longer want to fight the employee's claim. Instead, it might want to settle for a small sum of money and move on, while you might want a full trial to "vindicate" your name. If a conflict like this arises, the same attorney can't represent you both. The attorney will likely continue representing the company, his or her original client, and leave you to find your own lawyer.

Sometimes, an individual manager is named as a defendant purely for legal or strategic reasons. For example, by naming an individual as a defendant, a plaintiff can avoid having his or her case transferred from state to federal court in certain cases where that otherwise would be allowed. (See "Why Supervisors Get Sued," in Chapter 2, for more information.) But even if you are plainly not the real target of the lawsuit, your personal assets are still at risk. It's important to take the claims against you seriously and make sure that the attorney representing you protects your interests. Even if no conflict of interest exists between you and the company at the beginning of a lawsuit, keep an eye out for conflicts that might emerge as the case proceeds.

TIP

Get a "second opinion" as to potential conflicts of interest. Although you might have no reason to doubt the judgment and ethics of the company's attorney, it's a good idea to consult with another lawyer privately and make sure there's no conflict of interest. Do this both at the outset of the lawsuit and at any later time when you think your interests might conflict with the company's.

Common Questions

Q: *My company and I personally have been sued by a job applicant who was interviewed and rejected by the hiring committee. While I was a member of the committee, the rejection decision was made by all of us together. I attended the deposition of another member of the hiring committee, and he testified that I made the final decision to reject the applicant. This is not true, and my deposition is coming up. Obviously, I'll tell the truth, but that's going to create problems for my company, isn't it?*

A: *It might, but there is a more immediate problem. You need to see an attorney who isn't affiliated with your company to find out whether you need your own lawyer. The committee member's testimony conflicts with yours in a way that puts the blame on you for the hiring decision. The company might simply be caught in the middle of the dispute between you and the other committee member, or the company might be trying to focus liability for any harm from the rejection decision on you. If the latter is the case, the company's attorney clearly cannot represent your interests and the interests of the company at the same time.*

Make an appointment with an employment lawyer right away to talk about the problem. If you can't schedule an appointment before your deposition, ask that the deposition be delayed until you are able to speak with an attorney.

If you need your own attorney, your company might be willing—or legally required—to pay for your separate attorneys' fees. Some states require employers to indemnify employees: to pay all costs associated with doing their jobs. In these states, employers might have to foot the bill for an employee's lawyer and the cost of a damages award against the employee, as long as the lawsuit stems from the employee's official duties. If the employee is accused of behavior that falls outside the scope of his or her job (such as sexually assaulting an employee), however, the employee wouldn't be entitled to indemnification. When you speak to a lawyer to find out if there are any conflicts of interest, ask whether the company might be required to pay for your attorneys' fees.

The company may elect to pay for your lawyer even if it isn't required to do so. For example, the company might simply want to help you out financially, it might have an insurance policy that covers such fees, or it might want to keep you on the team and make sure that you present the company in a positive light. This latter motive highlights the potential problem with allowing the company to pay your lawyer: An employer might want to exercise subtle (or not so subtle) control over you or your attorney by pulling the purse strings to compel you to support its case. Discuss the pros and cons of an arrangement like this with your own lawyer before agreeing to it.

Your Role as a Defendant

As long as no conflict of interest exists, you will work with the company's attorney in much the same way as you would if you were a witness in the suit, at least up to the point of trial. However, you need to stay on the lookout for possible conflicts of interest and seek outside advice if you're concerned that you aren't being adequately represented.

The plaintiff might be willing to settle his or her claims against you and proceed to trial only against the company. In that event, you likely take on the role of company liaison and witness, as discussed above.

If you're still a defendant when the trial starts, however, your role shifts significantly. As a witness and liaison, you only have to show up on the day that you are scheduled to testify and help company lawyers with trial preparations as necessary. As a party, you must attend every day of trial and sit at the defendants' table in front of the judge's bench. Although your active role during the trial is still restricted to testifying and helping behind the scenes, you have to sit there, in full view of the judge and jury, throughout the trial. This means you'll have to pay attention to your appearance and demeanor. Maintain your composure no matter what's going on around you. This can be quite difficult because you might hear accusatory, harsh, and even dishonest things said about you, to which you cannot respond or react.

A harassment or discrimination trial can last days and even weeks. Having to sit silently and passively for such a long stretch can be exhausting, even without the added stress of being personally attacked and at risk as a defendant.

TIP

Attend the depositions of the plaintiff's witnesses and read the transcripts. As a party to a lawsuit, you have the right to attend the depositions of witnesses. Although you might not want to attend all of them, sit in on those of witnesses who you know will testify about you or your actions. And, read the depositions of all witnesses before trial, so you're not surprised by what they say in court.

Limiting Your Exposure

Individual defendants are often dismissed from the lawsuit before trial. Compared to the company, individual managers are usually not viewed as having deep pockets filled with assets and resources to pay a large judgment. Throughout the litigation, your attorney will likely try to get you out of the lawsuit by filing motions, such as a motion to dismiss or a motion for summary judgment, as discussed above. Ask the attorneys about making such a motion as early as possible. Typically, a motion for summary judgment is not made until after some or all of the discovery is complete, but there might be enough evidence early on to prove that you can't be sued personally for your actions.

If you're jointly represented along with your employer, this is another potential source of conflict: You will naturally want to get out of the lawsuit as soon as possible, while the attorney might prefer to wait until he or she can make all of the defense arguments at once. If you sense resistance on the part of the company's lawyer, you should consult with another lawyer to assess the situation.

Settling Individual Claims

Plaintiffs often settle their claims alleged against individual defendants. In part, this is because individuals typically do not have the resources and assets to pay large verdicts. But dismissing an individual defendant might also make the plaintiff's case stronger. Juries could sympathize more with an individual defendant, but be more likely to award large damages against a faceless business. Dropping an individual defendant also helps the plaintiff focus on the strongest claims; because individuals are often sued for tactical reasons (rather than because they acted particularly badly), claims against them aren't likely to be the best in the bunch.

Talk to your lawyer (whether you're jointly or individually represented) about engaging in settlement talks with the plaintiff early and often throughout the litigation. If you're jointly represented and the attorney resists these requests, this might signal a conflict of interest. You should consider consulting an attorney unaffiliated with the company to make sure your interests are protected.

If you can't get out of the case, ask your company whether a damages award against you might be covered by insurance. Some employers offer insurance coverage for damage awards against company officers, directors, and other employees for actions they take in the course of their jobs. Early in the litigation, ask whether such coverage is available for you. If there is no such insurance available, talk to an outside lawyer about negotiating with the company to protect you in the event of an unfavorable judgment. For example, it might be possible to get the company to agree to pay for some or all of a damages award against you.

Dos and Don'ts

Do:

- Prepare a chronology of events and document index for the initial meeting with lawyers.
- Create a litigation calendar, and consult it often.
- Prepare questions for lawyers prior to testifying at deposition or in court.
- Sit in on and review the transcripts of the depositions of other witnesses.
- If you're named as a defendant in the lawsuit, consult with a lawyer unaffiliated with the company to make sure that the company's interests don't conflict with yours.

Don't:

- Panic—a cool head works better!
- Hesitate to ask the lawyers about what to expect at all stages of a lawsuit.
- Try to help your company or yourself by hiding the truth.
- Be bashful about reminding company lawyers to keep you in the loop regarding dates and scheduling.
- Let your emotions get the best of you at your deposition or in court.
- Answer a question unless you know what's being asked, when testifying.
- Ignore potential conflicts of interest if you're named as a defendant: You have a lot at stake, and you must act quickly to protect yourself.

State Laws on Discrimination and Harassment

State Laws Prohibiting Discrimination in Employment

Alabama

Ala. Code §§ 25-1-20, 25-1-21

Law applies to employers with: 20 or more employees

Private employers may not make employment decisions based on:
- Age (40 and older)
- Refusal to provide pay history

Alaska

Alaska Stat. §§ 18.80.220, 18.80.300, 39.20.520, 47.30.865

Law applies to employers with: One or more employees

Private employers may not make employment decisions based on:
- Age
- Ancestry or national origin
- Physical or mental disability
- Gender
- Marital status, including changes in status
- Pregnancy, childbirth, and related medical conditions (accommodations required; includes parenthood)
- Race or color
- Religion or creed
- Mental illness

Arizona

Ariz. Rev. Stat. §§ 36-2813, 41-1461, 41-1463, 41-1465

Law applies to employers with: 15 or more employees

Private employers may not make employment decisions based on:
- Age (40 and older)
- Ancestry or national origin
- Physical or mental disability
- AIDS/HIV
- Gender
- Pregnancy, childbirth, and related medical conditions
- Race or color
- Religion or creed
- Genetic testing information
- Certified medical marijuana use

Arkansas

Ark. Code §§ 11-4-601, 11-5-116, 11-5-403, 16-123-102, 16-123-107

Law applies to employers with: Nine or more employees

Private employers may not make employment decisions based on:
- Ancestry or national origin
- Physical, mental, or sensory disability
- Gender
- Pregnancy, childbirth, and related medical conditions (accommodations required)
- Race or color
- Religion or creed
- Genetic testing information

California

Cal. Gov't. Code §§ 12920, 12926, 12926.1, 12940, 12941, 12945; Cal. Lab. Code § 1101, 432.3

Law applies to employers with: Five or more employees

Private employers may not make employment decisions based on:
- Age (40 and older)
- Ancestry or national origin
- Physical or mental disability
- AIDS/HIV
- Gender
- Marital status

State Laws Prohibiting Discrimination in Employment (continued)

- Pregnancy, childbirth, and related medical conditions (including breast-feeding and other accommodations)
- Race or color (including hairstyles)
- Religion or creed
- Sexual orientation
- Genetic testing information
- Gender identity, gender expression
- Medical condition
- Political activities or affiliations
- Status as victim of domestic violence, sexual assault, or stalking
- Military and veteran status
- Salary history, unless voluntarily disclosed

Colorado

Colo. Rev. Stat. §§ 24-34-301, 24-34-401, 24-34-402, 24-34-402.3, 24-34-402.5, 27-65-115; 3 Colo. Code Regs. §§ 708-1:60.1, 708-1:80.8

Law applies to employers with: One or more employees; 25 or more employees (marital status only)

Private employers may not make employment decisions based on:

- Age (40 and older)
- Ancestry or national origin
- Physical, mental, or learning disability
- AIDS/HIV
- Gender
- Marital status (applies only to marriage to a coworker or plans to marry a coworker)
- Pregnancy, childbirth, and related medical conditions (accommodations required)
- Race or color (including hairstyles)
- Religion or creed
- Sexual orientation, including perceived sexual orientation

- Lawful conduct outside of work
- Mental illness
- Transgender status
- Wage differential based on sex, or salary history
- Domestic abuse or stalking victimization

Connecticut

Conn. Gen. Stat. §§ 31-40z, 31-51ss, 46a-51, 46a-60, 46a-81a, 46a-81c

Law applies to employers with: Three or more employees

Private employers may not make employment decisions based on:

- Age
- Ancestry or national origin
- Present or past physical, mental, learning, or intellectual disability
- Gender
- Marital status, including civil unions
- Pregnancy, childbirth, and related medical conditions (accommodations required)
- Race or color
- Religion or creed
- Sexual orientation, including having a history of such a preference or being identified with such a preference
- Genetic testing information
- Ethnic traits historically associated with race (hairstyle, headwraps, etc)
- Gender identity or expression
- Arrests or convictions that have been erased, pardoned, or rehabilitated
- Status as a veteran
- Salary history, unless voluntarily disclosed
- Status as victim of domestic violence or stalking

State Laws Prohibiting Discrimination in Employment (continued)

Delaware

Del. Code tit. 19, §§ 710, 711, 711A, 724

Law applies to employers with: Four or more employees

Private employers may not make employment decisions based on:

- Age (40 and older)
- Ancestry or national origin
- Physical or mental disability
- AIDS/HIV
- Gender
- Marital status
- Pregnancy, childbirth, and related medical conditions (including breast-feeding; accommodations required)
- Race or color
- Religion or creed
- Sexual orientation
- Genetic testing information
- Gender identity
- Status as victim of domestic violence, sexual offense, or stalking
- Family responsibilities
- "Reproductive health decisions"
- Salary history

District of Columbia

D.C. Code §§ 2-1401.02, 2-1401.05, 2-1402.11, 2-1402.82, 7-1703.03, 32-531.08

Law applies to employers with: One or more employees

Private employers may not make employment decisions based on:

- Age (18 and older)
- Ancestry or national origin
- Physical or mental disability
- Gender, including reproductive health decisions

- Marital status, including domestic partnership
- Pregnancy, childbirth, and related medical conditions, including parenthood and breast-feeding
- Race or color
- Religion or creed
- Sexual orientation
- Genetic testing information
- Enrollment in vocational, professional, or college education
- Family duties
- Personal appearance
- Political affiliation
- Gender identity or expression
- Status as unemployed
- Tobacco use
- Credit information
- Victim of domestic violence, sexual offense, or stalking

Florida

Fla. Stat. §§ 448.075, 760.01, 760.02, 760.10, 760.50

Law applies to employers with: 15 or more employees

Private employers may not make employment decisions based on:

- Age
- Ancestry or national origin
- "Handicap"
- AIDS/HIV
- Gender
- Marital status
- Pregnancy, childbirth, and related medical conditions
- Race or color
- Religion or creed
- Sickle cell trait

State Laws Prohibiting Discrimination in Employment (continued)

Georgia
Ga. Code §§ 34-1-2, 34-5-1, 34-5-2, 34-6A-1 and following

Law applies to employers with: 15 or more employees (disability); ten or more employees (gender) (domestic and agricultural employees not protected); one or more employees (age)

Private employers may not make employment decisions based on:
- Age (40 to 70)
- Pregnancy, childbirth, and related medical conditions (Accommodations only)
- Physical, mental, or learning disability
- Gender (wage discrimination only)

Hawaii
Haw. Rev. Stat. §§ 378-1 and following; Haw. Admin. Rules §§ 12-46-107, 12-46-182

Law applies to employers with: One or more employees

Private employers may not make employment decisions based on:
- Age
- Ancestry or national origin
- Physical or mental disability
- AIDS/HIV
- Gender
- Marital status
- Pregnancy, childbirth, and related medical conditions (includes breast-feeding; accommodations required)
- Race or color
- Religion or creed
- Sexual orientation
- Genetic testing information
- Arrest and court record (unless there is a conviction directly related to job)
- Credit history or credit report, unless the information in the individual's credit history or credit report directly relates to a bona fide occupational qualification
- Gender identity and gender expression
- Status as a victim of domestic or sexual violence (if employer has knowledge or is notified of this status)
- Salary history, unless voluntarily disclosed

Idaho
Idaho Code §§ 39-8303, 67-5902, 67-5909, 67-5910

Law applies to employers with: Five or more employees

Private employers may not make employment decisions based on:
- Age (40 and older)
- Ancestry or national origin
- Physical or mental disability
- Gender
- Pregnancy, childbirth, and related medical conditions
- Race or color
- Religion or creed
- Genetic testing information

Illinois
410 Ill. Comp. Stat. § 513/25; 775 Ill. Comp. Stat. §§ 5/1-102, 5/1-103, 5/2-101, 5/2-102, 5/2-103, 5/2-109; 820 Ill. Comp. Stat. §§ 105/4, 180/30; Ill. Admin. Code tit. 56, § 5210.110

Law applies to employers with: One or more employees

Private employers may not make employment decisions based on:
- Age (40 and older)
- Ancestry or national origin

State Laws Prohibiting Discrimination in Employment (continued)

- Physical or mental disability
- Gender
- Marital status
- Pregnancy, childbirth, and related medical conditions (accommodations required)
- Race or color
- Religion or creed
- Sexual orientation
- Genetic testing information
- Citizenship status
- Military status
- Unfavorable military discharge
- Gender identity
- Arrest record
- Victims of domestic violence
- Order of protection status
- Lack of permanent mailing address or having a mailing address of a shelter or social service provider
- Salary history

Indiana

Ind. Code §§ 22-2-14-2, 22-9-1-2, 22-9-2-1, 22-9-2-2, 22-9-5-1 and following

Law applies to employers with: Six or more employees; one or more employees (age only); 15 or more employees (disability only)

Private employers may not make employment decisions based on:
- Age (40 to 75)
- Ancestry or national origin
- Physical or mental disability
- Gender
- Race or color
- Religion or creed
- Status as a veteran
- Off-duty tobacco use

- Sealed or expunged arrest or conviction record
- Pregnancy, childbirth, and related medical conditions (accommodations only)

Iowa

Iowa Code §§ 216.2, 216.6, 216.6A, 729.6

Law applies to employers with: Four or more employees

Private employers may not make employment decisions based on:
- Age (18 or older)
- Ancestry or national origin
- Physical or mental disability
- AIDS/HIV
- Gender
- Pregnancy, childbirth, and related medical conditions (accommodations required)
- Race or color
- Religion or creed
- Sexual orientation
- Genetic testing information
- Gender identity
- Wage discrimination

Kansas

Kan. Stat. §§ 44-1002, 44-1009, 44-1112, 44-1113, 44-1125, 44-1126, 65-6002(e)

Law applies to employers with: Four or more employees

Private employers may not make employment decisions based on:
- Age (40 or older)
- Ancestry or national origin
- Physical or mental disability
- AIDS/HIV
- Gender

State Laws Prohibiting Discrimination in Employment (continued)

- Pregnancy, childbirth, and related medical conditions (accommodations required)
- Race or color
- Religion or creed
- Genetic testing information
- Military service or status

Kentucky

Ky. Rev. Stat. §§ 207.130, 207.135, 207.150, 342.197, 344.010, 344.030, 344.040

Law applies to employers with: Eight or more employees

Private employers may not make employment decisions based on:
- Age (40 or older)
- Ancestry or national origin
- Physical or mental disability
- AIDS/HIV
- Gender
- Pregnancy, childbirth, and related medical conditions (accommodations required)
- Race or color
- Religion or creed
- Occupational pneumoconiosis with no respiratory impairment resulting from exposure to coal dust
- Off-duty tobacco use

Louisiana

La. Rev. Stat. §§ 23:301 to 23:368

Law applies to employers with: 20 or more employees; 25 or more employees (pregnancy, childbirth, and related medical conditions only)

Private employers may not make employment decisions based on:
- Age (40 or older)

- Ancestry or national origin
- Physical or mental disability
- Gender
- Pregnancy, childbirth, and related medical conditions (accommodations may be required)
- Race or color
- Religion or creed
- Genetic testing information
- Sickle cell trait
- Being a smoker or nonsmoker

Maine

Me. Rev. Stat. tit. 5, §§ 19302, 4552, 4553, 4571 to 4577; tit. 26, § 833; tit. 39-A, § 353

Law applies to employers with: One or more employees

Private employers may not make employment decisions based on:
- Age
- Ancestry or national origin
- Physical or mental disability
- AIDS/HIV
- Gender
- Pregnancy, childbirth, and related medical conditions (accommodations may be required)
- Race or color
- Religion or creed
- Sexual orientation, including perceived sexual orientation
- Genetic testing information
- Gender identity or expression
- Past workers' compensation claim
- Past whistle-blowing
- Medical support notice for child
- Salary history, unless voluntarily disclosed
- Genetic predisposition

State Laws Prohibiting Discrimination in Employment (continued)

Maryland

Md. Code (State Government) §§ 20-101, 20-601 to 20-608; Md. Code (Lab. & Empl.) § 3-1407; Md. Code Regs. § 14.03.02.02

Law applies to employers with: 15 or more employees/contractors; one or more employees/contractors (harassment only)

Private employers may not make employment decisions based on:

- Age
- Ancestry or national origin
- Physical or mental disability
- AIDS/HIV
- Gender
- Marital status
- Pregnancy, childbirth, and related medical conditions (accommodations required)
- Race or color (including hairstyles)
- Religion or creed
- Sexual orientation
- Genetic testing information
- Civil Air Patrol membership
- Gender identity
- Organ donation
- Wage history
- Genetic identity

Massachusetts

Mass. Gen. Laws ch. 149, §§ 24A, 105A; ch. 151B, §§ 1, 4; 804 Code Mass. Regs 3.01

Law applies to employers with: Six or more employees

Private employers may not make employment decisions based on:

- Age (40 or older)
- Ancestry or national origin

- Physical or mental disability
- Gender
- Pregnancy, childbirth, and related medical conditions (including breast-feeding; accommodations required)
- Marital status
- Race or color
- Religion or creed
- Sexual orientation
- Genetic testing information
- Military service
- Arrest record
- Status as a veteran
- Salary history
- Sealed or expunged criminal record

Michigan

Mich. Comp. Laws §§ 37.1103, 37.1201, 37.1202, 37.2201, 37.2202, 37.2205a, 750.556

Law applies to employers with: One or more employees

Private employers may not make employment decisions based on:

- Age
- Ancestry or national origin
- Physical or mental disability
- AIDS/HIV
- Gender
- Marital status
- Pregnancy, childbirth, and related medical conditions
- Race or color
- Religion or creed
- Genetic testing information
- Height or weight
- Misdemeanor arrest record
- Civil Air Patrol membership

State Laws Prohibiting Discrimination in Employment (continued)

Minnesota

Minn. Stat. §§ 144.417, 181.81, 181.9414, 181.974, 363A.03, 363A.08

Law applies to employers with: One or more employees; 21 or more employees (pregnancy and childbirth accommodations)

Private employers may not make employment decisions based on:
- Age (18 to 70)
- Ancestry or national origin
- Physical, sensory, or mental disability
- Gender
- Marital status
- Pregnancy, childbirth, and related medical conditions (accommodations required)
- Race or color
- Religion or creed
- Sexual orientation, including perceived sexual orientation
- Genetic testing information
- Gender identity
- Member of local commission
- Receiving public assistance
- Familial status (protects parents or guardians living with a minor child)

Mississippi

Miss. Code § 33-1-15

Law applies to employers with: One or more employees

Private employers may not make employment decisions based on:
- Military status
- No other protected categories unless employer receives public funding

Missouri

Mo. Rev. Stat. §§ 191.665, 213.010, 213.055, 375.1306

Law applies to employers with: Six or more employees

Private employers may not make employment decisions based on:
- Age (40 to 70)
- Ancestry or national origin
- Physical or mental disability
- AIDS/HIV
- Gender
- Race or color
- Religion or creed
- Genetic testing information
- Off-duty use of alcohol or tobacco

Montana

Mont. Code §§ 49-2-101, 49-2-303, 49-2-310

Law applies to employers with: One or more employees

Private employers may not make employment decisions based on:
- Age
- Ancestry or national origin
- Physical or mental disability
- Gender
- Marital status
- Pregnancy, childbirth, and related medical conditions
- Race or color
- Religion or creed

Nebraska

Neb. Rev. Stat. §§ 20-168, 48-236, 48-1001 to 48-1010, 48-1102, 48-1104

Law applies to employers with: 15 or more employees; 20 or more employees (age only)

State Laws Prohibiting Discrimination in Employment (continued)

Private employers may not make employment decisions based on:
- Age (40 and over)
- Ancestry or national origin
- Physical or mental disability
- AIDS/HIV
- Gender
- Marital status
- Pregnancy, childbirth, and related medical conditions (accommodations required)
- Race or color
- Religion or creed
- Genetic testing information (applies to all employers)

Nevada
Nev. Rev. Stat. §§ 608.0193, 608.0198, 613.310 and following, 613.4353

Law applies to employers with: 15 or more employees

Private employers may not make employment decisions based on:
- Age (40 or older)
- Ancestry or national origin
- Physical or mental disability
- AIDS/HIV
- Gender
- Pregnancy, childbirth, and related medical conditions (including breast-feeding; accommodations required)
- Race or color
- Religion or creed
- Sexual orientation, including perceived sexual orientation
- Genetic testing information
- Use of service animal
- Gender identity or expression
- Opposing unlawful employment practices

- Credit report or credit information (with some exceptions)
- Requesting leave or reasonable accommodation due to status as victim of domestic violence (applies to all employers)

New Hampshire
N.H. Rev. Stat. §§ 141-H:3, 354-A:2, 354-A:6, 354-A:7

Law applies to employers with: Six or more employees

Private employers may not make employment decisions based on:
- Age
- Ancestry or national origin
- Physical or mental disability
- Gender
- Marital status
- Pregnancy, childbirth, and related medical conditions
- Race or color
- Religion or creed
- Sexual orientation
- Genetic testing information
- Victims of domestic violence, harassment, sexual assault, or stalking
- Off-duty use of tobacco products
- Gender identity

New Jersey
N.J. Stat. §§ 10:5-1, 10:5-4, 10:5-4.1, 10:5-5, 10:5-12, 10:5-29.1, 34:6B-1, 43:21-49

Law applies to employers with: One or more employees

Private employers may not make employment decisions based on:
- Age (18 to 70)
- Ancestry or national origin

State Laws Prohibiting Discrimination in Employment (continued)

- Past or present physical or mental disability
- AIDS/HIV
- Gender
- Marital status, including civil union or domestic partnership status
- Pregnancy, childbirth, and related medical conditions (including breast-feeding; accommodations required)
- Race or color
- Religion or creed
- Sexual orientation, including affectional orientation and perceived sexual orientation
- Genetic testing information
- Atypical heredity cellular or blood trait
- Military service
- Accompanied by service or guide dog
- Gender identity
- Unemployed status
- Liability for service in the U.S. Armed Forces
- Familial status
- Salary history (job applicants)

New Mexico

N.M. Stat. §§ 24-21-4, 28-1-2, 28-1-7, 50-4A-4; N.M. Admin. Code § 9.1.1

Law applies to employers with: Four or more employees; 50 or more employees (marital status only)

Private employers may not make employment decisions based on:
- Age (40 or older)
- Ancestry or national origin
- Physical or mental disability
- Gender
- Marital status
- Pregnancy, childbirth, and related medical conditions

- Race or color
- Religion or creed
- Sexual orientation, including perceived sexual orientation
- Genetic testing information
- Gender identity
- Serious medical condition
- Domestic abuse leave
- Criminal arrest or conviction
- Cultural or religious headdresses
- "Protective hairstyles" and traits historically associated with race such as hair texture or length

New York

N.Y. Exec. Law §§ 292, 296; N.Y. Lab. Law §§ 201-d, 201-g

Law applies to employers with: One or more employees

Private employers may not make employment decisions based on:
- Age (18 and older)
- Ancestry or national origin
- Physical or mental disability
- Gender
- Marital status
- Pregnancy, childbirth, and related medical conditions (accommodations required)
- Race or color
- Religion or creed
- Sexual orientation, including perceived sexual orientation
- Genetic testing information
- Lawful recreational activities when not at work
- Military status or service
- Observance of Sabbath
- Political activities
- Use of service dog

State Laws Prohibiting Discrimination in Employment (continued)

- Arrest or criminal accusation
- Domestic violence victim status
- Familial status
- Gender identity and transgender status
- Reproductive health decision-making

North Carolina

N.C. Gen. Stat. §§ 95-28.1, 95-28.1A, 127B-11, 130A-148, 143-422.2, 168A-5

Law applies to employers with: 15 or more employees

Private employers may not make employment decisions based on:
- Age
- Ancestry or national origin
- Physical or mental disability
- AIDS/HIV
- Gender
- Race or color
- Religion or creed
- Genetic testing information
- Military status or service
- Sickle cell or hemoglobin C trait
- Lawful use of lawful products off site and off duty

North Dakota

N.D. Cent. Code §§ 14-02.4-02, 14-02.4-03, 34-01-17

Law applies to employers with: One or more employees

Private employers may not make employment decisions based on:
- Age (40 or older)
- Ancestry or national origin
- Physical or mental disability
- Gender
- Marital status

- Pregnancy, childbirth, and related medical conditions (accommodations required)
- Race or color
- Religion or creed
- Lawful conduct outside of work
- Receiving public assistance
- Keeping and bearing arms (as long as firearm is never exhibited on company property except for lawful defensive purposes)
- Status as a volunteer emergency responder

Ohio

Ohio Rev. Code §§ 4111.17, 4112.01, 4112.02

Law applies to employers with: Four or more employees

Private employers may not make employment decisions based on:
- Age (40 or older)
- Ancestry or national origin
- Physical, mental, or learning disability
- AIDS/HIV
- Gender
- Pregnancy, childbirth, and related medical conditions
- Race or color
- Religion or creed
- Military status
- Caring for a sibling, child, parent, or spouse injured while in the armed services

Oklahoma

Okla. Stat. 10A § 1-2-101; tit. 25, §§ 1301, 1302; tit. 36, § 3614.2; tit. 40, § 500; tit. 44, § 208

Law applies to employers with: One or more employees

State Laws Prohibiting Discrimination in Employment (continued)

Private employers may not make employment decisions based on:
- Age (40 or older)
- Ancestry or national origin
- Physical or mental disability
- Gender
- Pregnancy, childbirth, and related medical conditions (except abortions where the woman is not in "imminent danger of death")
- Race or color
- Religion or creed
- Genetic testing information
- Military service
- Being a smoker or nonsmoker or using tobacco off duty
- Reporting child abuse or neglect

Oregon
Or. Rev. Stat. §§ 659A.030, 659A.122 and following, 659A.303, 659A.357; 2019 Or. Laws Ch. 139

Law applies to employers with: One or more employees; six or more employees (disability and pregnancy, childbirth, and related medical conditions accommodations).

Private employers may not make employment decisions based on:
- Age (18 or older)
- Ancestry or national origin
- Physical or mental disability
- Gender
- Marital status
- Pregnancy, childbirth, and related medical conditions (accommodations required)
- Race or color
- Religion or creed
- Sexual orientation

- Genetic testing information
- Parent who has medical support order imposed by court
- Domestic violence victim status
- Refusal to attend an employer-sponsored meeting with the primary purpose of communicating the employer's opinion on religious or political matters
- Credit history
- Whistle-blowers
- Off-duty use of tobacco products
- Salary history, unless voluntarily disclosed.

Pennsylvania
43 Pa. Const. Stat., §§ 954 to 955

Law applies to employers with: Four or more employees

Private employers may not make employment decisions based on:
- Age (40 to 70)
- Ancestry or national origin
- Physical or mental disability
- Gender
- Pregnancy, childbirth, and related medical conditions
- Race or color
- Religion or creed
- GED rather than high school diploma
- Use of service animal
- Relationship or association with a person with a disability

Rhode Island
R.I. Gen. Laws §§ 12-28-10, 23-6.3-11, 28-5-6, 28-5-7, 28-6-18, 28-6.7-1

Law applies to employers with: Four or more employees; one or more employees (gender-based wage discrimination only)

State Laws Prohibiting Discrimination in Employment (continued)

Private employers may not make employment decisions based on:
- Age (40 or older)
- Ancestry or national origin
- Physical or mental disability
- AIDS/HIV
- Gender
- Pregnancy, childbirth, and related medical conditions (includes breast-feeding; accommodations required)
- Race or color
- Religion or creed
- Sexual orientation, including perceived sexual orientation
- Genetic testing information
- Domestic abuse victim
- Gender identity or expression
- Homelessness

South Carolina
S.C. Code §§ 1-13-30, 1-13-80

Law applies to employers with: 15 or more employees

Private employers may not make employment decisions based on:
- Age (40 or older)
- Ancestry or national origin
- Physical or mental disability
- AIDS/HIV
- Gender
- Pregnancy, childbirth, and related medical conditions (accommodations required)
- Race or color
- Religion or creed

South Dakota
S.D. Codified Laws §§ 20-13-1, 20-13-10, 60-12-15, 60-2-20, 62-1-17

Law applies to employers with: One or more employees

Private employers may not make employment decisions based on:
- Ancestry or national origin
- Physical or mental disability
- Gender
- Race or color
- Religion or creed
- Genetic testing information
- Preexisting injury
- Off-duty use of tobacco products

Tennessee
Tenn. Code §§ 4-21-102, 4-21-401 and following, 8-50-103, 50-2-201, 50-2-202

Law applies to employers with: Eight or more employees; one or more employees (gender-based wage discrimination only)

Private employers may not make employment decisions based on:
- Age (40 or older)
- Ancestry or national origin
- Physical, mental, or visual disability
- Gender
- Pregnancy, childbirth, and related medical conditions (accommodations required)
- Race or color
- Religion or creed
- Use of guide dog
- Volunteer rescue squad worker responding to an emergency

State Laws Prohibiting Discrimination in Employment (continued)

Texas

Tex. Lab. Code §§ 21.002, 21.051, 21.101, 21.106, 21.402; Tex. Fam. Code § 261.110

Law applies to employers with: 15 or more employees

Private employers may not make employment decisions based on:
- Age (40 or older)
- Ancestry or national origin
- Physical or mental disability
- Gender
- Pregnancy, childbirth, and related medical conditions (accommodations required)
- Race or color
- Religion or creed
- Genetic testing information
- Reporting child abuse or neglect

Utah

Utah Code §§ 26-45-103, 34A-5-102, 34A-5-106

Law applies to employers with: 15 or more employees

Private employers may not make employment decisions based on:
- Age (40 or older)
- Ancestry or national origin
- Physical or mental disability
- AIDS/HIV
- Gender
- Pregnancy, childbirth, and related medical conditions (includes breast-feeding; accommodations required)
- Race or color
- Religion or creed
- Sexual orientation
- Genetic testing information
- Gender identity

Vermont

Vt. Stat. tit. 18, § 9333; tit. 21, §§ 305, 495, 495d, 495m

Law applies to employers with: One or more employees

Private employers may not make employment decisions based on:
- Age (18 or older)
- Ancestry or national origin
- Physical, mental, or emotional disability
- AIDS/HIV
- Gender
- Pregnancy, childbirth, and related medical conditions (accommodations required)
- Race or color
- Religion or creed
- Sexual orientation
- Genetic testing information
- Gender identity
- Place of birth
- Credit report or credit history
- Salary history
- Status as crime victim

Virginia

Va. Code §§ 2.2-3900, 2.2-3901, 2.2-3905, 40.1-28.6, 40.1-28.7:1, 51.5-41

Law applies to employers with: 15 or more employees; six or more for unlawful discharge and disabilities; and six or more but fewer than 20 for unlawful discharge based on age

Private employers may not make employment decisions based on:
- Age (40 and older)
- Ancestry or national origin

State Laws Prohibiting Discrimination in Employment (continued)

- Physical or mental disability
- AIDS/HIV
- Gender
- Marital status
- Pregnancy, childbirth, and related medical conditions (accommodations required)
- Race or color (including hairstyles)
- Religion or creed
- Genetic testing information
- Military status
- Arrest or conviction for marijuana possession
- Sexual orientation

Washington

Wash. Rev. Code §§ 38.40.110, 49.44.090, 49.44.180, 49.58.020, 49.58.040, 49.60.030, 49.60.040, 49.60.172, 49.60.180, 49.76.120; Wash. Admin. Code § 162-30-020

Law applies to employers with: Eight or more employees; one or more employees (gender-based wage discrimination only); 15 or more employees (pregnancy and childbirth accommodations).

Private employers may not make employment decisions based on:
- Age (40 or older)
- Ancestry or national origin
- Physical, mental, or sensory disability
- AIDS/HIV
- Gender
- Marital status
- Pregnancy, childbirth, and related medical conditions (including breast-feeding; accommodations required)

- Race or color (including hairstyles)
- Religion or creed
- Sexual orientation
- Genetic testing information
- Hepatitis C infection
- Member of state militia
- Use of a trained service animal by a person with a disability
- Gender identity
- Domestic violence victim
- Salary history
- Immigration

West Virginia

W. Va. Code §§ 5-11-3, 5-11-9, 15-1K-4, 16-3C-3, 21-5B-1, 21-5B-3

Law applies to employers with: 12 or more employees; one or more employees (gender-based wage discrimination only)

Private employers may not make employment decisions based on:
- Age (40 or older)
- Ancestry or national origin
- Physical or mental disability, or blindness
- AIDS/HIV
- Gender
- Pregnancy, childbirth, and related medical conditions (accommodations required)
- Race or color
- Religion or creed
- Off-duty use of tobacco products
- Membership in the Civil Air Patrol (for employers with 16 or more employees)

State Laws Prohibiting Discrimination in Employment (continued)

Wisconsin

Wis. Stat. §§ 111.32 and following

Law applies to employers with: One or more employees

Private employers may not make employment decisions based on:

- Age (40 or older)
- Ancestry or national origin
- Physical or mental disability
- Gender
- Marital status
- Pregnancy, childbirth, and related medical conditions
- Race or color
- Religion or creed
- Sexual orientation, including having a history of or being identified with a preference
- Genetic testing information
- Arrest or conviction record
- Military service
- Declining to attend a meeting or to participate in any communication about religious matters or political matters
- Use or nonuse of lawful products off duty and off site

Wyoming

Wyo. Stat. §§ 19-11-104, 27-9-102, 27-9-105

Law applies to employers with: Two or more employees

Private employers may not make employment decisions based on:

- Age (40 or older)
- Ancestry or national origin
- Disability
- Gender
- Pregnancy, childbirth, and related medical conditions
- Race or color
- Religion or creed
- Military service or status

State Laws That Regulate Lactation Breaks

Arkansas
Ark. Stat. Ann. § 11-5-116

Covered Employers: One or more employees

Break Provided: Employer must provide reasonable unpaid breaks to express breast milk; if possible, break time to run concurrently with other breaks.

Other Requirements: Employer must make reasonable efforts to provide a private and sanitary room or location near the employee's work area, other than a toilet. Employee must make reasonable efforts to minimize disruption to employer's business.

Exceptions: Employer not required to provide breaks if doing so would impose an undue hardship on the employer.

California
Cal. Lab. Code §§ 1030, 1031, 1032, 1033

Covered Employers: One or more employees

Break Provided: Employer must provide reasonable unpaid breaks to each time the employee needs to express milk; if possible, break time to run concurrently with other breaks.

Other Requirements: Employer must provide a private room or location, other than a bathroom, that meets certain criteria near the employee's work area.

Exceptions: An employer that employs fewer than 50 employees may be exempt if it can demonstrate that a requirement would impose an undue hardship by causing the employer significant difficulty or expense when considered in relation to the size, financial resources, nature,

or structure of the employer's business. If that employer can demonstrate that the requirement to provide an employee with the use of a room or other location, other than a bathroom, would impose such undue hardship, the employer shall make reasonable efforts to provide the employee with the use of a room or other location, other than a toilet stall, in close proximity to the employee's work area, for the employee to express milk in private. An employer is not required to provide break time if to do so would seriously disrupt the operations of the employer.

Colorado
Colo. Rev. Stat. Ann. §§ 8-13.5-101 and following

Covered Employers: One or more employees

Break Provided: Employer must provide separate reasonable unpaid breaks or allow employee to use meal or rest breaks to express breast milk for up to two years following childbirth.

Other Requirements: Employer must make reasonable efforts to provide a private break room or location, other than a toilet stall, near the employee's work area.

Exceptions: Employer not required to provide breaks if doing so would impose an undue hardship on the employer.

Connecticut
Conn. Gen. Stat. Ann. § 31-40w

Covered Employers: One or more employees

State Laws That Regulate Lactation Breaks (continued)

Break Provided: Employer must allow employee to use meal or rest breaks provided by employer to breast-feed or express breast milk.

Other Requirements: Employer must make reasonable efforts to provide a private break room, other than a toilet stall, near the employee's work area. Employer may not retaliate against employees who exercise their rights to express breast milk at work.

Exceptions: Employer not required to provide private break room if doing so would impose an undue hardship on employer.

Delaware
Del. Code Ann. tit.19, § 710 and following

Covered Employers: Four or more employees

Break Provided: Employer must provide sufficient break time and appropriate facilities for expressing breast milk unless accommodation imposes an undue hardship.

Exceptions: "Undue hardship" means a significant difficulty or expense when considered against enumerated factors.

District of Columbia
D.C. Code Ann. §§ 2-1402.11, 2-1402.82, 32-1231.01 to 32-1231.03

Covered Employers: One or more employees

Break Provided: Employer must provide reasonable unpaid breaks to express breast milk. Break time runs concurrently with other breaks provided by the employer.

Other Requirements: Employer must make reasonable efforts to provide a private break room or location, other than a toilet stall, near the employee's work area.

Exceptions: Employer not required to provide breaks if doing so would impose an undue hardship on the employer.

Georgia
Ga. Code Ann. § 34-1-6

Covered Employers: One or more employees

Break Provided: An employer shall provide break time of a reasonable duration to an employee who desires to express breast milk at the worksite during work hours.

Other Requirements: Employer must provide a private location, other than a restroom, at the worksite.

Exceptions: An employer that employs fewer than 50 employees is exempt from requirements that would impose an undue hardship by causing the employer significant difficulty or expense when considered in relation to the size, financial resources, nature, or structure of the employer's business.

Hawaii
Haw. Rev. Stat. §§ 378-2, 91, 92

Covered Employers: One or more employees

Break Provided: Employer must provide reasonable breaks to express breast milk for up to one year following childbirth.

State Laws That Regulate Lactation Breaks (continued)

Other Requirements: Employer must provide a private location, other than a restroom, that is sanitary, shielded from view and free from intrusion, for the employee to express breast milk. Employer may not discriminate or retaliate against employees who express breast milk at the workplace.

Exceptions: Employer with fewer than 20 employees not required to provide breaks if doing so would cause an undue hardship.

Illinois
820 Ill. Comp. Stat. §§ 260/5, 260/10, 260/15

Covered Employers: Six or more employees

Break Provided: Employer must provide reasonable breaks to an employee who needs to express breast milk for her nursing infant child each time the employee has the need to express milk for one year after the child's birth; break time may run concurrently with other breaks.

Other Requirements: Employer must make reasonable efforts to provide a private break room or location, other than a toilet stall, near the employee's work area.

Exceptions: Employer not required to provide breaks if doing so would create an undue hardship.

Indiana
Ind. Code Ann. § 22-2-14-1, 2

Covered Employers: 25 or more employees

Break Provided: Employee may use rest or meal breaks provided by employer to express breast milk.

Other Requirements: To the extent reasonably possible, employer shall provide: a private location, other than a toilet stall, for employees to express breast milk; and either provide a refrigerator for storage of breast milk or allow the employee to supply her own cold storage for breast milk.

Kentucky
Ky. Rev. Stat. Ann. §§ 344.030, 344.040

Covered Employers: 15 or more employees

Break Provided: Employers must make reasonable accommodation for nursing mothers and employees with pregnancy- or childbirth-related conditions. Accommodation may include more frequent or longer breaks and a private space other than a bathroom to express breast milk.

Exceptions: Employer not required to provide accommodations if doing so would impose an undue hardship on the employer's program, enterprise, or business.

Maine
Me. Rev. Stat. Ann. tit. 26, §§ 602 to 604

Covered Employers: One or more employees

Break Provided: Employer must provide adequate unpaid time to express breast milk, or allow employee to use rest or meal breaks provided by employer, for up to three years following childbirth.

State Laws That Regulate Lactation Breaks (continued)

Other Requirements: Employer must make reasonable efforts to provide a clean, private location, other than a restroom, to express breast milk. Employer may not discriminate against employees who express breast milk in the workplace.

Massachusetts

Mass. Gen. Laws Ann. ch. 151B, § 4

Break Provided: Employers must make reasonable accommodation for nursing mothers and employees with pregnancy-related conditions if the employee requests such an accommodation. Accommodation may include more frequent or longer breaks and a private non-bathroom space for expressing breast milk.

Exceptions: Employer not required to provide accommodation if doing so would impose an undue hardship.

Minnesota

Minn. Stat. Ann. § 181.939

Covered Employers: One or more employees

Break Provided: Employer must provide reasonable unpaid breaks to express breast milk; break time to run concurrently with other breaks if possible.

Other Requirements: Employer must make reasonable efforts to provide a private location, other than a toilet stall, with access to an electrical outlet and in close proximity to the employee's work area. Employer may not retaliate against an employee who exercises her right to express breast milk at work.

Exceptions: Employer not required to provide break time if doing so would unduly disrupt employer operations.

Mississippi

Miss. Code Ann. § 71-1-55

Covered Employers: One or more employees

Break Provided: Employer must allow employee to use meal or rest breaks provided by employer to express breast milk.

Nebraska

Neb. Rev. Stat. § 48-1102

Covered Employers: 15 or more employees

Break Provided: Employer must provide reasonable accommodation to nursing mothers, which may include breaks (unpaid, unless concurrent with paid breaks) and an appropriate location for expressing breast milk.

Exceptions: Employer not required to provide breaks if doing so would impose an undue hardship on the employer.

Nevada

Nev. Rev. Stat. Ann. § 613.335

Covered Employers: All employers. Employers with less than 50 employees are exempt if accommodations constitute undue hardship. Certain licensed contractors not required to comply where employees work at a construction job site at least three miles from the employer's regular place of business.

State Laws That Regulate Lactation Breaks (continued)

Break Provided: For mothers with a child under one year of age, reasonable break time with or without compensation, to express breast milk as needed; and a place, other than a bathroom, reasonably free from dirt or pollution, protected from the view of others, and free from intrusion by others.

Exceptions: If employer believes complying will cause an undue hardship, the employer and employee must engage in a timely, good faith and interactive process to determine an effective, reasonable accommodation. If the parties cannot reach an agreement, the employer can require the employee to accept the reasonable alternative selected by the employer, subject to the employee's right to appeal the decision to the appropriate authorities.

New Jersey
N.J. Stat. Ann. § 10:5-12

Covered Employers: All employers

Break Provided: Reasonable break time and a suitable room or other location with privacy, other than a toilet stall, in close proximity to the work area for the employee to express milk, unless employer demonstrates accommodation is undue hardship on the business operations.

Other Requirements: No time limit (e.g., child under one year, etc.), to requirement. Cannot treat a breast-feeding woman less favorable than other employees or penalize for requesting or using an accommodation.

Exceptions: "Undue hardship" factors include: overall size of the employer's business with respect to the number of employees, number and type of facilities, budget; the type of operations, nature and cost of accommodation; and extent that accommodation would involve waiver of an essential requirement of a job as opposed to a tangential or non-business necessity requirement.

New Mexico
N.M. Stat. Ann. § 28-20-2

Covered Employers: One or more employees

Break Provided: Employer must provide flexible unpaid breaks to express breast milk.

Other Requirements: Employer must provide a clean, private location, other than a toilet, near the employee's work area.

New York
N.Y. Lab. Law § 206-c

Covered Employers: One or more employees

Break Provided: Employer must provide reasonable unpaid breaks, or allow employee to use meal or rest breaks provided by employer, to express breast milk for up to three years after childbirth.

Other Requirements: Employer must make reasonable efforts to provide a private location near the employee's work area. Employer may not discriminate against employee who chooses to express breast milk at the workplace.

State Laws That Regulate Lactation Breaks (continued)

North Dakota
N.D. Cent. Code § 23-12-17

Covered Employers: Voluntary

Break Provided: Employer may use the designation "infant friendly" on promotional materials by adopting voluntary workplace breast-feeding policies including flexible work scheduling, and permitting work patterns that provide time for expression of breast milk.

Oklahoma
Okla. Stat. tit. 40, § 435

Covered Employers: One or more employees

Break Provided: Employer must provide reasonable unpaid breaks to breast feed or express breast milk; break time to run concurrently with other breaks if possible.

Other Requirements: Employer may make reasonable efforts to provide a private, sanitary location near the employee's work area.

Exceptions: Employer not required to provide break time if doing so would cause an undue hardship on the employer's operations.

Oregon
Or. Rev. Stat. Ann. § 653.077, Or. Admin. R. § 839-020-0051

Break Provided: Employer must provide reasonable rest period to express milk each time the employee has a need to express milk, for up to 18 months after childbirth. Break time to run concurrently with other breaks if feasible.

Other Requirements: Employer must make reasonable efforts to provide a

private location, other than a restroom, near the employee's work area. Employee must give reasonable notice of intention to express breast milk upon return to work.

Exceptions: Employer with 10 or fewer employees isn't required to provide breaks if doing so would impose undue hardship.

Rhode Island
R.I. Gen. Laws §§ 23-13.2-1; 28-5-7.4

Covered Employers: One or more employees

Break Provided: Employer must provide reasonable, unpaid break time to breast-feed or express breast milk; break time to run concurrently with other breaks if possible.

Other Requirements: Employer shall make reasonable efforts to provide a private, secure, and sanitary location in close proximity to the work area, other than a toilet stall.

Exceptions: Employer not required to provide break time if doing so would create undue hardship on employer's operations.

South Carolina
S.C. Code Ann. § 41-1-130

Break Provided: Employer must provide reasonable unpaid break time or allow employee to use paid break or meal time to express breast milk. Employer must make reasonable effort to provide private location, other than toilet stall, in close proximity to the workplace. The break time must, if possible, run concurrently with any break time already provided to the employee.

State Laws That Regulate Lactation Breaks (continued)

Other Requirements: Employer does not have to provide break time if doing so would create an undue hardship on the operations of the employer.

Tennessee
Tenn. Code Ann. § 50-1-305

Covered Employers: One or more employees

Break Provided: Employer shall provide reasonable, unpaid break time to express breast milk; break time to run concurrently with other break time, if possible.

Other Requirements: Employer shall make reasonable efforts to provide a private room or other location in close proximity to the work area, other than a toilet stall.

Exceptions: Employer not required to provide break time if doing so would unduly disrupt employer's operations.

Texas
Tex. Health & Safety Code Ann. § 165.003

Covered Employers: Voluntary

Break Provided: Employers voluntarily implementing policies supporting worksite breast-feeding may designate themselves "mother-friendly."

Utah
Utah Code Ann. § 34A-5-106

Covered Employers: 15 or more employees. Does not apply to religious organizations or Boy Scouts.

Break Provided: Employer must provide reasonable accommodations for employee related to breast-feeding unless employer

demonstrates accommodation would create an undue hardship on the employer.

Exceptions: Employer cannot deny employment opportunities to employee based on the need to make reasonable accommodations related to breast-feeding unless employer demonstrates the accommodation would create an undue hardship on employer.

Vermont
Vt. Stat. Ann. tit. 21, § 305

Covered Employers: One or more employees

Break Provided: Employer shall provide reasonable breaks to express breast milk for up to three years following childbirth. Employer has discretion to make breaks paid or unpaid.

Other Requirements: Employer shall make a reasonable accommodation to provide a private space, other than a restroom, for employee to express breast milk. Employer may not retaliate or discriminate against employee who exercises her rights to express breast milk at the workplace.

Exceptions: Employer not required to provide breaks if doing so would substantially disrupt the employer's operations.

Virginia
Va. Code Ann. §§ 2.2-3905, 2.2-3909

Covered Employers: 6–14 employees

Other Requirements: Employer with more than five but fewer than fifteen employees may not terminate a female employee on the basis of lactation.

State Laws That Regulate Lactation Breaks (continued)

Washington
Wash. Rev. Code § 43.10.005

Covered Employers: 15 or more employees

Break Provided: Employer must provide reasonable break time for an employee to express breast milk for two years after the child's birth each time the employee has need to express the milk and providing a private location, other than a bathroom, if such a location exists at the place of business or worksite, which may be used by the employee to express breast milk. If the business location does not have a space for the employee to express milk, the employer shall work with the employee to identify a convenient location and work schedule to accommodate their needs.

Federal Law Requires Lactation Breaks

29 U.S.C. § 207

Covered Employers: Employers covered by the Fair Labor Standards Act (FLSA)

Break Provided: Employers shall provide reasonable, unpaid break time to express breast milk for a nursing child for one year after birth each time the employee needs to express milk.

Other Requirements: Employers are required to provide a private location, other than a restroom, that is shielded from view and free from intrusion from coworkers and the public, which may be used by an employee to express breast milk.

Exceptions: Employers with fewer than 50 employees not required to provide break time if such requirements would impose an undue hardship by causing the employer significant difficulty or expense when considered in relation to the size, financial resources, nature, or structure of the employer's business.

Forms

This book comes with files that you can access online at:
www.nolo.com/back-of-book/HDAB.html
You can open, edit, print, and save these RTF files with most word processing programs such as Microsoft *Word*, Windows *WordPad*, and recent versions of *WordPerfect*.

Editing RTFs

Here are some general instructions about editing RTF forms in your word processing program. Refer to the book's instructions and sample agreements for help about what should go in each blank. Forms may contain:

- **Underlines.** Underlines indicate where to enter information. After filling in the needed text, delete the underline. In most word processing programs you can do this by highlighting the underlined portion and typing CTRL+U.
- **Bracketed and italicized text.** Bracketed and italicized text indicates instructions. Be sure to remove all instructional text before you finalize your document.
- **Alternative text.** Alternative text gives you the choice between two or more text options. Delete those options you don't want to use. Renumber any numbered items, if necessary.
- **Signature lines.** Signature lines should appear on a page with at least some text from the document itself.

Every word processing program uses different commands to open, format, save, and print documents, so refer to your software's help documents for help using your program. Nolo cannot provide technical support for questions about how to use your computer or your software.

CAUTION
In accordance with U.S. copyright laws, the forms and files provided by this book are for your personal use only.

List of Forms

All the files listed below are available for download at:
www.nolo.com/back-of-book/HDAB.html

The following files are in RTF:

Form Title	File Name
Litigation Calendar	Calendar.rtf
Intake Form—Employee Complaint	IntakeForm.rtf
Policy Distribution Log	Log.rtf
Policy Prohibiting Discrimination and Harassment	Policy.rtf
Acknowledgment of Receipt of Policy	Receipt.rtf

Index

On Nolo.com you'll also find:

Books & Software

Nolo publishes hundreds of great books and software programs for consumers and
business owners. Order a copy, or download an ebook version instantly, at Nolo.com.

Online Forms

You can quickly and easily make a will or living trust, form an LLC or corporation,
apply for a provisional patent, or make hundreds of other forms—online.

Free Legal Information

Thousands of articles answer common questions about everyday legal issues,
including wills, bankruptcy, small business formation, divorce, patents,
employment, and much more.

Plain-English Legal Dictionary

Stumped by jargon? Look it up in America's most up-to-date source for
definitions of legal terms, free at Nolo.com.

Lawyer Directory

Nolo's consumer-friendly lawyer directory provides in-depth profiles of lawyers all
over America. You'll find information you need to choose the right lawyer.

HDAB5